MW01008267

Praise for

For Women Only

"Shaunti's signature message, which she has shared around the world with millions of listeners, is life changing and something every woman needs to hear. Every time I have given someone this book, I have seen lives and marriages changed!"

—Lysa TerKeurst, *New York Times* best-selling author of *Made to Crave*

"This one short little book brings a long-lasting, big impact on marriage—which is why I've been taking groups of women through a *For Women Only* study every year since I first read it. Shaunti's message has impacted my relationships personally, and I've seen some amazing transformation in the lives and marriages of others."

—Holly Furtick, lead pastor's wife, Elevation Church, Charlotte, North Carolina

"What an important book!"

—Beth Moore, Bible teacher, best-selling author of *So Long, Insecurity*

"In our weekly couples' study, we read and discussed both *For Women Only* and *For Men Only* over the course of several months. They were fascinating and very helpful. The findings in these books about how men and women think are so enlightening. My wife and I think these books should be required premarital reading!"

—Comedian Jeff Foxworthy

"You're about to gain some fresh insight into some of the mysteries of masculinity. *For Women Only* is a book that I believe will provide understanding and bring harmony to a lot of marriages."

—Bob Lepine, cohost of *FamilyLife Today*

"Ready for an eyeopener? Shaunti Feldhahn has uncovered a mountain of meaningful information for any woman wanting to understand men at a profound level."

—Drs. Les and Leslie Parrott, Seattle Pacific University; authors of *Love Talk*

"Men are in agreement on this one: *For Women Only* is one book every husband wishes his wife would read! It's a practical, thought-provoking message that will show you what you should do—and not do—when it comes to your relationship with the man in your life. Read it, and you're bound to have many 'aha!' moments that could revolutionize your relationship."

—Valorie Burton, best-selling author of *Successful Women Think Differently* and *What's Really Holding You Back?*

"*For Women Only* is the best book I have read for women, about men. Shaunti's research, facts, and stories in this little book create an incredible read for all women. Single, married, divorced, or not even allowed to date yet should all read this and come to understand the key truths that will help in your relationship with any man. I bought a copy, read it, was astonished, and then bought ten more and sent them to everyone on our team."

—Craig Gross, founder of XXXchurch.com

"This book is a treasure box that never seems empty of wisdom. Every time I dig in, my hands and heart emerge filled with tools that help me know myself better and relate to the people I love more effectively. If you've already read it, you should read it again. And if you are just opening these pages for the first time, buckle a seat belt over your soul and get ready for a ride you won't soon forget."

—PRISCILLA SHIRER, best-selling author of *One in a Million*

"We gave this book to every woman in our congregation for a special event. I interviewed Shaunti during all our worship services. The response was incredible. She has an engaging, compelling way of presenting her findings about how men think. It helped open the eyes of women to the real needs of the men in their lives, and it gave men a common language to talk with their wives. I urge churches and other groups to give her the opportunity to share this message."

—ANDY STANLEY, author of *Enemies of the Heart;* senior pastor, North Point Community Church, Alpharetta, Georgia

Praise for

For Men Only and *For Women Only*

"Whenever Shaunti Feldhahn appears as a guest on our radio program, we know that listener response will be enthusiastic. She has a way of connecting with the audience that is unique and compelling. We're thankful for the unique perspective she provides not only to the Christian community but to the culture at large."

—JIM DALY, president of Focus on the Family

"These are the books I pass out to people as the best on the subject. Shaunti Feldhahn has the rare ability to do impeccable research and then make her findings incredibly practical. There is something to learn on every page."

—Jim Burns, PhD, president of HomeWord; author of *Creating an Intimate Marriage*

"Whatever Shaunti Feldhahn researches, read. Actually, do more than read: study! Her ability to ask the right questions, find the right answers, and communicate the results clearly and practically sets her apart as a gifted researcher. Her content guides and changes lives."

—Emerson Eggerichs, PhD, best-selling author of *Love and Respect*

"Shaunti Feldhahn has a unique gift for helping men understand women, and women, men. Her books are the best I know at providing rich and practical gender understanding that can be used immediately. I highly recommend both all the time!"

—Robert Lewis, author of *Raising a Modern-Day Knight;* founder of Men's Fraternity

"Shaunti Feldhahn has the unique gift of communicating a Christian worldview in a language everyone, Christian or secular, understands. Her experience and educational background qualify her to speak and write authoritatively about relationships and how people respond. I personally have seen and felt the impact of her research. She is the go-to person for our organization when we need insight."

—Phil Waldrep, founder, Women of Joy conferences and Phil Waldrep Ministries, Decatur, Alabama

Shaunti Feldhahn

for

What You Need to Know About the Inner Lives of Men

women

REVISED AND UPDATED EDITION

MULTNOMAH
BOOKS

For Women Only

Scripture quotations are taken from the following versions: The Holy Bible, English Standard Version, copyright © 2001 by Crossway Bibles, a division of Good News Publishers. Used by permission. All rights reserved. King James Version. The Holy Bible, New International Version®, NIV®. Copyright © 1973, 1978, 1984 by Biblica Inc.™ Used by permission of Zondervan. All rights reserved worldwide. www.zondervan.com. The Holy Bible, New Living Translation, copyright © 1996. Used by permission of Tyndale House Publishers Inc., Carol Stream, Illinois 60188. All rights reserved.

Details in some anecdotes and stories have been changed to protect the identities of the persons involved.

Hardcover ISBN 978-1-60142-444-0
eBook ISBN 978-1-60142-210-1

Cover design by Mark D. Ford

Published in association with the literary agency of Calvin Edwards, 1220 Austin Glen Drive, Atlanta, GA 30338.

Published in the United States by Multnomah, an imprint of the Crown Publishing Group, a division of Penguin Random House LLC, New York.

Multnomah® and its mountain colophon are registered trademarks of Penguin Random House LLC.

Library of Congress Cataloging-in-Publication Data
Feldhahn, Shaunti Christine.
For women only : what you need to know about the inner lives of men / Shaunti Feldhahn. — Revised and Updated Edition.
pages cm
Includes bibliographical references.
ISBN 978-1-60142-444-0 — ISBN 978-1-60142-210-1 (electronic)
1. Man-woman relationships—Religious aspects—Christianity. 2. Man-woman relationships. 3. Men—Psychology. 4. Marriage—Religious aspects—Christianity. 5. Marriage. I. Title.
BT708.5.F455 2013
248.8'435—dc23

2012044949

Printed in the United States of America
2018—Revised Edition

10

Special Sales

Most Multnomah books are available at special quantity discounts when purchased in bulk by corporations, organizations, and special-interest groups. Custom imprinting or excerpting can also be done to fit special needs. For information, please e-mail specialmarketscms@penguinrandomhouse.com or call 1-800-603-7051.

For Jeff.
My beloved, my friend.

Song of Solomon 5:16

Contents

LIGHT BULB ON!

How I Woke Up to What I Didn't Know About Men

The other half of the people on the planet already know what you're going to read in this book.

As newlyweds, my husband and I lived in Manhattan, and like all New Yorkers, we walked everywhere. But I quickly noticed something strange. Quite often we'd be strolling hand in hand and Jeff would abruptly jerk his head up and away. We'd be watching in-line skaters in Central Park or waiting to cross the street in a crowd, and he would suddenly stare at the sky. I started to wonder, *Is something going on at the tops of these buildings?*

Turns out, something *was* going on, but it wasn't up in the buildings.

Have you ever been totally confused by something the man in your life has said or done? Looking at your boyfriend's rapidly departing back, have you ever wondered, *Why did that make him so angry?* Have you ever been perplexed by your husband's defensiveness when you asked him to stop working so much? Yeah? Me too.

But now, after interviewing and surveying thousands of men, I can tell you that the answers to those and dozens of other common perplexities are all related to what is going on in your man's inner life. Most are things he wishes you knew but doesn't know how to tell you. In many cases, they're things he has no idea you don't know. This book will share those interviews and those answers. But be careful. You might be slapping your forehead a lot!

I can tell you that the answers to dozens of common perplexities are related to what is going on in your man's inner life.

HOW IT ALL STARTED

Let me tell you how I got here. It all started with the research for my second novel, *The Lights of Tenth Street.* One of my main characters was a devoted husband and father. Because I had to put thoughts in his head, but had no idea what a guy would be thinking in a given situation, I interviewed my husband, Jeff, and many other male friends and colleagues. ("What would you be thinking if you were the character in this scene?") It took me a while to figure out how to handle what I found.

You see, in many cases, what I heard stunned me. Not just because what the men were thinking was so surprising but because it was so foundational. These weren't feelings that popped up every few months but were deep fundamental needs, fears, doubts, and thought patterns that occur in men every single day. It didn't matter whether the man I was talking to was old or young; what his racial or cultural background was; whether he was married or single, a churchgoer or an atheist, a corporate executive or a factory line worker—I kept hearing similar things.

For example, the character in my novel was a good guy who loved his wife and kids, was a devoted churchgoer and godly man, and a successful businessman. But he struggled with his thought life, especially the visual temptations that beckoned from every corner, from the secret traps of the Internet to the overt appeal of the miniskirt walking down the street. So, in short—and this is what shocked me—I discovered that instead of being unusual, my character was like almost every man on the planet. Including the faithful husbands I was interviewing.

That revelation led to a host of others, and following those trails led me to the thousands of personal and written interviews with men—including several professional, nationally representative surveys—that form the core of this book. I interviewed close friends over dinner and strangers in the grocery store, married fathers at church and the single student sitting next to me on the airplane. I talked to CEOs, attorneys, pastors, technology geeks, business managers, the security guard at Costco, and the guys behind the counter at Starbucks. I even interviewed a professional opera singer, a household-name movie star, and a former NFL offensive tackle with a Super Bowl ring. No one was safe.

Light Bulb On!

As I learned about what was going on at their secret inner core, I discovered that there were many things I thought I understood about men—but really didn't. Once I got below the surface, everything changed. I felt like a cartoon character who suddenly had a light bulb over my head.

Even better, it turned out that those revelations were mostly about things that my own husband always wished I knew but that he couldn't figure out how to explain. And that was a common refrain from most of the men I talked to. Although I still make many mistakes in my relationship with my husband—and will continue to—finally grasping these things has helped me to better appreciate and support him in the way that he needs.

These revelations were mostly things that my own husband always wished I knew but that he couldn't figure out how to explain.

And I'm not alone.

This is the second edition of this book, which originally came out in 2004. If I was surprised at these revelations about men, it was nothing to how surprised and grateful I was to see how much this message helped so many other women, men, and marriages! My team and I were flooded with thousands of e-mails from women and men sharing how simple "aha moments" had changed everything. Divorces had been canceled. Relationships were restored. How couples understood each other was changing—all because suddenly they knew one or two things they hadn't known before. This research was talked about on hundreds of media outlets and rapidly went all over the world. *For Women Only* sold more than a million copies in twenty-two different languages, precisely because these truths about men are so important and so universal.

In response to requests, Jeff and I researched and wrote the companion project, *For Men Only: A Straightforward Guide to the Inner Lives of Women,* which came out a few years later. Eventually we followed that one up with a few others in the "Only" series.

Over the last few years, we've been amazed and humbled to

see the sheer reach and impact of this research on so many women, men, teens, and families. And it all started because of a few simple, surprising, research-based truths that are updated and expanded for the second edition.

For this new edition, I have incorporated several new elements, including research I've done and new surprises I've uncovered since the original book released, as well as some key truths learned by brain scientists in recent years that often help explain why men think the way they do. I have even added an entirely new chapter—"The Thinker"—which unwraps a truth about men that I was so perplexed by before but found to be life changing once I understood what was going on. I hope you find all these "light bulb *on*!" moments to be life changing for you as well.

Why Was This Surprising?

When all this started, I and countless women I talked to were surprised to be so…surprised. Why? I think it's because we women assume we already know plenty about a man's inner life. But that may be one of our problems. Most men *know* they are confused about women. But because we don't tend to feel as confused about them, we can go for years without knowing what we don't know.

Let me give you an example. We have all heard that men are visual, but what exactly does that mean?

We all know, for example, that men are visual, but what exactly does that mean?

It turns out that what that means *in practice* is the key thing—the specific insight that can help each of us be a better wife, girlfriend, or mother. The difference is vast between having the vague notion that men are visual and knowing that the sexy commercial that just flashed across the screen might become a mental time bomb that explodes on him the next day. Or, on a different topic, the difference is vast between helplessly wondering why something made him so upset and having the insight of thousands of men to help us understand not only what is going on but also how to prevent that problem from arising in the first place.

Actually, there was a kind of double surprise in this research. When I interviewed men and drew some conclusions, they would often say, "But women already know that. Surely they know *that.*" All too frequently I found myself replying, "Well, *I* didn't know that." Thousands of other women, I've learned, don't either. And since the same is true on the men's side, no wonder we have misunderstandings and conflict!

Yet the solution is often simple. Both Jeff and I have been astounded to discover that the majority of relationship problems do not stem from the big, intractable issues. Instead, they tend to spring from basic human cluelessness. From simple, avoidable misunderstandings. From a "light bulb *on*!" moment that never happened.

EIGHT REVELATIONS

So here are the revelations this book is going to deliver—eight insights that will take you from "surface level" to "in practice" in your relationships with a husband, boyfriend, or son.

As with us women, the inner life of a man comes as a package, with all these elements melded together and wrapped up inside. Every area affects every other area, and I'm only covering those few areas that I thought were the most important, surprising, and helpful.

Our Surface Understanding		What That Means in Practice
"Men need respect."	→	*Men would rather feel unloved than inadequate and disrespected.*
"Men are insecure."	→	*Despite their "in control" exterior, men often feel like impostors and are insecure that their inadequacies will be discovered.*
"Men avoid issues by 'checking out.'"	→	*Men address issues by first pulling away to process and think—so they can better talk about them later.*

Our Surface Understanding	What That Means in Practice
"Men are providers."	→ Even if you personally made enough income to support the family's lifestyle, it would make no difference to the mental burden he feels to provide.
"Men want more sex."	→ Your sexual desire for your husband profoundly affects his sense of well-being and confidence in all areas of his life.
"Men are visual."	→ Even happily married men struggle with being pulled toward live and recollected images of other women.
"Men are unromantic."	→ Actually, most men enjoy romance (sometimes in different ways than women) and want to be romantic—but hesitate because they doubt they can succeed.
"Men care about appearance."	→ You don't need to be a size 3, but your man does need to see you making the effort to take care of yourself—and he will take on significant cost or inconvenience in order to support you.

THE SURVEYS

Although some of these revelations may be hard to believe, each has been repeatedly tested and carefully validated with highly reliable evidence—including, at last count, four groundbreaking professional, nationally representative surveys of more than sixteen hundred men. Two sets of experts have assisted me: Chuck Cowan at Analytic Focus, who is the former chief of survey design at the US Census Bureau, along with the survey team at the internationally respected firm, Decision Analyst. The surveys we developed together were meticulously planned and executed, and designed to deliver reliable results (the surveys had a 95 percent confidence level, ±3.5). In total, the anonymously surveyed men, ranging in age from twenty-one to seventy-five, answered several dozen questions about their lives and about how they think, what they feel, and what they need. The surveys stressed that we weren't dealing with outward behavior as much as with the inner thoughts and emotions that led to their behavior.

I also conducted multiple, more informal surveys, often to follow up with specific groups—for example, with a group of four hundred anonymous churchgoing men, and another of male business executives. Amazingly, across all these surveys there were very few differences.

After all the surveying, the results of my personal interviews were confirmed—when this whole thing started, I hadn't just happened to interview the weirdest men on the planet! Instead, all the anecdotes and quotes you will read in the pages ahead are backed up by statistically valid evidence.

BEFORE WE START: GROUND RULES

You're probably rarin' to turn the page. But first I'd like to offer some ground rules:

- If you're looking for male bashing or proof that your husband or boyfriend is indeed a cad, you won't find it here. I honor the men who shared their hearts with me, and I hope that by sharing their insight, more women might come to understand and appreciate the wonderful differences between us.

  If you are looking for male bashing or proof that your husband is indeed a cad, you won't find it here.

- This book is not an equal treatment of male-female differences. Nor do I deal at all with how your man should relate to *you.* Yes, we women obviously also have needs, but since the theme is the inner lives of men and my space is limited, I'm focusing entirely on how women relate to men, not the other way around. (That is also why the personal-relationship surveys did not poll gay men.) You and your man can find the "other half of the story" in *For Men Only.* (That said, if you and your mate are reading both books, one great tip is to read the book about *you* first—in other words, he reads this book and you read *For Men Only.* Highlight and make notes in the margins about which points matter most to you. Then when you trade books, you are each reading a personalized copy.)

- Realize there are exceptions to every rule. When I say that "most men" appear to think a certain way, realize that "most" means exactly that—most, not all. You or your mate may actually find that you are more like the opposite sex in some areas. The key is to sincerely look for what matters most to *your* man.
- Some readers will be dealing with serious issues beyond the scope of this book. If you or the man in your life fall in that category, please get the experienced and specialized help you need. (You can also go to forwomenonlybook.com to explore more resources.) Fortunately, understanding these points about men can make for a helpful starting point on your road to healing.
- These findings reveal how men normally think and feel, not necessarily what is right behavior. You may find some insights distressing because they affect

your view of the men in your life and your view of yourself. It would have been more comfortable for me to exclude certain statements, but I realized I was hearing things men often want us to understand but may not be willing or able to say directly to their spouses or girlfriends. Please realize that in most cases, these comments have little to do with *us*—they just reflect the way men are wired. And we should celebrate that fact. After all, it is because he is wired as a man that you love him.

- You'll notice a faith-based thread in these pages. Thousands of churches now require couples planning to get married to read this book and *For Men Only*. I also spend a lot of time speaking in the faith arena. That said, we surveyed men regardless of cultural background or religious belief, and my aim is for this book to be accessible and helpful to everyone.

The more we understand the men in our lives, the better we can support and love them in the way they need to be loved.

Finally, and most important, I hope that this journey is not just about learning intriguing new secrets. The more we understand the men in our lives, the better we can support and love them in the way they need to be loved. In other words, this revelation is supposed to change and improve *us.* In the last ten years, I've seen that in almost every case, if we are willing to do that (even if it is one-sided at first), the other outcome we so deeply desire—a more satisfying relationship with the men we love—is sure to follow.

So read on, ladies, and join me as we journey into the fascinating inner lives of men.

YOUR LOVE IS NOT ENOUGH

Why Your Respect Means More to Him than Even Your Affection

Men would rather feel unloved than inadequate and disrespected.

When I was a year or two out of college, I went on a retreat that profoundly impacted my understanding of men. The theme of the retreat was "Relationships," which as you can imagine was of great interest to a group of single young adults. For the first session, the retreat speaker divided the room in half and placed the men on one side, women on the other.

"I'm going to ask you to choose between two bad things," he said. "If you had to choose, would you rather feel alone and unloved in the world *or* would you rather feel inadequate and disrespected by everyone?"

I remember thinking, *What kind of choice is* that*? Who would ever choose to feel unloved?*

The speaker then turned to the men's side of the room. "Okay, men. Who here would rather feel alone and unloved?"

A sea of hands went up, and a giant gasp rippled across the women's side of the room.

The speaker then asked which men would rather feel disrespected, and we women watched in bemusement as only a few men lifted their hands.

Then it was our turn to answer and the men's turn to be shocked when most of the women indicated that they'd rather feel inadequate than unloved.

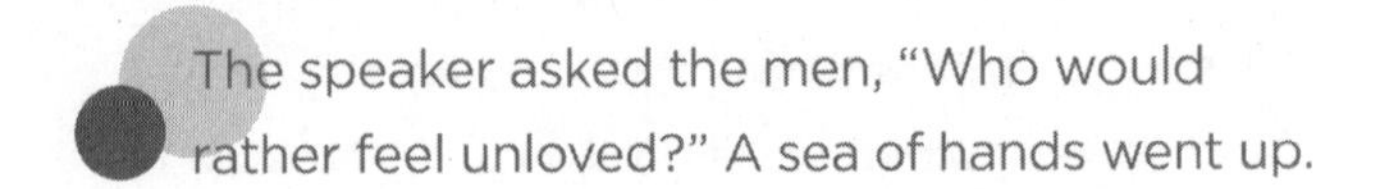

WHAT IT MEANS

While it may seem foreign to us, the male need for respect and affirmation, especially from his woman, is so hard-wired and so critical that *three out of four* men would rather feel unloved than disrespected or inadequate. In other words, if he had to choose, a man would give up feeling that his wife loved him, if he could just feel that she respected him! Look at the survey results:

Think about what these two negative experiences would be like: to feel alone and unloved in the world OR to feel inadequate and disrespected by everyone. If you were forced to choose one, which would you prefer? Would you rather feel...? (Choose one answer.)

Alone and Unloved	**74%**
Inadequate and Disrespected	**26%**

When I originally tested the survey questions, I discovered that many men had a hard time answering the "unloved versus disrespected" question. Chuck Cowan, my survey-design expert, warned me that might happen. *But why?* I wondered. *Those are two totally different things!*

Then one of my readers tested my survey questions on ten men who didn't know me. When I got the surveys back, only one note was attached: "A lot of the guys fussed over question 3 [the question above]. They did not feel the choices were different."

Finally the light bulb came on: *A man equates the two. If he feels disrespected, he is going to feel unloved.* And what that translates to is this: if you want to love your man in the way he needs to be loved, then you need to ensure that he feels your respect most of all.

The funny thing is, most of us *do* respect the men in our lives. But too often, it turns out, our words or actions convey exactly the opposite—without our ever intending it! Have you ever been totally perplexed when a man responded negatively to something and wondered, *What did I say?* Me too. As it turns out, this issue is often why.

A Disrespect Barometer

So how do we know when we've crossed the disrespect line? Thankfully, there is one easy barometer: our men's anger.

Before I elaborate, let me ask you: If you are in a conflict with the man in your life, do you think it is legitimate to break down and cry? Most of us would probably answer yes. Now let me ask another question: In that same conflict, do you think it is legitimate for your man to get really angry? Many of us have a problem with that. We'd think he's not controlling himself or that he's behaving improperly.

But Dr. Emerson Eggerichs, author of the groundbreaking book *Love and Respect,* has an entirely different interpretation. He told me, "In a relationship conflict, crying is often a woman's response to feeling unloved, and anger is often a man's response to feeling disrespected."

"Anger is often a man's response to feeling disrespected."

If a man can't articulate his feelings in the heat of the moment, he won't necessarily blurt out something helpful like "You're disrespecting me!" But rest assured, if he's angry at something you've said or done and you don't understand the cause, there is a good chance that he is feeling the pain or humiliation of your disrespect.

If you want confirmation of this, consider the response from the survey. More than *80 percent* of men—four out of five—said that in a conflict they were likely to be feeling disrespected. Whereas we girls are far more likely to be wailing, "He doesn't love me!"

Even the best relationships sometimes have conflicts on day-to-day issues. In the middle of a conflict with my wife/significant other, I am more likely to be feeling... (Choose one answer.)*

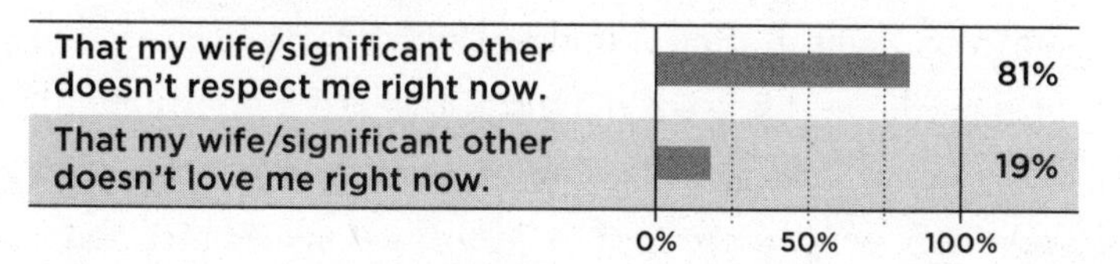

"Unconditional Respect"

Just as you need the man in your life to love you unconditionally, even when you're not particularly lovable, your man needs you to demonstrate your respect for him regardless of whether he's meeting your expectations at the moment.

"We've become such a love-dominated culture," Dr. Eggerichs says. "Like the Beatles said, 'All you need is love.' So we've come to think that love should be unconditional. But respect must be earned. Instead, what men need is unconditional respect—to be respected for who they are [that is, our husbands], apart from how they do."

Notice that in chapter 5 of the letter the apostle Paul wrote to the church in the city of Ephesus—one of the most frequently cited Bible passages on marriage—he never tells the wife to love her husband. And he never tells the husband to respect his wife (presumably because we already tend to give what we want to receive). Instead, in different ways, the passage repeatedly urges the husband to *love* his wife and the wife to *respect* her husband.

Often, we women will naturally say "I love you" but at the same time want to control things. Unfortunately, men tend to interpret this as disrespect and distrust (which it sometimes is). But marriage invites all of us to place the other person's needs above our own (he's required to do that too, remember), and it does tremendous things for your man to know that you are choosing to respect him—in other words, choosing to trust, appreciate, admire, believe in, and honor him.

It's a Choice!

And that reveals the most important aspect of demonstrating respect: It is a choice. A choice that we make out of reverence for God and love for our husbands. Just as our men can choose to demonstrate love toward us even if they don't feel it at the moment, so we can and should demonstrate respect toward them.

> Just as our men can choose to demonstrate love toward us even if they don't feel it at the moment, so we can and should choose to demonstrate respect.

What, then, is the woman to do who no longer respects the man in her life? While my surveys have found that this affects a relatively small percentage of marriages, there are certainly real issues out there. As a place to start, I encourage you to consider two factors that seem related:

First, you may be caught in what Eggerichs dubs the Crazy Cycle—the unfortunate dynamic where your man doesn't give enough love, so you don't give enough respect, so he feels slighted and doesn't give enough love...and on and on. Your choice to respect can break that cycle.

And second, feelings often follow words or actions, rather than the other way around. For example, if you regularly disparage your husband to him or to your friends, don't be surprised if you feel contempt. But your choice to show him respect can change your feelings. In fact, your choice to show respect can transform your entire relationship. I have seen and heard of thousands of lives and relationships changed by just such a one-sided choice.

IT'S NOT REAL UNLESS YOU SHOW IT

Which brings us to what respecting a man looks like in practice. You wouldn't believe the number of men who told me that they do recognize, deep down, that their mates respect, value, and appreciate them...but the problem is that their wives don't necessarily show it outwardly—or even know how.

Want to know what respecting your husband but not showing it feels like to him? Well, consider that awful joke: "Why do I have to tell my wife I love her? I told her that when we got married!" Just as a wife feels dreadful if her husband never expresses his love, so a husband feels dreadful if a wife never demonstrates her respect. To him, it's the very stuff of love and it's not negotiable.

Of course, the way he needs to feel your respect is quite different from the way you need to feel his love. Most women appreciate it when a husband says, "I love you." But, as I discovered pretty quickly, it just doesn't do it for a guy to hear his wife coo, "Oh, honey, I respect you *so* much." He *does* need to hear, "Honey, I'm so proud of you" and "I trust you" and "Thank you for what you did." But demonstrating through your day-to-day actions that you do truly respect him often means even more than words.

> The way a man needs to feel your respect is quite different from the way you need to feel his love.

The surveys came back with some practical insights on how we can do just that. Men's comments revealed six key needs.

Need 1: Respect His Judgment

The men were really touchy about this. A man deeply needs the woman in his life to respect his knowledge, opinions, and decisions—what I would call his judgment. No one wanted a silent wallflower (nor would I advocate becoming one!), but many men wished their mates wouldn't question their knowledge or argue with their decisions all the time. It's a touchy (and difficult) thing in these liberated days, but what it really comes down to is their need for us to defer to them sometimes.

I find that I can easily show respect on the positive side—for example, I can demonstrate that I respect Jeff by calling on his knowledge in a given subject. But sometimes it is a lot harder for me *not* to show *dis*respect. It takes a lot more effort to defer to his judgment when I want to seize control, since of course I think my way is right! In those scenarios, I can discover too late that my husband might have had a point—or I have argued an issue (and him) right into the ground. Can you relate?

Sadly, many men confessed that they felt as if their opinions and decisions were actively valued in every area of their lives *except* at home. In fact, several men explicitly told me that their comrades at work seemed to trust their judgment more than their own wives did. While a man's colleagues will rarely tell him what to do (asking, suggesting, or collaborating on the decision instead), more than one wife has fallen into the habit of ordering him around like one of the kids.

Early in my marriage, I unconsciously made that mistake far too many times. Jeff finally told me how stupid it made him feel, and hearing that was enough to shake me of the habit. On the surveys, many men said the one thing they wished they could tell their wives was to "show more trust in my decision-making abilities," which is code for (among other things) "I'm not stupid."

Need 2: Respect His Abilities

Another strong theme that emerged was that men want—even need—to figure things out for themselves. And if they can, they feel like they have conquered something and are affirmed as men. For some reason, spending hours figuring out how to put together the new DVD player is fun. Problem is, we want to help them. And guess how they interpret that? You got it: distrust. (It's a wonder *any* relationships work and that the human race didn't die out millennia ago!)

And, of course, our attention is not all benign. Sometimes we truly don't have confidence that our men can figure things out on their own. On the survey, one man wished he could tell his wife, "Have confidence in my general abilities of learning, application, fixing, rebuilding, repair, etc., without having to do it your way because you know it and think I do not."

Problem is, we want to help them. And guess how they interpret that? You got it: distrust.

"Honey, Will You Please Just Ask...?"

It turns out that the old joke about men never wanting to stop and ask for directions is based on this truth—that men love figuring things out for themselves. If they can find their way through the hazards of the concrete jungle with only a tattered map and their wits, they feel like they've conquered something. They feel affirmed, excited, encouraged, alive.

Realizing that, now put yourself in your man's shoes and listen to this phrase: "Honey, can we *please* just stop and ask for directions?" While your overwhelming impulse is simply to get practical help, his is to conquer Everest, thank you very much. And here you are telling him you don't believe he can do it. And remember how important it is to a guy that his mate believes in him! When you tell him to ask for directions, you're telling him point-blank that you don't trust him to figure it out for himself.

Now, if you're like me, you're probably saying to yourself, "You're right, I don't! How on earth could he know how to find the highway entrance in this maze of streets?"

Well, there you have it, don't you? Are you going to decide to trust him or not? This particular "Will I trust him?" question is just a metaphor for all the little trust choices we make. I've talked to dozens of men about this, and here is their near-unanimous opinion: "Let him do it."

Several men said something like, "I'm not an idiot, okay? If I didn't think I could find what I was looking for, why would I be trying?" One said, "I may have no idea where I'm going. But it's fun; it's a challenge to try to find my own way. And I'm not stupid—I've got a clock on the dashboard. I know whether we're going to be late or not."

Little Things Add Up to One Big Clue

We don't realize that the act of forcing ourselves to trust our men in these little things means so much to them. But it does. It's not a big deal to us, so we don't get that it's a big deal to them. We don't get that our responses to these little choices to trust or not trust—or at least act like we do—are interpreted as signs of our overall trust and respect for them as men.

The next time your husband stubbornly drives in circles, ask yourself which is more important: being on time to the party or his feeling trusted? No contest.

Next time your husband stubbornly drives in circles, ask yourself which is more important: being on time to the party or his feeling trusted?

Don't Tell Him How

The 1984 movie *The Natural* provides a powerful example of a woman's respect for a man.[1] Robert Redford plays an amazing baseball talent who, after mysteriously leaving his girlfriend and dropping out of sight for years, has finally gotten to the major leagues. After taking the world by storm, he suddenly hits a humiliating slump and starts doubting himself. In one powerful scene, his old flame watches from the stands as he strikes out again and again. When the dispirited Redford comes up for his final at bat, to scattered boos from the crowd, she suddenly stands up, alone, in the stands. Somehow he senses her presence, awakes from his slumber, and slams a home run, reigniting his passion and his game.

One man, explaining why he loves that scene, said, "She just stood up and supported him. She didn't come down from the stands and tell him what to do or how to fix what was wrong. She didn't tell him how to hold his bat. She just supported him and let *him* figure it out."

Another man agreed. "She stood up and publicly said, 'I know you can do it.' For any man, especially if he is in a season of self-doubt, that is exactly what he needs to be able to hit a home run in life."

"She stood up and publicly said, 'I know you can do it.' For any man, that is exactly what he needs to be able to hit a home run."

Ladies, it is so easy for us to bristle at this idea and say, "Why can't I tell him how to hold his bat? We're equal partners! What if I know how better than he does?"

Well, of course, you *can* tell him. Most of us are perfectly competent to advise our men in all sorts of areas. But remember, he's the one up to bat, with his feeling of competency on the line.

True advice usually isn't a problem. But advice can quickly become instruction, and there we are again, trying to get in the batter's box and do it for him, implying that he can't do it himself.

Even thinking about this makes me cringe because it reminds me of the times I've inadvertently sent the message that I don't believe in my husband. Too often during Jeff's times of self-doubt with his business, I have tried to "support" him with advice—good, constructive advice, mind you. But I noticed that often demoralizes more than helps. To him, it meant that the person who knew him best didn't believe he could do it. What he most needed was for me to simply stand up and say, "I know you can do it." (See? I've been studying men for ten years and still mess up too often. Maybe in year eleven this will finally click...)

Some of you might be wondering, *But what if my man has so disappointed me that I feel that supporting him would just condone his mistakes?* If so, consider what another man pointed out: "That movie scene is a powerful illustration of what can happen when a woman chooses to honor and respect her man publicly, even when he may not deserve it. Instead of that choice somehow being demeaning or unfair to her, her act of showing respect lifted them both up."

Need 3: Respect What He Accomplishes

Now that you see how painful it is to a man to feel disrespected, and how important it is to him to figure things out on his own, perhaps you can see that very few things are as powerful to a man as feeling that he has tried something, accomplished it, done it well—and someone noticed.

I didn't see how profound this need was until a few years after the original edition came out, when my friend Lisa Rice and I were researching *For Parents Only.* We found that girls and women tended to have deep, hidden questions like, *Am I special? Am I lovable?* and thus needed to feel special and worthy of being loved for who they were on the inside. But the men and boys really didn't have those questions. Instead, they worried, *Do I measure up? Am I any good at what I do?* In other words: they deeply need to feel noticed, able, and appreciated for what they do on the outside.

We women need to feel special and worthy of being loved for who we are on the inside. Men need to feel able and appreciated for what they do on the outside.

As strange as it sounds to us, saying "You did a great job at that meeting" or "You are such a great dad" is far more emotionally powerful to a man than hearing "I love you." In the survey for my upcoming book, *Seven Secrets of Highly Happy Marriages,* more than seven out of ten men said that if their wives simply noticed something and said thank you, it had a big impact on their happiness level.

When (or if) your wife does the [action] below, choose the impact [it] has on you, in terms of how happy or "filled up" it makes you:

Noticing when I do something and sincerely thanking me for it. (For example, "Thank you for mowing the lawn even though it was so hot outside" or "Thanks for playing with the kids, even when you were so tired from work.") (Choose one answer.)

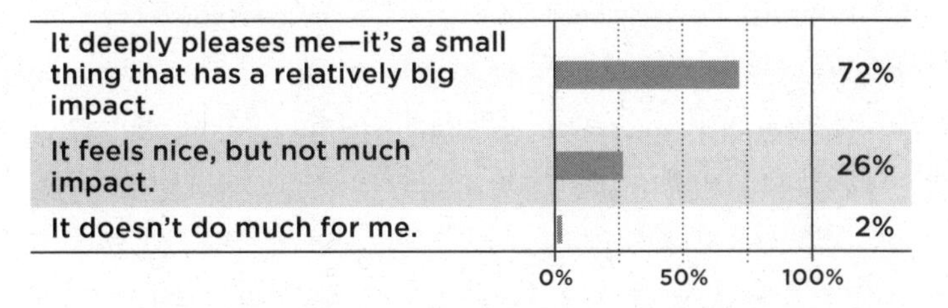

I cannot tell you the number of times a man has shared how secretly painful it is when his wife tries to thank him but instead sends the (accidental!) signal "But it wasn't good enough." As one man told me, "She'll come into the kitchen after I've finished wiping down all the countertops. I'm proud it looks so good, and she'll say, 'Thanks, honey. Oh, but you missed the crumbs under the toaster.' Under the toaster! I know she doesn't mean 'You've failed,' but privately it just kills me."

Many women have been confused about why their men would say, "Nothing I do is good enough for you." *Huh?* Well, guess what: that is a giant red flag. Without realizing it, we've been sending them the ultimate in painful messages: "You tried... and failed."

Thankfully, even simple appreciation (if it is undiluted by criticism) is powerful. One of my favorite speaking formats is when pastors interview me on these subjects at sermon time. One Sunday I was with Andy Stanley, pastor of North Point Community Church near Atlanta, when he relayed to the congregation something I'll never forget—a conversation where he told his wife, "If you never told me that you loved me again, but throughout our marriage you simply told me how proud you are...I'm not sure I would miss 'I love you' because of what it means in my heart to hear that you're proud of me. It is that big of a deal."

Need 4: Respect in Communication

Women wield incredible power in the way we communicate with our men (including our sons)—power to build up or to tear down, to encourage or to exasperate. Some things just push a man's buttons or are extremely painful in ways we don't realize. This goes beyond *what* we say, such as questioning a man's judgment or his abilities, and into *how* we say it (and *where* we say it, which is the subject of the next section).

Some things just push a man's buttons or are painful. This goes beyond what we say—and into how we say it.

In interviews, a large number of men said something like, "When my wife says something disrespectful, I often think, *I can't believe she doesn't know how that makes me feel!*" I had to reassure these men over and over that their wives probably didn't mean to disrespect them and were likely just clueless.

Let me give you several common examples of how a man might hear something negative where the woman never intended it.

Hearing Disrespect

At one point I was asking Jeff and one of his married colleagues about the dynamic of men wanting to do things for themselves. This man said, "Sometimes, if something breaks in the house, I want to try to take a crack at it before I call an expert. If my wife says, 'Well, you're really not a fix-it–type person,' I feel so insulted. She's not rude about it or anything, but it's like she doesn't respect me enough to believe that I can figure it out if I put my mind to it, even if it takes me a while."

This man's wife is one of my closest friends, and I know that she fully respects her husband. So it was an eyeopener to hear that what was (to her) an offhand remark was something he took extremely seriously—and, if I may delicately say so, extremely wrong.

Hearing Disappointment

In the survey, as in life, a sizable minority of men read something negative into a simple female reminder. I asked men what would go through their minds if their wives or significant others reminded them that the kitchen wall was damaged and it still had to be fixed. More than one-third of these men took that reminder as nagging or as an accusation of laziness or mistrust.

Early in the research, I met with my friend and book agent, Calvin Edwards, at Starbucks to start designing the original survey questions. When we saw a local pastor Calvin knew, I ran the "kitchen wall" question by him and asked what would go through his mind. Consider his illuminating response:

> *Pastor:* I'm irritated because I have to be reminded. I hate being reminded.
>
> *Calvin:* Why is that a problem? Look at your day planner

there—you set up systems to remind yourself of things all the time.

Pastor: Inherent in her reminder is a statement of disappointment. For me as a man, that is saying that I failed. I hate to fail. It's not the statement that bothers me; it's the implications of the statement.

Now, it's interesting that those who jumped to negative conclusions were still in the minority. A larger group—fully half of the men polled—simply didn't place as high a priority on the task as their wives did and said it would get done eventually.

Hearing Attacks

I got an excellent example of how our words can be misinterpreted as an attack when Chuck Cowan and I were discussing a survey question I had drafted: "Do you know how to put together a romantic event that your partner would enjoy?"

Chuck: That question won't work because you're starting off in attack mode.

Me: Huh?

Chuck: You're starting off suggesting the man is inept.

Me (thinking to myself): *Suggesting the man is inept? What is he talking about?*

Chuck: Soften it a bit—put it into a context that isn't so blatant.

Simply by adding a context sentence to the beginning—"Suppose you had to plan an anniversary event for your partner. Do you know how...?"—the question was softer and deemed just fine to not question a man's adequacy.

No matter what we think we are saying, in the end what matters is what the guy is hearing. Now, obviously, some people can be overly sensitive, and we can't walk on eggshells all the time. Nor do we want to pass up all opportunities to help men understand our communication wiring. But considering that most men appear to be highly sensitive to disrespect—including seeing it where none is intended—I would argue that it is not the average man who needs to be less sensitive to a woman's words, but the average woman who needs to be more sensitive to her man's feelings.

No matter what we think we are saying, in the end what matters is what the guy is hearing.

After all, don't we want our men to adjust to *our* sensitivities? Do you want your husband to publicly tease you about gaining ten pounds? It's all about loving each other the way the other person needs to be loved.

Need 5: Respect in Public

There is an epidemic of public disrespect for men today, and the biggest culprit is not television, movies, or other media but the women who are supposed to love their men most.

"The Most Fragile Thing on the Planet"

Dozens of men told me how painful it is when their wives or girlfriends criticize them in public, put them down, or even question their judgment in front of others. One very representative man on the survey said that the one thing he wished he could tell his wife was that "at a minimum, she should be supportive of me in public."

Dozens of men told me how painful it is when their wives or girlfriends criticize them in public.

Consider this statement, which I have heard (in essence) from many men: "My wife says things about me in public that she considers teasing. I consider them torture."

One married man put it starkly: "The male ego is the most fragile thing on the planet. Women have this thought that *He's got such a huge ego that I need to take him down a peg.* No way. The male ego is incredibly fragile."

We women often think of this as male pride—but that isn't

it. What is at stake isn't his pride as much as his secret feelings of inadequacy as a man. There's a big difference between feeling prideful and feeling adequate. What happens in public isn't that his "inflated" pride is brought down to ground level but that something made him feel inadequate and humiliated as a man. Disrespect in public is so painful that men will avoid it at any cost. In fact, many unmarried men described it as a major (if unseen) factor leading to a breakup instead of marriage. As one twenty-something man told me, "I don't want to live with that for the rest of my life."

Teasing Can Be Torture

Even good-natured teasing can sometimes be humiliating, not to mention more pointed jabs. Many of us have wondered why men who normally have a great sense of humor get upset by a little public joking at their expense. I was writing the original version of this chapter at my computer one day over the holidays, and my parents were around. I asked my dad a question, and my husband came into the office as we were talking. The resulting discussion was so fascinating—and foundational—that I started typing it into my file. Here is a portion:

> *Me:* What sort of teasing might a man take wrong?
>
> *Dad:* Anything that seems to show that the man is not somehow in control or not getting respect from his

wife. A man would never take that from another man, unless he wanted a fight.

Me: But what if she's truly teasing? Like they're out with friends, and the wife says, "Oh, the dishwasher broke," and she teases her husband about wanting to fix it when he's not a handyman?

Dad: Oh, that's terrible. You never want to do that. The guy is the protector, provider, and is supposed to take care of everything. This sort of teasing lets everyone know that he doesn't know how to take care of everything. It also lets everyone know how the wife feels about him—she's making light of something that is really important to him! But if a guy feels that he ought to be able to do something as the provider and he can't, he never makes light of it in his heart.

Jeff: It all depends on whether that particular guy already feels inadequate in that area. That same thing may not hit another man wrong.

Me: Does it make a difference if the wife is teasing him in front of men or women?

Dad: Oh, it's much worse in front of men. After an incident early on in our marriage, I asked your mom, "Please don't *ever* embarrass me in front of another man."

Me: Why?

Dad: Guys are always in competition with one another.

Your wife is the person who knows you better than anyone, and if she doesn't respect you, how can you expect another man to?

Jeff: It's also humiliating to know that the other guy feels sorry for me because my wife doesn't respect me.

Dad: Even worse, if the other man doesn't know you well, it is a sign of weakness. The other man is thinking, *If this guy's own wife doesn't respect him, he's nothing. We'll run him over the next time we do a deal together.* If you belittle your husband in front of another man, you can even ruin his career. I'm not kidding. Because any man he works with will now see him as weak.

Me: Back to the teasing question…

Dad: You have to understand—men don't let down their guards easily, particularly with other men, unless they are very close. Most men probably crave a situation where they can, but they aren't naturally made that way—it's all a competition instead. The only time a guy's guard is completely down is with the woman he loves. So she can pierce his heart like no one else.

"The only time a guy's guard is completely down is with the woman he loves. So she can pierce his heart like no one else."

Showing Public Respect Goes a Long Way

Learning how important public respect is to men, I have become much more sensitive to how often we talk negatively about them behind their backs. Not just because it matters to them, but because it affects how we feel about them: the more we express dissatisfaction, the more deeply it lodges in our hearts. I have a dear friend who loves her husband but also regularly complains about him. I'm convinced that's one of the main reasons she can't shake a nagging dissatisfaction with their relationship—a dissatisfaction that then affects him.

But on the positive side, just as your man is hurt by public disrespect, so will he think you are the most wonderful woman in the world if you publicly build him up. This is not artificial; you simply take those little opportunities to honestly praise him or to ask his opinion in front of others. Do you think he's a great father? Tell your dinner guests a story about something he did with the kids yesterday that proves it. Are you impressed with his managerial acumen? Brag on the way he solved a crisis at work. Did he take the kids out and let you sleep in Saturday morning? Tell your book club and make the other girls jealous.

Trust me—from the men I've talked to, that is the equivalent of his coming home to you with a dozen roses and a surprise date night without the kids. He will feel *adored*.

Need 6: Respect in Our Assumptions

Unfortunately, in one area, men have every right to read something negative into what we say. Listen to what you say to him or assume about him over the next few days. You may be astounded at how often you assume something bad. See if any of these negative assumptions ring a bell.

We Assume He Needs to be Reminded

To us, repeatedly asking "Have you done it yet?" doesn't seem like a big deal. But inherent in the question is our assumption that guys need the reminder—that they are either incapable of remembering on their own or that they remember but need our prodding to do the job. It's no wonder many men hate being nagged. What they are accurately hearing is "I don't trust you."

Instead, what if we were to assume the best of them rather than the worst? For example: *I asked him to do it. He hasn't done it. I trust my husband. Therefore, there's a* reason *he hasn't done it.*

Just realize, although his reason for not doing the task may be different from yours, that makes it no less legitimate. Remember, half the men on the survey indicated that sometimes they just have different priorities than their wives do. Or they could just be unable to handle one more thing. Remember the "kitchen wall" question I posed to the pastor at Starbucks? Here's how he put it:

I've revealed something about my preferences and priorities by *not* fixing it for a week. If I come home with the world on my shoulders—if a couple at church is divorcing or I'm worried that a key employee might leave—and my wife is in her house mode and says the living room fern is dying, that is hard for me to engage in. The brutal truth is that it's not as important to me. My first response is, "Get a fern doctor." But Scripture says that as a husband, I have to lay down my life for my wife, so sometimes I have to talk about the fern. But we have a little code now, where I'll tell her it's "fern doctor stuff" to let her know that sometimes my brain just doesn't go there.

We Assume He's Choosing Not to Help

A marriage counselor shared this example: "If my husband doesn't help with the kids or the cleaning, I shouldn't assume that he sees it and is choosing not to help. I should start with the assumption that he doesn't see it."

It turns out that avoiding this assumption is important for more than just our man's well-being. In my recent research, I found that one of the main reasons happy couples are so happy is because they always try to assume that their spouses have good intentions toward them.

We Assume It's Because of Him

Finally (and this may be a shocking thought), some things are not his fault—*they're ours.* We can assign unloving motives to our men for actions that can actually be traced back to something we have inadvertently said or done. For example, a wife who is constantly critical of her husband may spur him to withdraw emotionally to protect himself, thereby becoming unloving where he wasn't before.

"Men are not stupid," says Dr. Eggerichs. "They are not Neanderthals. Sometimes these behaviors that appear to be unloving are not unloving at all. They are reacting that way because they interpret something as disrespect. Even if sometimes they shouldn't."

SO WHAT SHOULD WE DO?

We as women hold incredible power. And responsibility. And opportunity. We have the ability to either build up or tear down our men. We can either strengthen or hobble them in ways that go far beyond our relationship, because respect at home affects every area of a man's life. There is something in how a man approaches the world that makes his inner, home-fired feelings of personal adequacy absolutely foundational to everything else.

So what should we do? As one man powerfully put it, "Always assume the best, and you will find it easier to show respect." Simple as it sounds, from now on we can choose to show that we appreciate, trust, and respect the men in our lives, and choose *not* to demonstrate disrespect, starting with never humiliating them in public.

If there are areas in which you find it difficult to trust your man, realize that you can be respectful even when you are wrestling with a real area of concern. Don't ignore problems, but find things you can appreciate and applaud regardless. The apostle Paul advised the Christians in Philippi to choose to "rejoice" by focusing on whatever is good and worthy of praise.

In fact, given how positively motivated a man is by his woman believing in him, and how demotivated he is by the sense that she doesn't, verbally praising the positives is *especially* vital for a man who needs to overcome past failure.

And when we realize that *we* have messed up—maybe for years—we can acknowledge our fault and ask for forgiveness. In my years of speaking on the importance of respect to a man, I have been so touched to see how forgiving most men are when wives or girlfriends suddenly get it. I have had dozens of men come up to me in private, with tears of gratitude, to tell me something like, "She came home last night and said, 'I'm so sorry. I had no idea how much I was hurting you.' I can't tell you how much that meant to me."

As we move forward, we'll inevitably blow it sometimes. We'll see the anger or withdrawal that signals our men are suffering the pain of our disrespect. But when that happens, men recommended we avoid saying, "I'm sorry I made you *feel* XYZ" (since, as one man put it, "That implies 'I wasn't disrespectful, and you shouldn't feel that way' "). Instead, they recommended simply saying something like, "I'm really sorry I said that—it was disrespectful. I know I can trust you."

It's Not Just for Them, but for Us

Consider this man's plea: "She has to make me feel respected so that I can command respect out in the world. If she defeats me emotionally, I can't win the race and bring home the prize for her."

Another man told me, "You know that saying 'Behind every good man is a great woman'? Well, that is *so true.* If a man's wife is supportive and believes in him, he can conquer the world—or at least his little corner of it. He will do better at work, at home, everywhere. By contrast, very few men can do well at work *or* at home if their wives make them feel inadequate."

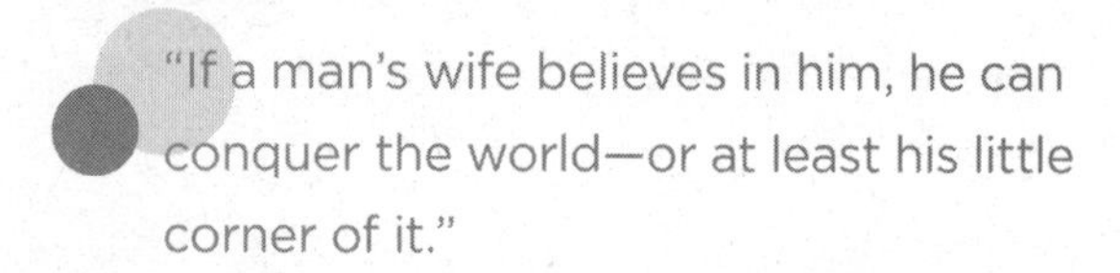

As you now have glimpsed, inside their confident exterior many men are vulnerable and even insecure. That is the subject of the next chapter.

---

* To avoid confusion, be aware that I am using the words *girlfriend, significant other,* and *partner* interchangeably, with no particular meaning as to age, seriousness of the relationship, or living arrangements. For consistency, I used the words *wife / significant other* throughout the surveys.

THE PERFORMANCE OF A LIFETIME

Why Your Mr. Smooth Looks So Impressive but Feels Like an Impostor

Despite their "in control" exterior, men often feel like impostors and are insecure that their inadequacies will be discovered.

At the risk of admitting that I am a closet Trekkie, let me take you to an old episode of *Star Trek: The Next Generation.*[2] The confident captain, Jean-Luc Picard, and his friend Dr. Beverly Crusher are (of course) stuck on a dangerous and unfamiliar planet. And their predicament has an interesting twist: because of some alien meddling, the two can hear each other's thoughts.

As the captain leads them toward help, he scans the unfamiliar horizon, motions in a particular direction, and says, with his usual commanding certainty, "This way."

Since she can hear what he is actually thinking, the doctor stares at him and says, "You don't really know, do you? You're acting like you know exactly which way to go, but you're only guessing!" Then, with growing amazement, she asks, "Do you do this all the time?"

He gives her a look, then answers, "There are times when it is necessary for a captain to give the appearance of confidence." Dr. Crusher had just discovered what most of us never grasp—that the men in our lives are hiding a deep sense of self-doubt.

> Dr. Crusher had just discovered what most of us never grasp—that the men in our lives are hiding a deep self-doubt.

This inner uncertainty leaves even the most confident-seeming man dreading the moment when he will be exposed for who he really is—or at least believes himself to be.

An impostor.

"THEY ARE GOING TO FIND ME OUT!"

Most men have an inner vulnerability that we don't even know is there, stemming from a set of competing core needs and fears.

Something deep inside them wants to tackle a great challenge and try difficult things...but at the same time, they find the idea of failing excruciating. One of their greatest emotional needs is to feel competent and successful at what they do, especially in front of others...but at the same time, they have a deep conviction that what they do is always being watched and judged. Hence the reason for this deep, unseen insecurity: they so deeply want to succeed but feel that they are one mess-up from being found out.

In all my surveys, no matter how I asked the question, no matter how successful a man was, and no matter how secure they looked on the outside, around three-fourths admitted to this insecurity about whether they could hack it and what others think of them. Whether it was about being a good husband, father, mechanic, businessman, or student, they deeply wanted to do well, and tried to look confident but felt insecure.

Look at the stark results from the national survey I conducted for my workplace book *The Male Factor* when I asked if the men ever instinctively felt certain ways:

"I am not always as confident as I look."

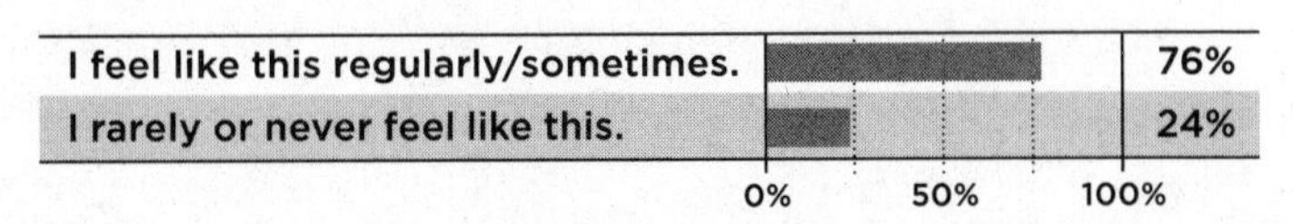

Just as the heart cry of a woman tends to be, *Am I loveable?* the secret heart cry of a man is, *Do I measure up?* And he is looking to those around him—especially the woman who knows him best—for clues to the answer to that question.

In one follow-up survey I did with four hundred churchgoers, 72 percent of the men said, "I try to perform well and look as competent as possible, when inside I sometimes feel insecure and am concerned about others' opinion of me and my abilities."

To compensate for his insecurity—and his feeling of being watched—a man may feel the need to work long hours to prove to his wife that he can provide for his family. Or he may get emotionally worn down by the constant need to look on the ball at work.

One thing is certain: the idea of someone thinking he can't cut it is humiliating—a feeling every man wants to avoid at all costs. So he puts up a good front so others will think he's highly competent. And there we are, back at the beginning. In the spotlight stands a man—maybe your husband—feeling sure that if anyone (even his wife) really knew him for what he was, they'd know the truth. The truth that—at least some of the time—he is not what he appears to be.

The idea of someone thinking he can't cut it is humiliating—a feeling every man wants to avoid at all costs.

WHAT'S DRIVING HIM?

You and I watch the men in our lives go off to work every day, joke with friends, and take physical risks without flinching. And if you're like me, it never once crosses your mind that he lacks confidence, that deep inside he feels like a poser. *I have full confidence in him and his abilities,* you think. *Why wouldn't* he*?* But the facts show that he doesn't. Here's what the surveys show he's really feeling.

"I'm Always Being Judged"

Men told me they are hard enough on themselves without any external pressure. Add in the conviction that the eyes of the world are critically trained on them, and you suddenly see how uncomfortable and insecure they might feel. One man put it this way: "We think about what others think about us *all the time.*" One male friend shared an amusing anecdote that perfectly captured this myopic male certainty:

> When I was in college, I drove one of the school transit buses part-time to earn money. Sometimes, when I had no one on board, I drove—um—rather quickly. One day I came hurtling around a corner, and there was an elderly man standing at the bus stop, shaking his head no at me.

> It irritated me that he was disapproving of my driving! Years later I lived in New York City, and one day I shook my head no to tell an approaching bus driver not to stop because I didn't need his particular route. Suddenly it hit me: All those years ago that elderly man had just been saying no, he didn't need my route. Instead, I built up this whole assumption that he had examined my performance and found me wanting. That is a silly example, but it's what every guy does.

This man went on to clarify, "It's your abilities *and* you that are being judged. Men aren't always as sure of themselves as they look. That's why, when your wife makes a joke at your expense in front of other people, it's a knife."

"I Have No Earthly Idea How to Do This"

Another male friend illustrated the impostor complex with this story:

> A young friend of mine had just gotten a job as a college professor. He had never done these particular lesson plans, so he was running to stay one step ahead of his students. Often he would literally be one day ahead of them in the textbook. One evening, one of his students ran into him

> on campus and said she was looking forward to his class in the morning. She said, "I wish I knew as much as you do about this stuff." He smiled and nodded, but inside he was thinking, *Tomorrow, you will!*

My friend said, "That is a perfect description of how many men feel as they go through life, especially whenever they do something unfamiliar—which most of us have to do all the time. A client may be asking me to do something new, and I may be smiling and nodding, but in the back of my mind, I'm thinking, *I have no earthly idea how to do this, and I hope I can learn it before they find out.*"

What was startling about this conversation is that I have worked with this man for years, and he is an extremely competent businessman. I had originally thought that maybe this dynamic only affected younger, less-experienced men. But hearing the same thing from those who are highly accomplished helped me realize just how deep-seated this vulnerability is.

"But I Want to Do This!"

The doubt our men experience regarding their ability to pull things off has an interesting partner—their deep desire to take on something new and exciting. These two feelings may seem contradictory, but they are all part of the male package. Men want to conquer Everest (or at least the mean streets of the city), but they also know they risk taking a humiliating tumble on the way. One man put it this way:

> When a guy does something that he's never done before and he's being paid for it, he thinks, *I* can *do this, but what if they find out this is my first time?* There's a joke among some guys that you're going to be talking in front of a group sometime, and your fourth-grade teacher's going to run in and say, "He doesn't know what he's talking about! He was a D student!" It's this irrational, debilitating fear that you'll publicly be found out. And sooner or later, every man has to face it. Because if you want to move up, that will inevitably mean doing something new.

As you might guess, those times—whether at work or at home—are when men feel the shakiest and need the most encouragement from us.

THE IMPOSTOR AT WORK

A man's uncertainty about his adequacy on the job can take a huge toll. One man said, "We have incredible anxiety over where we stand at work. I start to think that the fact that my boss isn't communicating with me means that he's found me out. This creates intense anxiety and uncertainty."

"I Want to See You First Thing Monday Morning..."

Frank Maguire helped start Federal Express and earlier held an inside position in the Kennedy White House. His book *You're the Greatest* takes us inside the unique torture of a man's workplace anxiety.

Every Friday as he left the FedEx office, Maguire called his good-byes to FedEx founder, Fred Smith, and Fred would call back, "Thanks for going the extra mile this week." Maguire always left with a bounce in his step.

Then came the Friday when his cheery good-bye was met with, "Frank, I want to see you first thing, Monday morning."

"I had a lousy weekend," Maguire said. "Not only me, but my wife, my kids, even Thor, the wonder dog. We all had a miserable weekend."

On Monday, when he nervously asked Fred, "What did you want to talk to me about?" he was met with a puzzled look. "Oh, I forgot. It wasn't important."

You can guess why Frank Maguire had a miserable weekend—he was expecting to be fired. But why would he think that? He was a successful, valued executive at a fast-growing business. He had even been trusted by the president of the United States. So why did he assume a neutral comment was a portent of woe?

Because inside he felt like an impostor. And he was sure he had just been found out.

Inside he felt like an impostor. And he was sure he had just been found out.

Maguire wrote, "I've been around many powerful leaders. On the surface, they looked totally secure. You would never guess there was even one ounce of fear. But my experience has also convinced me that no matter what your title or position in life is, we all, no exceptions, carry our treasures in fragile containers."[3]

"We're All on the Replacement List"

One of the most revealing interviews I conducted was with Ken Ruettgers, a former all-pro offensive tackle with the Super Bowl champion Green Bay Packers. He now helps retiring athletes make the difficult transition into well-balanced, regular lives.

When I told him the subject of this chapter, he jumped on it. "I've never seen so many insecurities as in the locker room," he said. Surprised, I asked him why. Here's his explanation:

> Because the guys are naked on the field. They have two or three hours to prove themselves, and there's no fooling the camera. Once you look through the mask, you've got the most insecure guys ever. They try to put up a great front, but once they know each other really well, they'll ask, "How'd I do on that play?" They are just looking for affirmation.
>
> And it's not just the camera—it's the knowledge that some guys are going to get cut. [Another all-pro football player] put it this way: "We're all on the replacement list. You just want to stay off the top of it."
>
> You know, sports is like corporate America—there's a "What have you done for me lately?" attitude. It's incredibly draining, and there is a huge, unspoken fear of failure.

Ken went on to make an important point. "Keep in mind that guys can use that fear of failure for good. It gets you out of bed in the morning. It gets you to the gym when you wouldn't go otherwise."

Ken's words helped me realize why so many men—talented, effective men—work such long hours. Sometimes the long hours are a necessity for the job. But not always. Sometimes they are (in the guy's mind) an insurance against fear—fear of falling behind, fear of being cut from the team.

THE IMPOSTOR AT HOME

One of the things that surprised me the most in all my research was that a man's performance anxiety doesn't, as one man put it, "just end when we walk through the front door." Many feel just as inadequate at home. The majority of men do want to be good husbands. But in the same way they worry that they may not know everything about being a good employee, they secretly worry that they don't know how to succeed at being a good husband, father, provider, or handyman.

"At least at work," one man told me, "I have an idea of how to succeed—work hard, get ahead, complete assignments, and get in good with the boss. At home, what is the measure of success? How do I know whether I am a success or a failure?"

Not surprisingly, men said they judge themselves—and feel that others judge them—based on the happiness and respect of their wives.

If a man feels like he's trying to bluff his way through this being-a-husband thing, you can imagine his relief when he can tell that his wife feels loved and happy, or when she publicly honors him and his "husband abilities." And conversely, you can imagine the trepidation he feels when he receives the cold shoulder confirmation that he got it wrong again, that he is indeed an impostor, that he doesn't know what he's doing in his personal life. One man wrote me a note about this:

I don't know one man who thinks he has all the answers when it comes to being a good father or husband. If we've had good fathers, then we try and remember what our fathers would do in the situation. If we didn't have good fathers, we feel like we're making it up as we go. If my wife often challenges my decisions or appears displeased with me as a husband—it's the impostor all over again. It may even cause a man to withdraw from taking an active role in the lives of his wife and kids if he doesn't think he can do it well or be affirmed in it. That's not a rational or Christlike approach by the man, for sure, but that is how some guys feel.

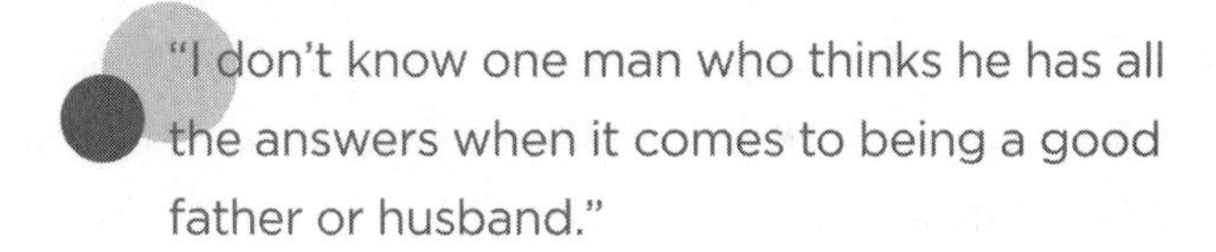

"I don't know one man who thinks he has all the answers when it comes to being a good father or husband."

WHAT SHOULD WE DO?

So what on earth can we do about this? You and I aren't responsible for changing how a man is wired. But we can certainly affect how he feels about his ability to make his way in the world. In particular, as you have probably guessed by now, men's private doubt about whether they measure up is the reason why our respect (chapter 2) matters so much to them. Once we understand what our husbands secretly feel and think, our words and actions can make a huge difference.

"Affirmation Is Everything"

Have you ever noticed how the adulterous woman in the book of Proverbs seduces the unwitting young man? It's not with sex (okay, not *just* with sex); it's with flattery. "She threw her arms around him...and with a brazen look she said, 'I've offered my sacrifices and just finished my vows. It's you I was looking for!'.... With her flattery she enticed him. He followed her at once."

Flattery is simply a seductive counterfeit for affirmation. As one marriage counselor told me, "Affirmation is everything. When a man is affirmed, he can conquer the world. When he's not, he is sapped of his confidence and even his feeling of manhood. And believe me, he will, consciously or unconsciously, seek out places where he receives affirmation."

Fortunately for us, home is by far the most important place for a man to be affirmed. If a man knows that the person who knows him best believes in him, he is empowered to do better in every area of his life. A man tends to think of life as a competition and a battle, and he can go duke it out if he can come home to someone who supports him unconditionally, who will wipe his brow and tell him he can do it. As one of our close friends told me, "It's all about whether my wife thinks I can do it. A husband can slay dragons, climb mountains, and win great victories if *he* believes his *wife* believes that he can."

Don't Tear Him Down!

If, instead of affirming, a wife reinforces her husband's feelings of inadequacy, it can become a self-fulfilling prophecy. For example, if she focuses her attention on what he is doing wrong in the relationship, she can unwittingly undermine what she most wants—for him to do it right.

Of the men I surveyed, only one man in four felt actively appreciated by his family.

But I discovered a dismaying fact. Of the men on my main survey, only one man in four felt actively appreciated by his family. And 44 percent of men actually felt unappreciated at home. More pointedly, men in their prime years of responsibility for home, children, and work—men between the ages of thirty-six and fifty-five—felt even less appreciated.

I'll bet that many of the wives or girlfriends of these men would be surprised to learn that they didn't feel appreciated. My guess is that most of us *do* appreciate our men but don't show it enough.

If a man isn't convinced that his woman thinks he's the

greatest, he will tend to seek affirmation elsewhere. He may spend more hours at work, where he feels alive and on top of his game, or he may spend too much time talking to the admiring female associate. He may immerse himself in watching or playing sports, feeling the thrill of the competitive rush. Or he may retreat to his workshop or his home office, feeling as if he can control things there even if he feels inadequate and clumsy elsewhere.

"Why else do you think so many men take sports so seriously?" one man asked me. "It's something they feel good at, something they've practiced. They are admired and encouraged by other men on the field. People say 'Good hit!' or 'Good shot!' or show by tightening their defense that they know you're about to smoke them. There's nothing like that feeling. But I feel that same way at home when my wife applauds me for bringing in a big business deal or brags to her friends about what a good father I am. It's that same feeling."

During my clinical research for *The Lights of Tenth Street,* several experts told me that the chronic feeling of not measuring up is a major reason men fall into pornography addiction. For whatever reason, they feel like less than a man, so they seek—and find—affirmation in pornography. As one man pointed out, "All those women in the men's magazines and porn sites convey one message: 'I want *you,* and you are the most desirable man in the world.' My wife may be nagging me at home, the kids may be disobedient, and I may be worried about messing up at work, but looking at the woman in that picture makes me feel like a *man*."

> "All those women in the men's magazines convey one message: 'I want you, and you are the most desirable man in the world.'"

If affirmation does indeed carry so much power, why should a man have to look for it in other places when he has a wife who loves and respects him? There's nothing wrong with work, sports, or hobbies—it's wonderful for him to feel alive and encouraged in those pursuits. But they shouldn't have to be a retreat from an *un*affirming home life.

Create a Safety Zone

Obviously, if many of our men spend their workdays feeling like they are always being watched and judged, it is no wonder that they want to come home to a totally accepting environment, where they can safely let their guard down. Men need a place where they can make their mistakes in peace and not constantly worry that they are one misstep away from being exposed.

If we don't realize this, then it is so easy in the day-to-day hustle and bustle to notice only our men's mistakes ("I can't believe you forgot the dry cleaning *again*"). If that becomes a pattern, we risk creating a situation that is the opposite of what we want. Most of us want our men to be able to relax and truly open up to us. But in many ways, it is up to us to create the intimate, safe environment that makes that possible.

We may think that the adage "His home must be his haven" is antiquated and unnecessary these days, but that is far from the truth. In fact, as the workplace has gotten harsher and less loyal, more demanding and less tolerant of mistakes, I'd say it's even more important that a man's home be a haven. Most of the men I talked with crave a retreat from the daily pressure of always having to perform.

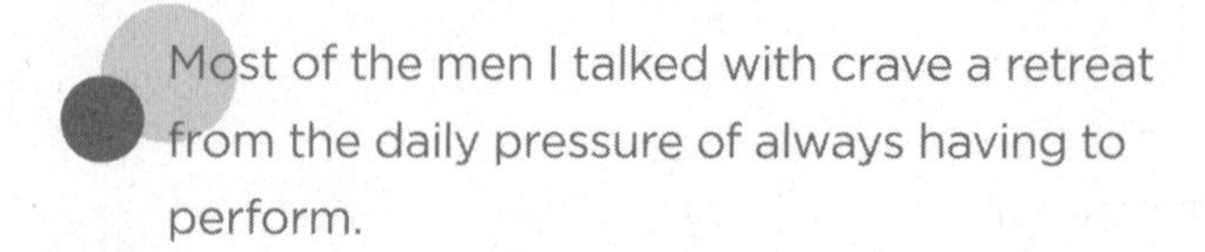

Supportive Sex

Okay, girls, don't keel over from surprise when I tell you that this particular type of affirmation came up again and again. We'll talk more about how men view sex in a separate chapter, but I owe it to the many husbands who commented on its importance to mention it here.

"Sex plays a *hu-u-u-u-uge* role in a man's self-confidence!" reported one husband via e-mail. "A man can be having a horrible time at work, rejection in his industry, and every other area can be going rotten—but if his wife wants him physically and affirms him in bed, he can handle the rest of the world, no problem. Conversely, if he gets the same impostor message at home ('You don't measure up. Don't touch me'), it will devastate him far worse than any career blow."

Another man said, "The role of sex cannot be overstated. A great sex life will overshadow and overcome a multitude of impostor messages from the world."

THE GIFT OF CONFIDENCE

I heard from many men, "Men put a lot of pressure on themselves." On the survey, one husband pleaded, "I want my wife to know and understand my weaknesses, failings, shortcomings, and still want me. I need her to be my number-one source of encouragement to become the man God created me to be." We might think we wouldn't have the ability to change our men's feelings of workplace inadequacy, but we would be wrong. By staunchly supporting our men, showing that we believe in them, and providing an emotionally safe environment to come home to, we can help give them confidence to dive back into the workplace fray.

In his autobiography, Jack Welch, the famous chairman and CEO of General Electric, provides an insight for businessmen that is important for every wife—and mother—to hear. Speaking about his mother, he wrote,

> Perhaps the greatest single gift she gave me was self-confidence. It's what I've looked for and tried to build in every executive who has ever worked with me. Confidence gives you courage and extends your reach. It lets you take greater risks and achieve far more than you ever thought possible. Building self-confidence in others is a huge part of leadership. It comes from providing opportunities and challenges for people to do things they never imagined they could do—rewarding them after each success in every way possible.[4]

It's about sending the men we love into the world every day, alive with the belief that they can slay dragons.

A wife can give her husband that confidence. It's not about being the supportive "little woman." It's about realizing that, despite their veneer of confidence, our men really do "carry their treasures in fragile containers," and they crave our affirmation for whether they "done good." It's about sending the men we love into the world every day, alive with the belief that they can slay dragons.

THE THINKER

When Checking Out Is Actually Checking In

Men address issues by first pulling away to process and think—so they can better talk about them later.

A few years after the original edition of this book was released, I was at my desk working when the phone rang. It was a dear friend in another city, seven months pregnant with her second child, in tears after an argument with her husband. Each of them had hurt the other's feelings, and when the conflict escalated, her husband had quietly left the house and driven away.

"I can't handle this anymore—he's done this several times," she sobbed. "How can he do this to me? He must not love me very much."

One thing about writing these books about the inner lives of men is that I sometimes find myself very able to see things from the guy's point of view—and it's not always comfortable. Feeling like a traitor, I asked my friend, "Um, when you and he had your first big conflict, did he end up leaving the room?"

I could hear the sniffles on the other end of the line. "Yes. Can you believe that? I told him exactly how he made me feel, and instead of talking about it, he wanted to walk away! I know he was upset with me too, but he wouldn't even explain why!"

"Uh…and did you follow him and continue to ask him questions about what he was thinking?"

"Yes! But he wouldn't answer me. He said he didn't want to talk yet. He just seemed to shut down—like he didn't even care that he hurt my feelings."

I told her that I was pretty sure why he had left the house and that it had nothing to do with him not caring. She listened in surprise as I shared my guess that he had probably left *because* he cared about her but couldn't figure out how to respond in the moment. Her emotions had probably flustered him. Then he probably got angry that he was flustered and couldn't think clearly. And then, I suggested, he most likely felt he couldn't risk saying or doing *anything* for fear of hurting her even more. All he could do was escape.

The next day she told me that when her husband had returned, he had explained it in almost that exact way—and she realized he had tried to get the point across plenty of times before, but she had never really understood what he was saying.

Much to my friend's surprise, I laughed. "Join the club!"

WHAT I DIDN'T SEE BEFORE

My husband is a thoughtful guy, but in the first half of our marriage, I often found myself completely baffled or hurt during a conflict by how Jeff communicated with me. Or didn't.

A typical scenario might have gone something like this: We'd stumble into a disagreement or misunderstanding. We'd each try to make—and win—our point. Temperatures would rise. Soon I'd feel hurt (he would too). But more than anything, I'd feel a huge need to talk things out.

Right then, though, Jeff would want to step away.

But why? We'd both been told in premarital counseling how dangerous it was to *not* communicate when there was conflict!

My reaction would be to pursue him. Upset, I'd follow him down the hallway, asking him something like, "Well, what do you think about what I just said? Don't leave before we've worked this out! At least tell me what you're feeling!"

But instead of talking, he would head downstairs, face tight, aiming for the solace of his home office. "I don't know what I'm thinking, and I just can't talk about it," he'd say and disappear, leaving me shattered that my usually loving husband suddenly didn't care enough to engage on such an important issue.

Any of that sound familiar?

As our research continued, Jeff and I realized that a big truth was hiding underneath the stormy surface of these conflicts. A truth that applies not just to conflict but to all areas of verbal communication—and can dramatically reduce how often conflict happens in the first place.

You see, caring husbands or boyfriends want to communicate with the women they love. But how they need to go about it is likely to be very different from the way you or I automatically prefer. Understanding that difference offers great promise for our relationships, and that difference is what this chapter—new for this edition—is all about.

Men want to communicate with the women they love, but how they need to go about it is likely to be very different.

READING HIS SIGNALS IN A NEW LIGHT

We've all heard comments similar to these from a husband, boyfriend, or son:

- (frustrated) "I don't know what I'm thinking right now!"
- (wearily) "I just need a few minutes to decompress before you hit me with your day."
- (angrily) "I figured it out already, okay!"
- (pleading) "Can we *please* talk about this later?"
- (in front of the television) "Sorry, honey... Did you say something?"

No matter how they strike us at the time, these are not necessarily signals of a lack of care or a lack of desire to address important issues. More than likely, they are signals of one of four significant differences in the way men seem to process and talk about thoughts and emotions—differences largely related to the wiring of the male brain.[5]

Processing Difference 1: Men Often Have to Think Something Through Before They Can Talk It Through

Women tend to be verbal processors—we usually think something through by talking it through. We have lots of connections between the left and right hemispheres of the brain, allowing us to do fast, surface-level processing—and talk about—many thoughts and feelings at the same time.

For example, if I need to figure out how to handle an upsetting situation with the kids, thinking out loud and talking it through with someone helps me deepen and clarify my thoughts. As I circle through the options (probably several times), I get more and more clarity. I also feel better because I have talked through—and thus processed—all those feelings.

For most men, however, that process can be bewildering—and is certainly the polar opposite of their own. Men tend to be internal processors. In most cases (although not all), it is actively difficult for a man to think something through by talking it through. He can *choose* to do so, but the more important or emotionally demanding the issue, the more difficult that becomes. A man's brain is wired to process one thing at a time, going deep within each one, rather than having all the interhemisphere connections that easily juggle many functions at once. So he's more inclined to (a) talk about something, or (b) think about it, or (c) feel something about it. His brain will tackle each task deeply over a period of time, but it won't easily do any of them together. (That is, if it is something requiring any thought. Rhapsodizing on his team's last-second win doesn't count.)

In most cases, it is actively difficult for a man to think something through by talking it through.

In practice, then, if someone (ahem) presses your husband, son, or boyfriend to talk, that makes it harder for him to think things through. If feelings are swirling around, he'll struggle even more. That's why many men have learned that it usually works far better to get some distance to think about something first.

Let's say *he's* wondering how to handle a tricky situation with the kids. Here's how guys have described it to me: He will think through each option deeply, finish that thought, with all its implications, and then move on to the next one. Then, perhaps, he'll move on to exploring his feelings about the matter. Only when he has processed the issue internally will his brain be able to move on to the next item in line, which is being able to talk about it. And only then will he feel capable of the type of robust and multilayered discussion that is likely to occur when he finally does talk with his mate.

"I don't know what I'm thinking or feeling yet—but I will once I process it for a while."

I often was skeptical of Jeff's heat-of-the-moment comments such as, "I don't know what I'm thinking" and "I don't know what I'm feeling." *How can you not know what you're thinking or feeling?* I would wonder. But now I realize that he was essentially saying, "I don't know what I'm thinking or feeling *yet*—but I will once I process it for a while."

The truth of this was clear on the second national survey. I asked the men what happened when they'd had a tiff and their wives wanted to talk about it and they didn't. Less than a third said it was because they were simply mad and didn't want to talk. Instead, more than seven out of ten gave answers that fell into the category of needing the space to process it and figure out a solution before they could talk coherently, or so they didn't say something in anger that they'd regret later.

Think about several instances when you've had a tiff with your wife/significant other and she has wanted to talk about it. In a situation where you don't want to talk about it, please check ALL the reasons why. (Choose all correct answers.)

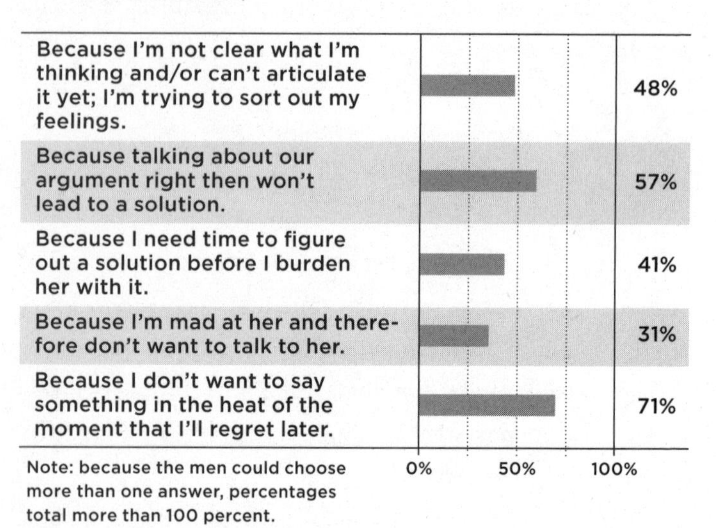

Note: because the men could choose more than one answer, percentages total more than 100 percent.

Thinking to Talk? Or Just to Think?

Now, it is important to note another piece of this truth: if a man is going to actually talk about something important, he has to *know* he's going to talk about it, so he can include that in his processing. As one young man told me,

> I can think something through deeply, in order to decide on the right course of action, and still not be able to articulate it. I can have done the entire internal chess match in my head, and have thought through all the variables, but if I didn't think about needing to *explain* them, I am sometimes totally stumped when my girlfriend asks, "Why?" It's like I did the math problem in my head, not on paper, so I can't show her the steps—even though I actually did do them.

He went on to say that he's fine as long as he knows ahead of time that he'll need to explain why: it simply means that "part of my thinking has to include how to do that."

The Frustrating Reality

Now that you see the male need to think things through first, you can understand how uncomfortable guys must feel when we press them to talk before they've done that, especially when emotions are running high. Consider this back-and-forth exchange between Trevor and Alec, two men I was interviewing together, as they described what happened as emotions began heating up and their wives pressed them to talk about their feelings.

Trevor: She follows me around the house and says, "Why did that upset you? What are you thinking?" And she doesn't realize it'll take me half an hour to work through everything that just happened and figure out what I'm thinking!

Alec: Exactly.

TREVOR: And then you try and try, and finally you blurt out, "I'm feeling this way."

Alec: And then she says, "But why?"

Trevor (looking exhausted): It's all I can do to get the *first* level out, and the immediate question "Why?" is *impossible*!

Alec: Women interpret that as lacking emotions. It's not lacking them; it's not being able to interpret them. Or articulate them. For women, emotions seem to enhance their ability to articulate clearly with words, but for men, emotions inhibit their ability to articulate.

Combine this reality with the fact that women's brains are simply more wired to talk about things, while men's brains are more geared to act on those things, and there's even more frustration. Men feel just as much inside as we do, but they can't always put those feelings into words right away. In most cases, they can *do* something about their feelings much more easily than they can *talk* about them.

Men can do something about their feelings much more easily than they can talk about them.

As Jeff and I were driving to pick up our daughter from a remote overnight camp, he likened a man's need to feel prepared for a conversation to my need to have directions for a trip.

> Guys don't like to talk through things on the fly. That is not comfortable, because I don't really know where it is going. I like to have a road map of what I've thought through and thus know where the conversation is going. I think for a woman, part of the joy of communication is the discovery. But as a guy, I don't like to discover things in the communication, because I don't trust that it will cover all the nuances I need to think through. So not knowing where the conversation is going creates discomfort, whereas for you, it's part of the adventure.
>
> It's actually the reverse of what happens when we're

> driving somewhere. Men don't want to ask for directions, because figuring it out as we go along is where we have that sense of adventure. We love that feeling! Whereas for you, if we were just driving without directions right now, you wouldn't feel real great because you don't know where we're going. That's exactly what it feels like for a guy sometimes when he is unprepared for a conversation.

Processing Difference 2: Men Need Time to Do This

Not surprisingly, the solution for a man to thinking things through is time apart. Men can think and talk about baseball, politics, cooking dinner, chores, or rebuilding the deck with no time delay. But on issues of emotional importance, most men simply need time and space for internal processing. And that may mean a few hours or (for the really big issues) a few days.

While there is no set amount of time that always works (it depends entirely on the guy and the issue), I have heard over and over again that men felt better able to talk about something big the next day. In fact, in his excellent book *What Could He Be Thinking?* Michael Gurian relays what brain scientists have discovered: "Men can take up to *seven hours longer* than women to process complex emotive data." While there are exceptions, Gurian explains, "Men more than women will not know what they feel at the moment of feeling and will take longer to figure it out.

[And] men more than women may not be able to put their feelings into words in the moment and will tend to take longer to express feelings in words than women do."[6]

I'm betting you have seen this seven-hour processing time in practice without knowing what you were seeing. Perhaps you had an argument over dinner, and your man escaped to the gym or the big-screen television in the basement—but the next morning, he was able to talk about it. He wasn't checking out in the way we think *(He doesn't care about me… He's trying to avoid the issue).* Instead he was checking out to get space to do that internal processing.

In most cases, he was probably doing it *because* he cared about you! Here's how one man on the second survey put it: "During a confrontation or argument, I need the cooling period before I can rationally come to an agreement or solution to whatever is wrong. I can't get her to understand that I am not running away from the situation. I have to have some space to gather my thoughts because I might say something that I will regret later… I don't ever want to take a chance of that happening."

> He was probably checking out because he cared about you!

Of course, some men do truly check out, whether out of laziness or to avoid conflict. But in my research that seemed to happen only rarely. Most men care deeply about their wives. From the thousands of stories I've heard, it is clear that we will get a far better outcome and the productive conversation *we* need if we are able to give our men the processing time *they* need.

Processing Difference 3: Men Think Through Everything

Our lack of awareness of this truth is a main reason we have conflict in the first place. It's not that men just need internal processing on those specific things that they decide to think through. It turns out men think everything through. But because they don't do it out loud, it is too easy for us to assume they weren't thinking at all.

> Because men don't think out loud, it is easy for us to assume they weren't thinking at all.

So when our man does something that confounds us, we think (or even say), "What was he thinking!" Well, fess up, girls —the translation of that is "He wasn't thinking." It's synonymous with "Well, that was a boneheaded move, and he did it because he clearly wasn't thinking."

But I discovered that men tend to think through *e-v-e-r-y-t-h-i-n-g.* Including our potential objections to whatever they just did! I was so shocked when I started realizing this that I tested it.

For a whole year, whenever Jeff and I were with another couple and witnessed a situation where the wife was clearly puzzled, or upset with something the husband had done, I would ask permission to jump in (our friends are used to this by now) and ask him about his reasoning. In every single case, the guy relayed a string of well-thought-out decision variables, leaving his wife—and usually me—with our mouths hanging open.

In one such example, Tess watched in horror as her husband, Robert, swiped a dish rag from their sparkling-clean sink and used it to clean mud from his shoes.

Tess: Robert, what on earth are you doing?

Me: Wait! Robert, what were you thinking just now?

Robert: Well, I was thinking that I only had a minute before I had to run to my meeting, that we're out of paper towels in the kitchen, and that this dish rag is getting kind of ratty and it would get the dirt off better than a paper towel anyway. Then I was thinking that I would throw this in the laundry on the way out the door and that it would be a perfect buffing rag for when I wax the car tomorrow.

Tess: Oh.

Now, you and I may or may not agree with Robert's reasoning, but there clearly was reasoning behind a ridiculous-looking action. During this yearlong experiment, not once, when I asked what the man had been thinking, did a guy figuratively scratch his head and answer, "Uh, I dunno." Even if it was a split-second judgment, and even if I personally would not have agreed with it, there was always specific reasoning behind it.

More than eight out of ten men on the second national survey agreed that in such a situation, they likely had thought about things ahead of time, with more than a third saying they had even considered their wives' potential objections!

Suppose you are doing some minor project, and it's not something you discussed with your wife/significant other. She gets that "What were you thinking?" look on her face and clearly has a question about what you're doing. Choose the situation that happens most frequently. (Choose one answer.)

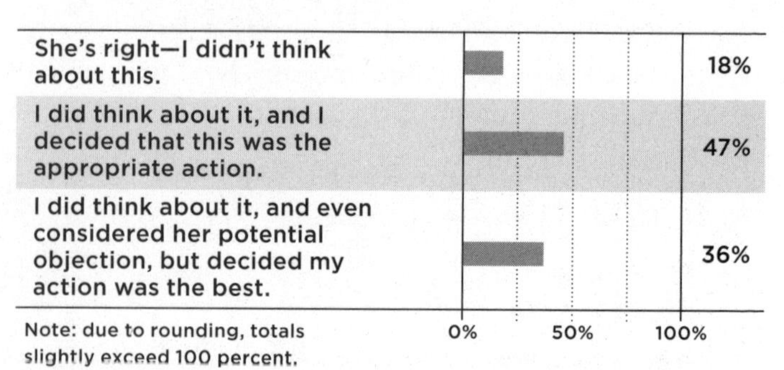

As a survey taker put it, "I want her to know that I have often already considered and thought about her potential objections before she voices them."

As you can tell, this ultimately comes back to the respect issue. When confronted by an action that we find inexplicable, do we respect our men, or are we each subconsciously assuming, *That was a boneheaded move, because he wasn't thinking*?

One representative survey taker said the one thing he most wanted his wife to know was, "Sometimes my ideas might not work right, but that doesn't mean I was trying to screw up." He emphasized, "I'm generally trying to do what I think is best for our family."

But Mistakes Are Inevitable

And that brings up a key point: a man's ideas won't always work right any more than ours will. Just because a man thinks something through deeply doesn't mean that his judgment is correct or that he has all the information or experience needed to make a smart decision. (For example, in the dish-rag incident mentioned earlier, how different would it have been if the husband had been unaware that those particular dish towels were the last gift to his wife from her favorite aunt?)

Although many issues are minor ones—on which husbands would love their wives to just trust them—many men emphasized that discussion and even disagreement about important issues is healthy and necessary. We just need to do it with the best assumptions of our mates rather than the worst.

Processing Difference 4: After All That Thinking and Talking, Men Need to Think About Nothing

Sometimes a man isn't stepping back in order to think something deeply through but because he needs time when he doesn't think about anything at all. Many of us have been hurt when, at the end of a long day, we really want to talk about something, and all our husbands want to do is collapse on the couch and surf all 375 channels.

But it turns out that the same brain wiring that requires men to process something deeply before they talk about it also requires mental space to off-load the day's existing inputs before they can take in anymore. Many men described it as feeling like their brain was a sort of container into which stuff poured all day long—and at some point they feel completely full. Doing something completely mindless—such as sitting on the back deck and listening to an iPod, watching television, or even mowing the lawn—allowed some of those things to seep out of their brains and make room for more. Here's how one man put it:

> When I get home from work, if my wife tries to talk about the kids or her budget problems at work, it's like she's trying to pour more into an already full bucket. Whatever she's pouring just spills over and I'm not actually taking in what she's saying. But a few years ago we realized that if she can give me just thirty minutes, that is enough for me to let go of some of what is already in the bucket and create enough space for whatever she's wanting to talk about. Sometimes that thirty minutes is torture for her, but she's seen it really does work. So she finally believes that it's not that I'm trying to get away from her.

Working with It, Not Against It

I have seen in my own life—and in researching thousands of couples—that we'll be so much happier when we work *with* the way our men are wired in this area rather than expecting them to have wiring that they simply do not have and getting upset that they don't.

This doesn't mean that men shouldn't make an effort to work with our wiring and those things that are important to us. In *For Men Only,* Jeff and I help male readers understand how women's brains are wired and how to listen in a way that will make us feel cared for. Each of us can adapt and do things that are important for our mates, even when they don't come naturally.

We'll be so much happier when we work *with* the way our men are wired rather than expecting them to have wiring that they simply do not have.

But since some brain-wiring realities simply don't change, we'll be far happier when, for example, we give them the time they need to process, before expecting them to talk about items of importance. Or give them the mental space to unload full-up brains before expecting them to listen with interest to more.

The best way to learn your man's wiring is to just ask. For example, "When we are in the middle of a conflict and you need time to process it, when do you usually feel able to talk about it? Does that mean a few hours later? the next day?" This has the dual benefit of also validating to him that he's wired differently—and that's okay.

I shared the brain science behind this issue at a recent marriage conference and later overheard two guys talk about how *liberating* the information had been to them. Surprised, I asked Jeff why they might have used that word. He responded,

> Well, this difference in how we process things hits all our insecurities as men. When I'm flustered and I can't talk as well as you can during conflict, I think I'm not as smart as

> you are. I can't win in communication with you. And if I can't win, it makes me want to shut down and not even try. So it makes a huge difference for a guy to know "I am smart, I can solve things—I'm just doing it differently than she does." And that will make a guy more willing to engage, because he doesn't feel like a failure. If he knows this is how he is wired, he won't feel stupid anymore.

Dadthink v. Momthink—A Family Story

I was in Colorado speaking at a women's retreat one chilly fall weekend, and I called Jeff on the way to a final dinner. Because of the time difference, it was a couple of hours later at home and Jeff already had put our then six-year-old son to bed. He mentioned offhand that our little boy had wanted to go to bed wearing only his pajama bottoms, so he had let him. I knew Jeff was (like many dads) more inclined to let kids try things, but I couldn't believe Jeff let him go to bed in cold weather without his pajama top! What was he thinking? Didn't he know our little guy would end up freezing and probably wake up crying?

I almost went off on him, then stopped myself. (I know this is lame, but I literally thought to myself, *Respect. Remember the respect chapter.*) I asked, as calmly as I could, "I'm confused. Won't he get cold?"

Jeff chuckled. "Of course. He's been asking to do this the last two nights you've been gone, and I kept telling him, 'You'll be too cold, buddy.' But he kept asking. So I figured, okay, better for him to learn this lesson now than when it is full winter. So I let him do it, but had him sleep in our bed, so when he wakes up because he's too cold, I'll put his top on. And he probably won't want to do that again!"

I instantly was so convicted that I had automatically assumed Jeff didn't know what he was doing—but grateful I had approached it the way I had. And I was determined from then on to make the best assumption rather than the worst.

Recognizing and working with how men process things has eliminated so much unnecessary conflict and made us so much happier in my home, and I'm betting it will do the same in yours.

THE LONELIEST BURDEN

How His Need to Provide Weighs Your Man Down, and Why He Likes It That Way

Even if you made enough income to support the family's lifestyle, it would make no difference to the mental burden your husband feels to provide.

In my interviews I was startled to hear the explicit mental certainty most men had about their roles as family providers. Whatever a man's wife felt about it, whatever she did or didn't earn, he felt that providing was his job. Period. Echoed by many, one man stated it this way: "I love my wife, but I can't depend on her to provide. That's my job."

In several interviews, the man's wife was sitting right next to him. One wife, shocked, turned to her husband and said, "But I've always worked! I've always contributed to the family budget!"

His gentle response: "You working or not is irrelevant. Not to the family budget—it does ease some of the financial pressure. But it is irrelevant to my need to provide."

"IT'S MY JOB"

We have all heard that men want to be providers. Each man wants to club the buffalo over the head and drag it back to the cave to his woman. But what few women understand is that this is not just an issue of "wanting to." Rather, it is a burden that presses heavily on men and won't let up.

Consider the stunning results from the survey: a man's need to provide goes so deep that even if you did bring home enough money to nicely support the whole family, your man would probably still feel compelled to provide.

Suppose your wife/significant other earned enough to support your family's lifestyle. Would you still feel a compulsion to provide for your family? (Choose one answer.)

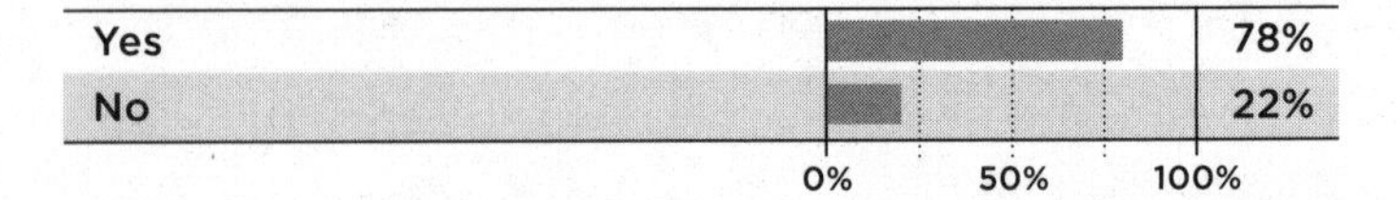

It didn't matter whether the men were married or single, religious or not, old or young—nearly eight in ten felt this compulsion. The only major difference was an ethnic one: the compulsion was stronger among minority groups.

> For most men, the drive to provide is so deeply rooted that almost nothing can relieve them of their sense of duty.

Does the big picture here surprise you as much as it did me? Popular culture often portrays men as willing freeloaders. What they really want to do, we're told, is park on the recliner and command the remote. But in reality, for most men the drive to provide is so deeply rooted that almost nothing can relieve them of their sense of duty. It appears to be nothing less than an obsession—similar in some ways to women's obsessive body insecurity ("I wish I could lose weight!").

"And It's My Job All the Time!"

The second thing the survey revealed is that men don't merely carry this burden; they carry it constantly. There's no respite—the knowledge of their responsibility is always there, pressing down on them. Look at the data:

Under what circumstances do you think about your responsibility to provide for your family? (Choose one answer.)

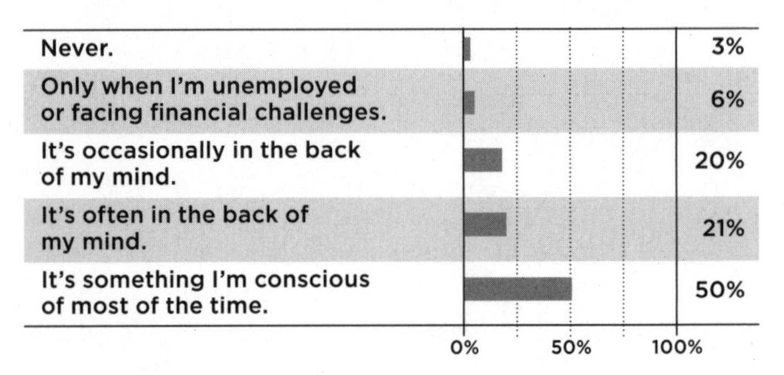

Stop for a second and read those results slowly, until they sink in. A large majority of men (71 percent) say that their responsibility to provide is always or often on their minds. Think about what it must feel like to be conscious of this burden most of the time!

An employee at my local Costco described the provider impulse this way: "It's always in the back of my mind that I need to provide. A man won't feel like a man if he doesn't."

"Is it ever *not* in the back of your mind?" I asked.

"Nope," he declared. "If you're going to be the man, that's just the way it is."

THE INNER LIFE OF A PROVIDER

What drives this compulsion to provide? And since this need appears to be unchanging—despite our modern dual-income culture in which a wife can often provide for herself, thank you very much—what must we learn to recognize and (for the most part) accept about the way our men are wired?

Providing Is at the Core of a Man's Identity

Being a provider appears to be at the core of a man's identity as a male and as a person of worth: he feels that to be a man, he needs to be a provider. Even single men feel this way. On one long plane trip, I asked the unmarried man sitting next to me whether he felt a burden to provide even though he had no one to provide for. "It's still the same," he said. "You want to be in control of your life." He explained that if he didn't provide for himself, other people would have to, and he would no longer be in control.

Men feel powerful when they provide. And they want to be depended on.

In other words, being the provider isn't just a burden but a highly desirable goal. Men feel powerful when they provide. And they want to be depended on. The ability to take care of those they feel responsible for lies at the very center of their sense of personal significance. Providing for those he loves is not just what a man does for a living—in a unique way, it is an enormous part of who he is.

I was telling one man how surprised I was at how intense guys are about being the providers. "Maybe you should see this as the flip side of how we think about sex," he offered. "About sex, men are pretty utilitarian and women are emotional. About money, work, or providing, women are utilitarian, but men get emotional!"

Providing Is a Primary Way to Say "I Love You"

For a man, bringing home a paycheck is love talk, pure and simple. He has something to prove ("I can take care of you, I am worthy of you"), and he wants to deliver.

Even more pointedly, in a man's mind, providing for his wife is a central way of expressing his love. As one young man told me, "My job is to worry about providing so that my wife doesn't have to. That's one way I show her I love her."

It's ironic that we may complain about our man's work habits, not realizing that he thinks he is saying "I love you"—and we are complaining about it! This dynamic is both confusing and distressing for men.

A couple we know had recently read *The Lights of Tenth Street,* in which the main male character frequently travels and his wife at one point wonders whether he cares more about work than her. After reading this scene, our male friend—who also travels a lot—turned to his wife and asked, "Do *you* ever wonder that?"

Surprised, she answered, "Well, of course!"

Flabbergasted, he said, "Why do you think I do work this much? It's *because* I care about you!" He had been traveling for almost twenty-five years, and his wife had never understood that he viewed it as a sacrifice he made out of love and a desire to provide for her.

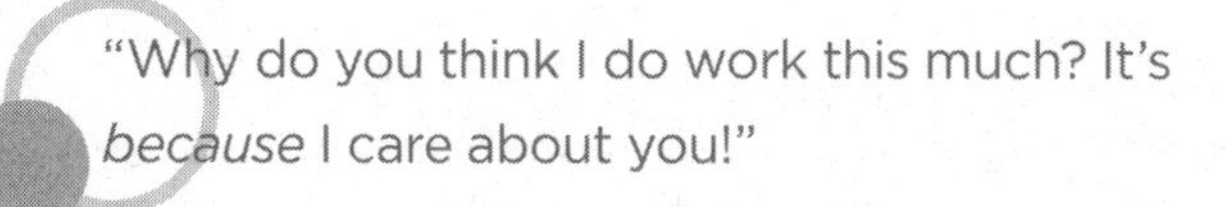

"Why do you think I do work this much? It's *because* I care about you!"

Providing Accompanies His Need to Succeed

Now, let's be honest—other motivations are also at work here. Many of the men I interviewed combined a selfless desire to provide with a powerful internal drive to succeed and find pleasure in their work. Half of the men surveyed agreed that if they worked a lot, it was because they felt, "I've got to work a lot to get ahead, and I want to get ahead" or "I want to be working this much because I enjoy work" or both.

On the survey, one man echoed the feelings of many men I interviewed. He said the one thing he wished his wife knew was "that I enjoy my career and that being successful is important for me and for us."

Just as women can have multiple reasons for doing the things we value, including work, so men do too. We should appreciate our mates' drive to work, provide, and succeed as long as they maintain some balance and the home relationships remain strong. In particular, we should be grateful if our mates are in the enviable position of loving what they do for a living.

Providing Carries an Ongoing Risk of Failure

Now let's make the connection between the provider impulse and an earlier topic—your man's deep insecurity that he may not cut it. It turns out that providing is *the* key arena where men experience the ongoing risk of failure.

Paul of Tarsus said that the man who doesn't provide for his family is "worse than an infidel." As a woman, I always assumed that was a command: "Provide for your family or you are worse than an infidel." What I didn't realize was that, although it may in fact be a command, it is also a description of how terrible men feel about themselves when times are tight and they are not doing a good job of providing.

Most men, as you now see, don't need that command. They are driven to provide no matter what. That statement could just as easily be read as a reflection of internal angst—the horrible feeling that one is truly "worse than an infidel."

"I Feel like My Skin Is Being Flayed Off"

Because of this dynamic, men constantly worry about failure at work, layoffs, or a downturn in business. Since a majority of men (61 percent) said they regularly felt unappreciated at work, it appears that many truly think they are at risk. But because we see our men as talented and effective, we may not understand this fear and therefore may not realize how strongly they feel about doing whatever is necessary to protect their jobs and provide for their families.

If the worst happens and the family encounters financial problems, your man feels like a failure. Even if the financial problems have nothing to do with him (say, for example, his biggest client went out of business), if the result is that you have to adjust your lifestyle, can't buy the children the birthday presents they asked for, or have trouble paying the mortgage, he suffers emotional torture.

One man, whose business is currently in a very difficult season, described it this way: "Every day, with every step I take, I feel like my skin is being flayed off."

Even without financial problems, men can still wrestle with a feeling of failure if they aren't bringing in most of the family income. An increasing number of men earn less than their wives or have become the primary caregivers for children. These men told me that even when it was a logical, mutual decision made with their wives, they still struggled at times. In some ways, they said, they had even *more* of a need to be respected and appreciated as providing—whether that meant being a great dad or covering an important share of the bills.

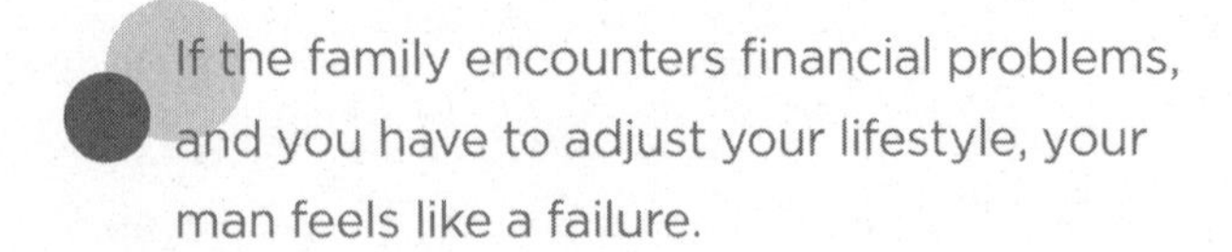

Providers Can Feel Trapped

Every day, providers can feel a strange tension between wanting to be depended on and feeling trapped by that responsibility. The vast majority of men who put in long hours do so not just because they want to get ahead but because they believe, as several men told me, "there is no other option." And they get frustrated when we don't understand that, particularly when they feel *we* are the source of some of the pressure.

For a man, today's version of dragging the buffalo home isn't just meeting the minimum bills. It's also about making his wife happy by giving her the things she wants. And without realizing it, we may send signals that we care more about the things than about how hard our men have to work to provide them.

One very direct survey response made me wince. This man wished he could tell his wife, "I feel confused. You want me home more (I travel each week and really wish I could be home), yet you want a new house, nice things, substantial income, etc. Please understand the Catch-22 I am in. Due to past cutbacks with previous employers, I had to take this job. I feel like I am pushing two big rocks uphill."

Because they want to make us happy, men are surprisingly sensitive to hearing pressure from us where none was intended. One man shared, "Yesterday my wife was annoyed at some stubborn old stains and said, 'I really don't like this carpet.' I felt so bad. Like I was failing her, that I wasn't able to give her the new carpet she wanted." He was shocked when I told him his wife was likely simply venting rather than stating her displeasure with his ability to provide.

Even without creating financial pressure, we can also inadvertently pressure our men in other ways, such as by complaining about their long work hours. Many of us secretly suspect that if our men would just tell their bosses no once in a while, they would be able to spend more time with us. Or we may worry that our men just don't want to be with us very much. So, on the survey, I just *had* to test these suspicions. You know how many men were actually thinking one of those two things? A tiny fraction (5 percent or less).

Instead, the vast majority (82 percent) had what I would characterize as an unselfish motivation, answering that if they didn't work that hard, they would let their families and/or the organizations down. Most of these men answered, "If I don't work this hard, I feel like my job might be at risk, and I do have to provide for my family" or "There is no way to support our family lifestyle without working this hard—I guess I could find a job with fewer hours, but it wouldn't pay enough." Furthermore, half of those men went out of their way to add that they didn't want to be away from their families so much.

Consider the response of one surveyed man, whose mate had probably challenged him about his priorities: "My priorities *are* my family. I wish I knew of some way not to work so much, or to be available more, but I don't know how to make this work otherwise. I wish she was more aware of this."

Don't get me wrong—I am the last person to advise sitting in silence if you're concerned about your man's time away from family. I tend to go too far in the other direction! But if you can put yourself in your husband's shoes and understand how he might feel trapped, he's more likely to see your concern as supportive rather than antagonistic.

Providing Means Earning Enough for Both Present and Future

For men, the need to provide for today is amplified by anxieties about also providing for the future. Essentially, they feel like they have to earn two incomes. One man wrote, "I wish my wife would understand that I am not only providing for the present, but I am trying to save for our golden years."

Many working men also mentioned anxiety at the idea of retirement's emotional consequences. They said that when a man gets a social security or pension check without feeling like he is earning it, he feels like he has lost his purpose.

This dynamic may partly explain why men who are unemployed or on welfare so often get depressed and lose motivation. They feel like they have failed at being a provider, and are less than a man.

SO HOW DO WE RESPOND?

Now that we grasp how overwhelming the provider impulse is, what should we do about it?

Reconsider Existing Areas of Conflict

Ladies, we must face the fact that our mates feel caught, with few options, on provider issues. And they probably also feel deeply misunderstood by us. We need to take a look at where both facts may have impacted our relationships.

For example, once I understood Jeff's provider burden, I suddenly grasped that an unwillingness to stand up to his boss wasn't some uncharacteristic weakness but a strong desire to continue to be able to pay the mortgage. Which meant that my primary response should be appreciation more than criticism.

We must face the fact that our mates feel caught, with few options, on provider issues.

Some women might suddenly realize the pressure they have inadvertently been putting on their husbands by coming home with new shopping bags every day—while others may grasp just how painful it is for their husbands to earn less than they do. Others may understand what one man described as "the stress of feeling that you are asking him to choose between one huge need (to provide financial security for you) and another (to show you he really does care about family time)."

Of course, just because we understand a man's viewpoint doesn't mean that we will always agree with it. But regardless, understanding where your man is coming from is essential to any kind of productive conversation.

Help Relieve the Pressure

Many of us have faced difficult financial seasons in recent years, and obviously that's hard for everybody. It is easy to get nervous and blame our husbands or pressure them to "do something." But most men don't need more pressure. They've got that in spades internally, and when we add to it, we're probably demotivating them instead of helping.

What they need instead is our steadfast belief that they will solve the problem ("I know you can do it") and our steadfast offer to help them do what it takes to stay afloat. That may mean showing our willingness to bring in more income ourselves or expressing excitement about staying with friends at the beach in the off-season instead of going on that romantic Caribbean vacation. (I say *excitement* rather than *willingness* because a man will internalize your disappointment as a personal failure to provide.)

During difficult financial seasons, they need our steadfast belief that they will solve the problem.

Several men have told me that the best thing their mate can do is to show that she realizes how tight things are by refusing to spend money unnecessarily. That, combined with our emotional support, does wonders for the man's feeling that "we can get through this."

But how can we be emotionally supportive when *we* need support? Having gone through an extremely difficult financial season ourselves, I can say that the answer is to cast our cares for provision on the Lord rather than on our men. In the end, it is His job to carry the burden.

In the conclusion to the Lord of the Rings movie trilogy, when the hero is completely exhausted from carrying his terrible burden, his best friend lifts him to his shoulders, crying, "I can't carry it for you...but I can carry you!"[7] By praying for our husbands and looking to the Lord rather than to our circumstances, we trust Him to carry both our husbands and their burdens. Then from the overflow of our hearts, we can give back to and encourage our men.

Encourage and Appreciate Him

One man gave a great summation of what a man needs most, whether a couple is "in plenty or in want": "Thank him regularly for providing. He forgets quickly."

Most of us want to support our men, and in this case being a support means understanding them, appreciating them, and helping to relieve the pressure they feel rather than adding to it.

Being a support means helping to relieve the pressure they feel rather than adding to it.

One husband put it this way: "Make sure he knows your pleasure in any financial progress so he knows all his obsessive hard work was worth it. And when he comes in really late from an extra-long day at the office, surprise him with a thank-you gift. Use your imagination."

SEX CHANGES EVERYTHING

Why Sex Unlocks a Man's Emotions (Guess Who Holds the Key?)

Your sexual desire for your husband profoundly affects his sense of well-being and confidence in all areas of his life.

It's not exactly a shocker to say that men want more sex. We've known that—and giggled about it with our girlfriends—since junior high. But do you know how strongly your man feels this need? And more to the point, *why*?

On each survey and in my random interviews around the country, an urgent theme emerged: Men want more sex than they are getting. And what's more, they believe that the women who love them don't seem to realize that this is a crisis—not only for the man, but for the relationship.

Why on earth is it a crisis? After all, a lot of other legitimate needs get in the way. Like sleep. Isn't sex just a biological urge that he really should be able to do without? Well...no. For your husband, sex is more than just a physical need. Lack of sex is as emotionally serious to him as, say, his sudden silence would be to you, were he simply to stop communicating with you. It is just as wounding to him, just as much a legitimate grievance—and just as dangerous to your marriage.

SEX FILLS A POWERFUL EMOTIONAL NEED

Although popular opinion portrays males as one giant sex gland with no emotions attached, that is the furthest thing from the truth. But because men don't tend to describe their sexual needs in emotional terms, we women may not realize that.

In a very deep way, your man often feels isolated and burdened by secret feelings of inadequacy. Making love with you assures him that you find him desirable, salves a deep sense of loneliness, and gives him the strength and well-being necessary to face the world with confidence. And, of course, sex also makes him feel loved—in fact, he can't feel completely loved without it.

At the most basic level, your man wants to be wanted. Look

at the overwhelming response from the second nationally representative survey.

With regard to sex, for some men it is sufficient to be sexually gratified whenever they want. For other men it is also important to feel wanted and desired by their wife. How important is it to you to also feel sexually wanted and desired by your wife? (Choose one answer.)

Response	%
Very important	66%
Somewhat important	31%
Not very important, as long as I get enough sex	2%
Irrelevant, as long as I get enough sex	<1%

This topic earned the highest degree of unanimity of any question: 97 percent of men said getting enough sex wasn't, by itself, enough—they wanted to feel wanted.

> At the most basic level, your man wants to be wanted.

One man I interviewed summed it up like this: "Everyone thinks women are more emotional than men. And everyone thinks that when it comes to sex, guys just want to 'do it' and women are more into the emotion and cuddling of it. So women think there are no emotions there. But there *are,* and when you say no, you are messing with all those emotions."

And it's not only a flat no that hurts. The survey showed that even if they were getting all the sex they wanted, three out of four men would still feel empty if their wives weren't both engaged and satisfied.

Imagine that your wife offers all the sex that you want but does it reluctantly or simply to accommodate your sexual needs. Will you be sexually satisfied? (Choose one answer.)

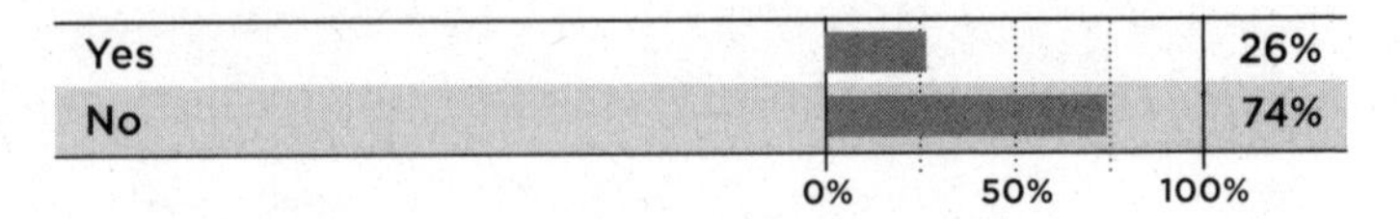

As one survey taker explained, "I think that my wife, after twentysome years of marriage, knows how important my need for sex is, but I wish she knew how important it is to me that she *needs* me sexually. She probably does not need sex so much, but I need her to want and need sex with me."

Reality Check!

I believe that most of us aren't manipulatively withholding something we know is critical to our husbands' sense of well-being.

Much more likely is that, after a long day at the office or with the kids, we just don't feel an overwhelming desire to rip off our husbands' clothes and go at it. I suspect we simply don't realize the emotional consequences of our responses (or lack of them) and view their desire for sex more as a physical desire or even an insensitive demand. Once we truly comprehend the truth behind our husbands' advances, we're more likely to *want* to respond.

WHY IS SEX SO IMPORTANT?

What kinds of emotional needs does your sexual interest meet for your man? In the written survey comments and in my interviews, I noticed two parallel trends—the great benefits a fulfilling sex life creates in a man's inner life and, conversely, the wounds created when lovemaking is reluctant or lacking.

Benefit 1: Fulfilling Sex Makes Him Feel Loved and Desired

Not surprisingly, the first thing that surfaced from the survey comments was that having a regular, mutually enjoyed sex life was critical to the man's feeling of being loved and desired. One plea captured it perfectly:

> I wish that my wife understood that making a priority of meeting my intimacy needs is the loudest and clearest

> way she can say, "You are more important to me than anything else in the world." It is a form of communication that speaks more forcefully, with less room for misinterpretation, than any other.

The reason why this message is needed is that many men, even those with close friendships, seem to live with a deep sense of loneliness that is quite foreign to us oh-so-relational women. And making love is the purest salve for that loneliness.

One man told me, "I feel like I go out into the ring every day and fight the fight. It's very lonely. That's why, when the bell rings, I want my wife to be there for me."

Another related that sentiment to the power of fulfilling sex. "A man really does feel isolated, even with his wife. But in making love, there is one other person in this world that you can be completely vulnerable with and be totally accepted and not judged. It is a solace that goes very deep into the heart of a man."

"Making love is a solace that goes very deep into the heart of a man."

Benefit 2: Fulfilling Sex Gives Him Confidence

Your desire for him goes beyond making him feel wanted and loved. As we touched on in the impostor chapter, your desire is a bedrock form of support that gives him power to face the rest of his daily life with a sense of confidence and well-being.

A few years back there were a series of television commercials for Viagra in which a man's colleagues and friends repeatedly stop him and ask what's different about him. New haircut? Been working out? Promotion? Nope, the man tells them all with a little smile.

One man I interviewed brought up those ads. "Every man immediately understands what that commercial is saying—it's all about guys feeling good about themselves. The ad portrays a truth that all men intuitively recognize. They are more confident and alive when their sex life is working."

On the survey, again, three out of four men agreed.

Imagine that your wife was an interested and motivated sexual partner, and you therefore had an active love life. How would having sex with her as often as you wanted affect your emotional state? (Choose one answer.)

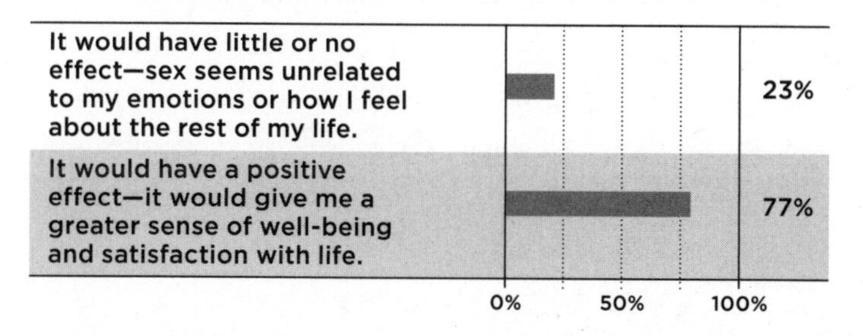

Once my eyes were opened to this truth, I realized how often I'd heard the "man code" for this fact but failed to understand it. When men had told me they felt better when they got more sex, I had just assumed they meant physically better. But as one husband told me, "What happens in the bedroom really does affect how I feel the next day at the office." Another wrote, "Sex is a release of day-to-day pressures...and *seems to make everything else better*" (emphasis mine).

Once we see how central a man's sex life is to his emotional well-being, we need to know what happens in his heart when he doesn't get what he's looking for.

"What happens in the bedroom really does affect how I feel the next day at the office."

Wound 1: "If She Doesn't Want to, I Feel Incredible Rejection"

As much as men want sex, most of them would rather go out and clip the hedges in the freezing rain than make love with a wife who appears to be responding out of duty. My husband, Jeff, explained: "The guy isn't going to be rejected by the hedges. And that's the issue. If she's just responding because she has to, he's being rejected by his wife."

Again, keeping in mind that what he wants most is for you to desire him, try to see this rejection issue from the man's point of view. If you agree, but don't make an effort to get really engaged with the man you love, he hears you saying, "You're incapable of turning me on even when you try, and I really don't care about what matters deeply to you." On the other hand, if you don't agree at all, but throw out the classic "Not tonight, dear," he hears, "You're so undesirable that you can't compete with my pillow...and I really don't care about what matters deeply to you."

Although you might just be saying you don't want sex at that point in time, he hears the much more painful message that you don't want *him.* Here's what the men themselves said on the survey:

- "She doesn't understand that I feel loved by sexual caressing, and if she doesn't want to, I feel incredible rejection."
- "When she says no, I feel that I am REJECTED. 'No' is *not* no to sex—as she might feel. It is no to me as I am. And I am vulnerable as I ask or initiate. It's plain and simple rejection."

"'No' is *not* no to sex—as she might feel. It is no to me as I am."

- "She doesn't understand how even her occasional dismissals make me feel less desirable. I can't resist her. I wish that I, too, were irresistible. She says I am. But her ability to say no so easily makes it hard to believe."

This feeling of personal rejection, and a sense that his wife doesn't really desire him, tends to lead a man into darker waters.

Wound 2: Your Lack of Desire Can Send Him into Depression

If your sexual desire gives your husband a sense of well-being and confidence, you can understand why an ongoing perception that you don't desire him would translate into a nagging lack of confidence, withdrawal, and depression.

The men I talked to scoffed at my tentative suggestion that a string of similar rejections wouldn't necessarily mean that their wives were rejecting them as men. They warned that any woman sending those signals would undermine the loving environment she wants most because, as one man said, "She is going to have one depressed man on her hands."

A man can't just turn off the physical and emotional importance of sex, which is why its lack can be compared to the emotional pain you'd feel if your husband simply stopped talking to you. Consider the painful words of this truly deprived husband—words that other men, upon reading them, call "heartbreaking":

> We've been married for a long time. I deeply regret and resent the lack of intimacy of nearly any kind for the duration of our marriage. I feel rejected, ineligible, insignificant, lonely, isolated, and abandoned as a result. Not having the interaction I anticipated prior to marriage is like a treasure lost and irretrievable. It causes deep resentment and hurt within me. This in turn fosters anger and feelings of alienation.

HOW CAN WE OVERCOME THE "SEX GAP"?

I can't tell you how often I heard a man's not-at-all-veiled appeal for his wife to not only desire him but to do something about it. Although every intimate relationship has its own story, here are a few ways to begin.

Choose to Love Him in the Way He Needs

Okay, if you're like me, you've probably been viewing your man's sexual need as mostly physical—important, yes, but probably also optional. By comparison, when you've been tugged on by little hands all day, your need for sleep can seem both important and immediately necessary. But once you realize that your man is actually saying, "This is essential to my feeling of being loved and desired by you, and is critical to counteract my stress, my fears, and my loneliness," well...that suddenly puts it in a different category. So how might you respond?

First, know that you're responding to a tender heart hiding behind all that testosterone. If at all possible, respond to his advances with your full emotional involvement, knowing that you're touching his *heart.* But if responding physically seems out of the question, let your words be heart words—reassuring, affirming, adoring. Do everything in your power—using words and actions your husband understands—to keep those pangs of personal rejection from striking the man you love. Leave him in no doubt that you love to love him.

And second, remember that if you do respond physically but do it just to meet his needs without getting engaged, you're not actually meeting his needs. In fact, you might as well send him out to clip the hedges. So enjoy God's intimate gift, and make the most of it!

Know that you're responding to a tender heart hiding behind all that testosterone.

Get Involved...and Have More Fun Too

One man on the churchgoers' survey was particularly blunt: "The woman needs to play an active role in the sex life. She needs to tell her mate what she needs, wants, and feels. Passive wife = boring life."

Whew!

I discovered that many men love the secret knowledge of having a wife who is sexually motivated. A few years ago, I overheard a thirty-year-old single friend telling Jeff what he wanted in a wife. "I want a wife who is a model of Christian virtue—godly, faithful, and always kind to others." A grin crept into his voice. "But when I get her home…!"

"It's like that song 'Behind Closed Doors' from the seventies," a married friend told me recently. "That's what every man wants—the girl next-door in the living room and a wildcat in the bedroom."[8]

Some of us may think that being a "wildcat" is a bit beyond us. Not so, say the men.

Now, some of us may laugh at that and think that being a "wildcat" is a bit beyond us. Not so, say the men. All that means, they say, is a wife who makes the first move once in a while and who brings all her attentions and passion for her man to bed with her. Do that, and watch your husband light up with delight!

If You Need Help, Get It

I recognize that some women might wish that they *could* respond more wholeheartedly to their husbands' sexual needs but feel stopped in their tracks for various personal reasons. I don't want to add any more frustration. I do, however, want to encourage you to get the personal or professional help you need to move forward. The choice to pursue healing will be worth it, both for you and for the man you love.

Make Sex a Priority

An excerpt from a *Today's Christian Woman* article by Jill Eggleton Brett captures this issue—and provides an important challenge to change our thinking. The author starts by admitting that, although her husband really wanted to make love more often, it "just wasn't one of my priorities." She then describes a subsequent revelation:

> I felt what I did all day was meet other people's needs. Whether it was caring for my children, working in ministry, or washing my husband's clothes, by the end of the day I wanted to be done need-meeting. I wanted my pillow and a magazine. But God prompted me: *Are the "needs" you meet for your husband the needs he wants met?* If our daughters weren't perfectly primped, he didn't complain. If the kitchen floor needed mopping, he didn't say a word. And if he didn't have any socks to wear, he simply threw them in the washer himself. I soon realized I regularly said "no" to the one thing he asked of me.

> I sure wasn't making myself available to my husband by militantly adhering to my plan for the day.... Would the world end if I didn't get my tires rotated? I'd been so focused on what I wanted to get done and what my children needed, I'd cut my hubby out of the picture.[9]

"I realized I regularly said 'no' to the one thing he asked of me."

Are the many other things that take our time and energy truly as important as this one? Now would be a good time to re-evaluate priorities with the help of our husbands so they know that we are taking this seriously.

Getting Those "Love Signals" Right

In closing, I thought it would be encouraging to look in on how one average husband and wife handled this issue. Mark and Anne had a good marriage in general. They had been married fifteen years when Mark noticed their sex life starting to wane. Anne was not responding the way she used to, was just not as interested, too busy, too tired. They didn't stop making love, but as Mark says, "It just seemed to be less of a priority for her."

Mark is a businessman, and he sometimes works long hours, which used to be a source of grief for Anne. Years earlier, she had sat down with him and explained that it wasn't so much the hours that hurt her but that he didn't come home when he said he would. She told him that he was a great husband, but that this one thing made her feel very uncared for. She told him that his willingness to tell her a realistic time when he'd be home and stick to it was—for her—one of the most important signals of his love. Mark understood and that became a top priority for him.

Now, years later, Mark sat down with Anne and told her that he was concerned about the drop-off in their sex life. He drew a parallel to Anne's need for him to be home when promised. He said, "I could be a great husband but not do this one thing that is really important to you, and I'd still fail at making you feel loved. Having sex like we used to, having you be responsive to me, is the same thing for me."

Anne had never understood it that way, and it was important for her to hear that she could be a great wife, but if she didn't respond to his need to feel desired—one of his most important "love signals"—she'd still fail at making him feel loved. As Mark now says, "It clicked for her. And that changed everything."

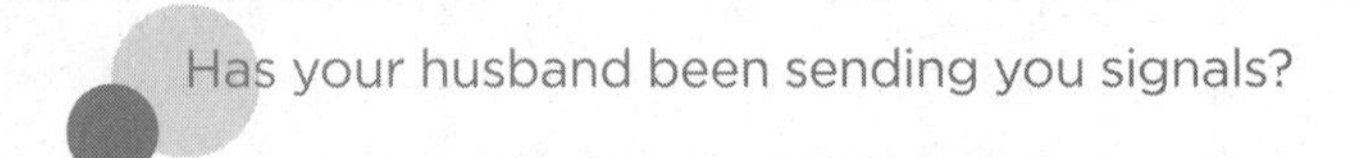

Has your husband been sending you signals?

Has your husband been sending you signals that he is unhappy about your responsiveness to him? It's possible that he may wish he could explain this to you but doesn't know how. Or maybe he's tried but you've discounted the importance of his request.

Having heard from so many men on this, I would urge you: Don't discount it. It is more important to him—and to your relationship and therefore your own joy in marriage—than you can imagine.

Now that you understand the tender places in your husband's heart, hopefully you have developed compassion for him and the way he is wired. Let's take that compassion and understanding with us as we examine the next area of his inner life.

KEEPER OF THE PHOTO FILES

Why It's So Difficult for Him Not to Look, and So Hard to Forget What He's Seen

Even happily married men struggle with being pulled toward live and recollected images of other women.

S*cene One:* Doug, a successful businessman with a wife and kids, has traveled to California for a business deal. The conference room fills with top executives, each one planning on giving him a presentation. The first executive, an attractive woman, walks to the whiteboard. She has a great figure, Doug notices, and her well-fitted suit shows it off tastefully. As she begins her presentation, the woman is friendly but all business.

Scene Two: I'm talking to a series of randomly selected Christian men who are serious about their faith and (if they're married) genuinely devoted to their wives. I describe scene one above and tell them it is straight out of my novel *The Lights of Tenth Street.* Then I ask each man a question: "If you were Doug, what would be going through your mind as the female executive makes her presentation?" Here are some of their answers:

- "Great body… Stop it! What am I thinking?"
- "I feel an instant tightening in my gut."
- "I bet she's using those curves to sell this deal."
- "Look at her face, look at her face, look at her face…"
- "It is hard for me to concentrate on her presentation because I'm trying so hard to look at her face and not her body."
- "I have to be ruthless about pushing back these images—and they keep intruding."
- "I wonder what's under that nice suit. Stop it! Concentrate on the presentation."

If you had been with me, listening to those men, what would you be thinking? I confess that their answers both amazed and dismayed me. Yet as I heard men I trusted reveal similar reactions over and over, I realized that this temptation must be normal. (And for this chapter in particular, remember that by "normal" I do not necessarily mean "easy to accept" or "what you would prefer" or even "right.")

Although I'd always heard that men are visual, I had never understood what that actually meant.

WHAT "MEN ARE VISUAL" MEANS

Here's the insight I stumbled on by accident, and which applies to even the most faithful of husbands: Regardless of whether they let this temptation into their thoughts (and many men work hard to avoid doing so), the unique wiring of the male brain creates an instinctive pull to visually consume the image of an attractive woman—and these images can be just as alluring whether they are live or recollected. Two areas of this "men are visual" thing surfaced that I, at least, didn't really get before:

- First, a woman who is dressed to show off a great body is an eye magnet that is incredibly difficult to avoid, and even if a man forces himself to not look, he is acutely aware of that woman's presence.
- Second, even when no such eye magnet is present, each man has a mental photo file of stored images that can intrude into his thoughts without warning, or be called up at will.

As I'll explain shortly, both are related to a type of brain wiring that is almost universal among men. Some women have this wiring too—and if you are one who does, these revelations may not seem surprising. But for the rest of us, it may seem a mystery—or worse. We might even experience it as a personal failure on our part (for not being enough of a woman to keep our man's attention) or as a personal betrayal on his (why would a loving and committed husband have to push back images of other women at all?).

Thankfully, as we delve deeper, discovering how hard-wired this compulsion and temptation is—and how little it has to do with us—puts those concerns in the right perspective and helps us support our men (including our sons) in this culture.

This book doesn't allow space to delve into a serious visually related issue like pornography addiction. Thankfully, many excellent resources do offer specialized help (several are listed at forwomenonlybook.com). In the meantime, let's look at what every woman should know about the visual wiring of men.

The Visual Wiring of the Male Brain

I have found that understanding the basics of brain science has been extremely helpful.[10] A man's brain structure and chemical mix wire him to be extremely visually oriented. That wiring makes him more likely to perceive attractive images as sexual, and triggers an initial reaction that is both instinctive and automatic. From there he can choose—if he opts to apply his willpower—how he will think and behave.

The most important wiring to understand is a small center

of the brain called the nucleus accumbens. It resides in the back of the brain—the area that controls stuff you don't consciously think about, like digestion and breathing. The nucleus accumbens is the part of the brain that automatically lights up when, for example, you are extremely hungry and you walk into a room to see a buffet of yummy-looking food. First, your brain draws you toward that food in a gut-level, automatic way. But then the cortical (thinking) centers in your brain kick in. Your ability to exercise your willpower kicks in. You might decide to start eating, or—thinking perhaps about your pocketbook, your schedule, or your waistline—you might force your thoughts (and your eyes) away.

Clinical studies show the same process happening in a man's brain when he sees an attractive woman dressed to call attention to a good figure (such as showing cleavage or wearing a tight skirt). The nucleus accumbens in his brain lights up, and he will most likely experience a primal, physical temptation to visually consume that image. But then his thoughts (and his will) kick in, and he can decide whether to continue to entertain that image or to wrench his thoughts away.

Most women don't understand this sequence because, on visual-sexual matters, our brains respond quite differently. In most cases, when we see an attractive man, our nucleus accumbens stays dark and instead our cortical centers light up. So we *think* to ourselves, "Wow, he's an attractive man." Since ours is a thinking-oriented response from the beginning, most of us simply have no idea what a man's initial, reflexive response feels like—or even that it exists.

Actually, brain scientists note two separate but related compulsions stemming from male brain wiring that greatly impact men in today's culture. Let's keep an open mind and look at them together.

Compulsion 1: A Man Can't Not Notice

In the survey, we created a scene similar to Doug's and asked men to predict their responses. Consider the results:

Imagine you are sitting alone in a train station and a woman with a great body walks in and stands in a nearby line. What is your reaction to the woman? (Choose one answer.)

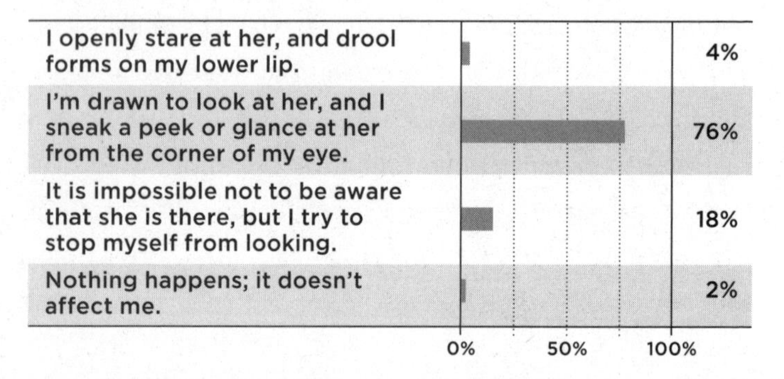

The first fact is that a whopping 98 percent of men put their response to an eye-catching woman in "can't *not* notice" categories (only 2 percent were unaffected by a woman with a great body). And the results were essentially the same among happily married and devoted Christian men—since they still had male brains.

Many men explained the power of this desire to look, even when they tried *not* to or when the attractive woman in question left their line of sight. One husband with a happy twenty-year marriage described a typical scenario: "My wife and I recently went out to dinner at a nice restaurant with some friends. The hostess was extremely attractive and was wearing formfitting clothes that showed off a great figure. For the rest of the night, it was impossible not to be aware that she was across the restaurant, walking around. Our group had a great time with our lovely wives, but I guarantee you that our wives didn't know that every man at that table was acutely aware of that woman's presence and was doing his utmost not to look in that direction."

In other words, the nucleus accumbens of the male brain had lit up, the biological impulse to visually consume that image had been triggered, and all the men were exerting their will to force their thoughts and their eyes away.

Of course, as you can tell from the survey, some men in that situation would sneak a peek instead. Even faithful, godly husbands who usually tried not to do that described sometimes giving in to an almost overwhelming curiosity. One faithful husband whom I highly trust confessed, "If I see a woman with a great body walk into Home Depot and I close my eyes or turn away until she passes, for the next half hour, I'm keenly aware that she's in there somewhere. I'm ashamed to say that, more than once, I've gone looking down the aisles, hoping to catch a glimpse."

Now think back to the very opening of this book. These examples clarify why Jeff would suddenly turn his head as we walked the streets of New York: He was choosing to honor me. He had just seen an attractive woman and was forcing himself to look away so the image would not linger.

And that brings us to the second fact.

Compulsion 2: A Man Has a Mental Photo File of Sensual Images

We've all heard that the male half of the population thinks about sex a lot. What I didn't realize was that they aren't exactly thinking about sex (as in, *I wonder if my wife will be in the mood tonight?*). Rather, they're picturing it, or picturing a sexual image. And those pictures aren't, unfortunately, always of their wives. They are often images that have been involuntarily burned in their brains just by living in today's culture—images that can arise without warning.

You might be wondering, *What kinds of images?*

Apparently just about anything: the memory of an intimate

time with you (good) or a memory from a *Playboy* magazine (bad). It could be a recollection of the shapely woman who walked through the parking lot two minutes ago or something he saw in a movie two years ago. As a result of his neural wiring, these images often arise in his brain without warning—even if the guy doesn't want them there. Or specific images can be recalled on purpose. As several men put it, "I have an unending supply of images in my head, stretching back to my teens."

Images often arise without warning, even if the guy doesn't want them.

The survey results were clear:

Many men have a mental set of sensual images that rise up or can be conjured up in their minds. Does this apply to you? (Choose one answer.)

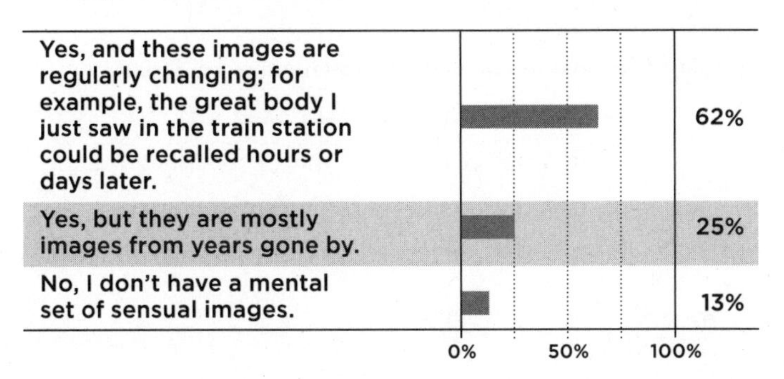

In total, 87 percent of men say these images pop up in their heads. When you break down the demographics, it is roughly the same across the board—whether men are old or young, happily married or single, religious or not.

The Tom Cruise Conversation

One day, shortly after the release of *Mission: Impossible II,* Jeff and I were riding in the car and talking over what I was discovering on this "visual" subject. Jeff confessed that he didn't understand why I was so surprised. Here's how our conversation went from there:

Jeff: But you knew men are visual, right?

Me: Well, yes, of course. But since most women aren't, I just didn't get it. I just don't experience things the same way you do.

Jeff: See, I'm not sure I really believe that.

Me: Well, it's true!

Jeff: Maybe we just use different language to describe it. For example, think of a movie star that you find physically attractive—Tom Cruise, say. After we've seen one of his movies, how many times will that attractive image rise up in your mind the next day?

Me: Never.

Jeff: I must not be explaining myself correctly. I mean, how many times will a thought of what he looked like with his shirt off just sort of pop up in your head?

Me: Never.

Jeff: Never as in *never*?

Me: Zero times. It just doesn't happen.

Jeff (after a long pause): Wow.

That was the end of that conversation, but it wasn't the end of the issue. When my husband then told this story to our small church group, he confessed that at first he thought I was embarrassed to admit that I really might have pictures of Tom Cruise in my head! It wasn't until he watched me tell the story to a group of women—and watched most of them say "never" right along with me—that the lightning bolt hit.

Our little exchange did more to teach Jeff and me how each of us is wired—and *not* wired—than almost anything else. And I hope my new understanding is helping me be more supportive and protective of my husband in today's culture.

Men in a Minefield

For those of us who aren't visual, it's hard to imagine that a man could have no control over those images popping up in his head. But as it turns out, there is a sort of shortcut for certain memories that bypasses the thinking centers of the brain.

Experts trace it to the amygdala, a part of the brain that acts as a kind of repository for memories that are tied to gut-level responses—such as a man's instinctive reaction to a provocatively dressed woman. Visceral memories from that kind of stimulation can bypass the thinking centers to involuntarily pop back up in a person's mind. While a woman's brain (more oriented toward processing emotion) is more likely to have emotional pop-up memories, men's pop-ups are more likely to be visual images.

Now, knowing about that brain wiring, imagine what today's sex-saturated culture must be like for a man. It is an environment filled with overt images that, biblically speaking, they were never supposed to have to face. The very act of living today for a man becomes an unasked-for walk through a minefield of possible triggers and unwanted images that can pop up again days or years later.

Consider this common example: A prime-time television commercial flashes a sensual two-second image—say, of a woman undressing—that is up on the screen and gone before the man can look away. *Boom,* nothing he can do. And it can end up in his mental photo files even if he doesn't want it there.

Mental Photo Files on Autoactivate

When I asked men how often a sensual thought or image barged into their consciousness, many of them said something like, "All the time." Of course, I wanted to know what "All the time" meant!

"If you're talking about a teenage boy, 'all the time' means *all the time,*" one forty-year-old man explained. "It would be fairly unusual for a teenage guy to go a couple of hours without an involuntary image—and then when he does, he could spend half an hour straight on the subject. A twenty-something man also has a pretty difficult time. Once you reach your thirties and forties, you're a little more settled and those thoughts are more often triggered by something."

And once those thoughts are triggered, he and others clarified, the man has to make a great effort to tear them down (if, that is, he is the type of man who wants to keep his thought life pure). They also said that the longer a man entertains the temptation, the more difficult it will be to get rid of.

THIS IS NORMAL?

Okay, let's take a deep breath for a second. For some of us, this is a lot to take in. For others, it's no big deal. Also, if you are visual, you may more readily understand the struggle experienced by a husband, boyfriend, or son. And don't worry—you're normal. But it's important for the rest of us to realize that our men are normal too. As the national survey showed, this temptation is common to nearly every man. And as my interviewees emphasized, it has no bearing on their devotion to their wives.

Before we go any further, we should make a critical distinction: temptations are not sins. The Bible states that Jesus was "tempted in every way, just as we are—yet was without sin." What we do with those temptations is the issue, and we'll get to that in a moment.

For now, remembering the brain wiring involved, let's sort out the progression of male responses to see which are involuntary and which most definitely are not.

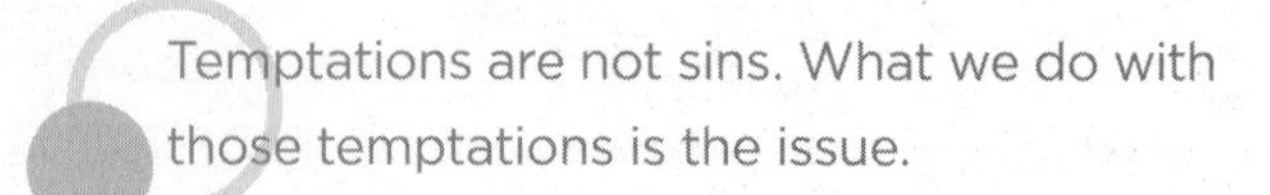

> Temptations are not sins. What we do with those temptations is the issue.

Step 1: For Every Man, Sensual Images and Thoughts Arrive Involuntarily

Daniel Weiss, media and sexuality analyst at Focus on the Family, told me, "I would emphasize to women that, yes, men do have these thoughts whether they want them or not."

In addition, if the stimulus is there (a great figure in a tight outfit), so is the response. As one man put it, "It doesn't even register that I thought *great body* until two seconds later!" Most men, it appears, cannot prevent that initial response.

Don't believe me? Let me illustrate.

Don't read this.

No really, don't read it. Just look at the letters.

Impossible, isn't it? There is no way to just notice the letters without reading the word. That's what it's like for a guy. His brain is wired to read "good body" without his even realizing it.

Step 2: Every Man's Involuntary Physical Impulse Is to Enjoy the Feelings Associated with These Thoughts and Images

Because men are hard-wired to be sexual hunters, every thought and image related to that pursuit comes associated with powerful feelings. When a sensual image enters a man's mind (or a great body enters his line of sight), it brings a rush of sexual pleasure—a short-term pleasure that, we must remember, was supposed to be tied to the only such images he would ever see...those of his wife! But in today's world of unavoidable tight-miniskirt and spaghetti-strap visuals, hopefully the man denies himself that short-term rush in order to honor God, his wife, or his mental purity and thus establish deeper pleasure down the road.

> Hopefully, the man denies himself the short-term pleasure in order to honor his wife.

But again, the initial physical sensation of enjoyment is involuntary. A few years after the original edition of this book came out, Jeff and I were at a crowded mall with our then six-year-old daughter and four-year-old son, and at one point we realized that our little boy was no longer at our side. Panicked, we ran back through the mall looking for him—only to find him standing stock-still in front of the Victoria's Secret window. There he was, staring thunderstruck at the life-size photographs of the models wearing...not much. Just as I thought to myself, *Oh shoot,* he raised his little arm and pointed. His voice held a note of awe.

"I like those ladies."

I nudged my husband, who bent down and said, "Yes, um, they are very pretty. What do you like about those ladies?"

"Their bare tummies," he said, and gestured to his own stomach. "Makes my tummy feel good." He was four years old and had no idea what sex was, but he still had a male brain.

One married man described the physical sensations associated with enticing thoughts and images this way: "When an image plays on a man's brain or he gazes at an attractive woman, it's not just pure lust. There's a thrill there. And a man can go back to that adrenaline rush by entertaining those images."

In my clinical research for *The Lights of Tenth Street,* I heard over and over again how enticing that visual sensation is for men and how difficult it is to resist. This factual insight into a man's inner life may help us understand why some men can make a series of wrong choices and end up struggling in some way with pornography.

Step 3: But Every Man Can Make a Choice—to Dwell on the Images and Thoughts or to Dismiss Them

This choice is the critical distinction between temptation and sin. Once an image intrudes in a man's head, either he can linger on it and possibly even start a mental parade into serious lust, or he can tear it down immediately and "take every thought captive," as the Bible puts it.

> Men I talked to make rigorous decisions to avoid unwanted visual invitations.

Most of the men I talked to take this choice extremely seriously. They make rigorous decisions to avoid unwanted visual invitations, to turn away from those that arise, and—when unwanted pictures arise anyway—to rip them down with all sorts of diversionary tactics. I hear that mentally running through baseball scores, household projects, and stored images of their wives were popular thought substitutes for many men. Honestly, it sounds exhausting.

So, although few men can stop an involuntary image from popping up in their heads, and few men can stop themselves from wanting to look, they can (and often do) exercise the discipline to stop themselves from actually doing so. On the survey, the biggest factor in whether a man made this choice wasn't whether he was older, married, or happy in his relationship (all of those mattered, but in small numbers). It was whether he regularly attended religious services. Confirming this, nearly half of the men on the follow-up churchgoers' survey said they would try to stop themselves from looking.

It is vital that we understand just how much strength and discipline that choice requires so that we can appreciate what our men try to do for us every day in this minefield of a culture.

AND NOW FOR SOME REASSURANCES...

After all these generalizations, it's vital to recognize the critical reassuring elements that are just as much a part of your man's inner life.

Reassurance 1: He Probably Wishes He Could Reserve His Visual Nature Just for You

Most men I spoke with said they enjoy being visual but wish they could reserve it entirely for their wives. They disliked having to face the temptations that abound today, the distractions at work, and the struggle to keep their thought lives pure. Many men echoed this husband's sentiment: "You have to realize: If men could, most would shut off their temptation to look at other women in a second. We loathe this temptation as much as our wives do!"

"Most men would shut off this temptation in a second if we could. We loathe this temptation as much as our wives do!"

Reassurance 2: He Can See a Beautiful Woman Without the Sexual Temptation

One distinction I heard repeatedly from men was that his "wanting to look" temptation often wasn't sexual at all. Instinctive? Yes. Physical? Sure. But not necessarily sexual.

One man told me, "What you may not realize is that a lot of this is simply about admiring beauty. It's like looking at a painting. You're not just thinking, *Let's go to a motel and shack up.* Women don't necessarily look at a man and admire him as a thing of beauty, but men will do that. It's like walking through an art gallery. A man might look, despite himself. But it's not necessarily a sexual thing."

Reassurance 3: Every Man Is Different—and Discipline Makes a Difference

Also, because every man is different, every man experiences a different level of visual temptation. For some men, an involuntary sensual image may be little more than a nuisance, while others might find it a real stumbling block.

Here's a comparison that some of us might recognize all too well. At a dessert party, I might struggle for two hours with the fact that a chocolate mousse cake is across the room, calling my name. But the person standing next to me might be able to put that temptation out of her mind. (Don't you just hate those people!) Similarly, the ongoing practice of self-discipline in turning away from the chocolate cake—or the provocative scene on the television screen—is likely to make that type of self-discipline easier next time. Many men I talked to have invested many years into taking "every thought captive" in this culture.

Reassurance 4: It's Not Because of You

Upon learning all of this, some of us may secretly wonder, *What's wrong with me? Am I not attractive enough?* I have gotten enough anguished e-mails to know that many women suspect that their husbands' struggles arise because of their flaws, not just because they are men. But hearing these truths from every man I interviewed made clear to me that this truly is—as the title of a popular book puts it—*Every Man's Battle.*[11]

In the biblical book of Job, the title character makes a telling statement: "I made a covenant with my eyes not to look with lust upon a young woman." Why would Job need to take such a step? After all, God describes him as "the finest man in all the earth" and "a man of complete integrity." Surely, the finest man in all the earth wouldn't even have this struggle!

But you see, Job had a male brain.

You love your husband as a man, and this is part of what makes him a man. Even if you were a bikini model, your husband would still have this vulnerability.

Reassurance 5: This Doesn't Impact His Feelings for You!

Finally, and most important, we must grasp this fact: a man's biological temptation has, as one man put it, "no impact whatsoever on my feelings for my wife." A man married more than twenty-five years explained,

> There is no relationship with the woman who catches your eye. With your wife, you have a deep and long and meaningful relationship. There is no competition there. Yes, your mind may make the observation that this other woman is twenty years younger and has never had two kids. But that is all it is—an observation. And that observation is immediately offset by other factors, such as the fact that you love your wife!

In one small-group interview, all the men agreed with that statement and added, in the words of one, "It is truly just an observation. There is nothing on earth that would be worth the price of going beyond that. I would *never* risk losing my wife."

SO WHAT'S A WOMAN TO DO?

For many of us, on these issues it would be so easy to move from understanding, to alarm, to the Charge of the Light Brigade—to get anxious or suspicious of our men and get all fired up to change them. But in the book's introduction, I said that these revelations are meant to change *us.* Of course, men can and should do things to keep their thought lives pure. Men should do whatever is necessary to honor the women they love. But many such books have been written and programs created for men by expert psychiatrists, counselors, and ministry leaders, including our challenge to the men in *For Men Only.* But this book is for us women, alone.

So what do we do?

Pray For Him—and For Yourself

Prayer is the most powerful and meaningful way to partner with the men in our lives, but it's often the most overlooked. There's a little verse in Psalm 127: "Unless the LORD protects a city, guarding it with sentries will do no good." We can work to help and protect our husbands and our marriages, but in the end, that's the Lord's job. So it is vital to cover your husband, boyfriend, or son in prayer from the onslaughts of this culture.

Similarly, if you are feeling despair at these revelations, or a desire to hound and punish your man for his wiring, that is *not* from the Lord. Just as men have to "take every thought captive," so do we have to take captive those worries that threaten to spiral out of control (which could deeply hurt our marriages). If you find yourself with any kind of insecurity about this, ask God to protect your heart as well.

Check Your Heart

Before we can truly support our men, we must first take stock of our willingness to support our men in the way they need to be supported. Consider this plea, from the follow-up churchgoers' survey:

> To accept the struggle I have with lust, and encourage me rather than freak out and conclude the worst about me. The more I can reveal my weaknesses without being judged or accused, or without a major crisis in our relationship resulting from my transparency, the more I know I am loved for who I am, not for who she wants me to be.

Do we love the men in our lives for who they are or for who we want them to be? Do we want to support our husbands or to change them?

The way you answer those questions makes a world of difference. And of course, the only person you can actually change is yourself. If you aren't sure you can address the issue with the right heart, you might want to spend some time praying and asking God for *His,* before you do anything.

Do we love the men in our lives for who they are or for who we want them to be?

That is especially important given the fact that men vary widely in how much they wrestle with this, and how ready they are to deal with it. When there is a real issue, I have seen how important it is for a wife to be able to handle it with maturity and care—even when she doesn't feel like it! And when there isn't a true problem, I've also seen how destructive it is for a wife to become hurt or suspicious when it is not warranted.

Become a Support

If you and your husband would like to work together, here are some ideas to get you started.

- *Let your husband know that you are willing to talk about this and that you understand the difficulties he must face every day.* Ask what you can do to help. Put yourself on his team to help him win this fight. Daniel Weiss gave me great insight on this:

> The best thing women can do to help their husbands is to practice two of the most crucial elements of a marriage—openness and honesty. Things that drive anyone dealing with sexual sin are shame, guilt, and secrecy. If the guy has secrecy, if there isn't a safe place to talk about what is a real temptation for guys, then chances are it's going to get worse. The best thing women can do is to let men know that it is all right for them to share their temptation if they want to.

- *Notice and appreciate your husband's efforts to honor you.* Keep your antenna up, and you'll be surprised by just how many daily choices he must make to keep his thought life pure in this culture.

Now that my radar is on, not only does my husband not resent my new awareness; he actually appreciates it. Because now I see the girl in the tight outfit—and I notice when Jeff is tense with the effort of not looking. And instead of being upset that he was attracted, I love him for the effort he is making to honor me.

- *Remember that, for a man, there's a fine line between your affirmation and humiliation.* No husband wants to be treated like your son ("What a good boy!"). But you *can* notice if your husband turns away from the latest provocative commercial, give him a quick grin, and say, "Thank you." Many women, when out with their men, will even say things like, "What a beautiful girl," relieving the stress of his effort to not look. (Of course, that only works if the attractive woman evokes admiration, not lust.)

- *Recognize the common factors that make it harder for a man to stay pure.* Several organizations mention the HALT checklist: Hungry, Angry, Lonely, Tired. When a man is working long hours, is out of sorts with the world (or you), feels unappreciated, feels like a failure, or is far from home on a business trip, he's likely to become more vulnerable. If you've ever found yourself eating the entire box of cookies when you feel unhappy, you understand this dynamic.
- *Know your limits.* Some men will have gone beyond normal struggles and into dangerous or addictive behaviors and need your encouragement as they seek specialized help (see forwomenonlybook.com for some starting points). Further, counselors in this area agree that while there needs to be an open husband-wife dialogue no matter what, if a true struggle has arisen, the husband's primary accountability partner must be male. One said, "It would be destructive if the wife becomes the police. Men don't need a critique but an encourager."

The key is to understand what is helpful in *your* marriage. Every man and every marriage is different. Ask him what makes him feel appreciated or makes his struggle easier, and then do it.

Champion Modesty in Yourself and Others

Let's face it, women and girls who are totally clueless about this problem can also thoughtlessly contribute to it. After all, the images in a man's mental photo files come from somewhere—and it's not just from pictures. The eye magnets on the street are choosing to dress the way they do.

> Women and girls who are clueless about this problem can thoughtlessly contribute to it.

Unfortunately, because many women don't have the same type of visual brain wiring, we may not understand what we are doing to the men around us—a fact that men find hard to believe, by the way. One father asked me why his normally cautious college-aged daughter dressed in a tight little top and skirt around a particular guy she found attractive. "Surely," this father said, "surely she knows what she's doing!"

"Yes," I agreed, "she knows she looks good. But she doesn't

realize what is actually going on in that guy's head. What she's smugly thinking is, *He thinks I'm cute.*"

"Cute has nothing to do with it!" the shocked father replied. "He's picturing her *naked*!"

And that is what we often don't get. Many women and teen girls are just longing for male love and attention, not realizing that the resulting attention is the wrong kind and has nothing to do with love.

After I researched *For Young Women Only,* one youth leader presented my findings on teen boys' visual wiring at a youth retreat. She e-mailed me to say that the girls talked to the boys about it during the entire bus ride home. When they arrived, they were so convicted about how they had unwittingly been causing the guys to stumble that they got off the bus, threw all their Soffe shorts into a Dumpster, and marched straight over to the mall to find outfits that were cute without being sexually tempting.

Unfortunately, I can also guarantee that many adult women reading this book are unwitting fodder for the mental photo files of some devoted married man just because of how they dress. It's natural to enjoy being noticed, but he doesn't want you in there. You're cluttering up a good husband's mind and tempting him to dishonor his wife.

It is our responsibility to ensure that, as much as it depends on us, this doesn't happen.

PUT IT IN PERSPECTIVE

Remember that, in God's plan, the only woman a man was ever supposed to see in an intimate way was his wife—and those pop-up visuals would make sure that, regardless of how far afield a man had to roam to feed his family (whether that meant ancient hunting trips or modern airplane trips), he'd have special images of his wife to keep him company and spur him to get back home.

It used to be that a man had to seek out visual temptations. Today they are impossible to avoid. So spend your energy helping him fight temptations instead of fighting him.

God doesn't make mistakes. One of my closest friends relates that, as a new bride of twenty-three, she was shaken to discover that her husband had this issue with his thought life. She cried out to God, "Why did You create him like this?" And then she realized: God *did* create him like this, and He said His creation was good.

God created men like this. And He said His creation was good.

We are all fallible, but we are also created the way we are for a purpose. Whether or not other things have gotten in the way, that good purpose is still there—for you and for the man you love.

CHOCOLATE, FLOWERS, BAIT FISHING

Why the Reluctant Romeo You Know Really Does Want Romance

Men enjoy romance (sometimes in different ways than women) and want to be romantic—but hesitate because they doubt they can succeed.

Our culture often depicts men as a bunch of clods who have no desire to be romantic. The husband who buys his wife a belt sander for Valentine's Day is the hilarious backbone of many a television sitcom or movie. One amusing example comes from the classic movie *When Harry Met Sally.* Harry (played by Billy Crystal) explains to Sally (Meg Ryan) what goes through his head immediately after a sexual encounter:

Harry: How long do I have to lie here and hold her....
Is thirty seconds enough?
Sally (shocked): That's what you're thinking?[12]

Are men really clods when it comes to romance—or do they just think about it differently than we do? Do they really write it off as a big waste of time? Or is it just something they're happy to put up with as long as they get sex afterward?

Are men really clods when it comes to romance—or do they just think about it differently than we do?

You might be in for a big surprise. According to my findings, most men feel that they *are* secret romantics who—like most of us—don't experience nearly as much intimacy in their primary love relationship as they'd like. Even more surprising, this desire is (in a way) quite apart from sexual intimacy. The great news is that our men long for connection, togetherness, and fun, intimate time...with us!

MEN WANT ROMANCE TOO

I have to confess, I truly was shocked to discover this. On my very first informal test survey of ten men, when I asked if they desired romance *for themselves,* every single respondent chose "Yes, very much"—and I realized that I had inadvertently bought into the popular notion that men really don't care.

As you can see from the survey, the vast majority of men actively enjoy and desire romance.

Regardless of whether you are able to plan romantic events, or whether your wife/significant other appreciates it, do you, yourself, desire romance? (Choose one answer.)

Answer	Percent
Yes, very much or yes, somewhat.	84%
I can take it or leave it.	14%
I don't care for it.	2%

Their answers held regardless of whether the men were old or young, married or unmarried. As one survey taker put it, "I wish my wife knew that I need romance, that I need touching and hugs as much as she does." Listen to what one man told me about one of those romantically awkward moments we all recognize:

> On our honeymoon, we were in the Caribbean and were at this dinner place with a dance floor, and no one was dancing. So of course my wife says, "Let's go dance." I'm risking humiliation, but I go. And within ninety seconds,

> the dance floor was full. Someone had to risk it. Most of the women in the restaurant probably thought that the other couples didn't think about dancing until we gave them the idea. But I guarantee every guy in that place *was* thinking about it and didn't want to risk it until someone else did.

Men want romance, just as we do. In the pages ahead, we'll talk about how to get past the awkwardness and misunderstanding and move in that direction. And we'll listen to the men (every last Cary Grant one of them) tell us how to do it.

WHY MEN DON'T MAKE A MOVE

When I've told women that they're probably married to a closet romantic, I usually hear the puzzled refrain, "Well, if they want to do romantic things, why don't they?"

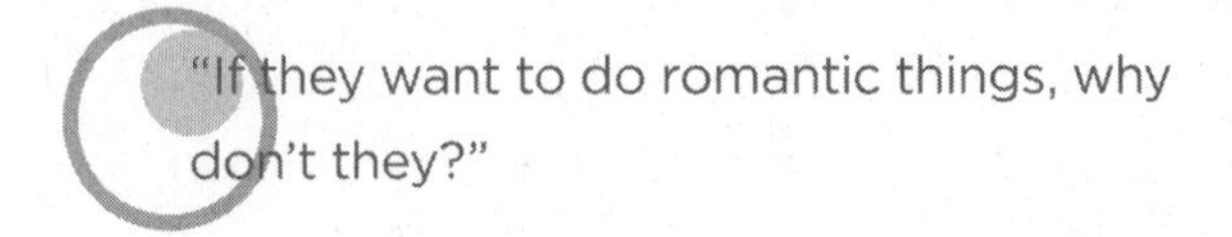

The male responses fall into two catchall categories: internal hesitation and the gender gap in definitions of romance. Consider the enlightening survey results:

Suppose you had to plan an anniversary event for your wife/significant other. Do you know how to put together a romantic event that you know your partner would enjoy? (Choose one answer.)

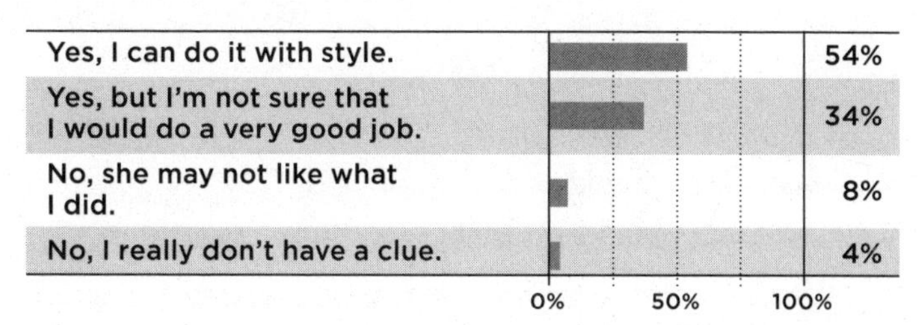

Notice that a huge majority (88 percent) felt they could probably put together a romantic event. So in addition to caring more about romance than we might have thought, these men also had a better idea (than, say, your average clod) of what romance might look like. But the survey also shows the problem: almost half (46 percent) feel unsure of themselves and aren't confident you'll like their romantic efforts.

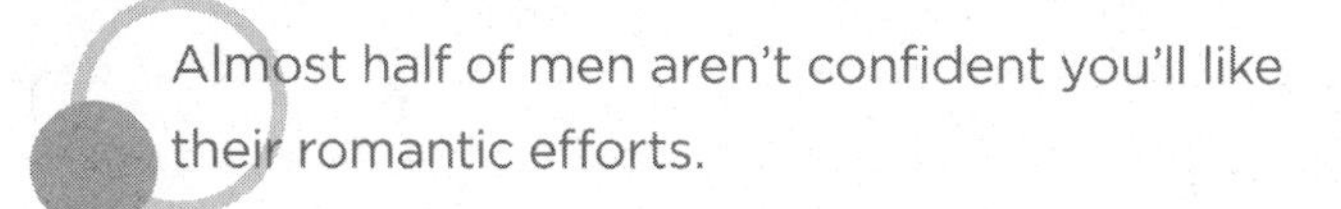

As I spoke with the men, I heard three distinct concerns that caused them to hesitate.

Internal Hesitation 1: "I Won't Do a Very Good Job"

Apparently, many of us have overlooked the most basic stumbling block to our men's romantic initiative: self-doubt. Many men just feel clumsy in romance. As one guy said, "We do feel like clods sometimes. It's like trying to write with your left hand."

A single man brought up the impostor issue: "I try to just do it without being found out," he said. "No guy really knows how—they just play the game like what they've seen."

When you factor in how performance oriented men are (how much they want to *do* things, do them well, and be affirmed for it), this self-doubt can translate into hesitation—or doing nothing at all—even if inside the man is yearning for romance.

One man described the tension: "The flip side of the need for respect is horror at the idea of humiliation. I'd rather burn at the stake. That's why a man won't risk trying to be romantic. I'm risking humiliation if I do it wrong."

Another man explained his anxiety this way: "The reason men practice sports so much is so they don't get embarrassed on the field—so they don't feel inadequate. But there's no way to practice romance. So if they don't know how, they figure it's best not to even approach it and risk being seen as inadequate."

Believe it or not, a man's willingness to take romantic risks may also be tied to how he's feeling about his job. A man who feels stressed and inadequate at work may feel particularly unable to risk feeling inadequate at home—in which case, it would feel safer for him to do nothing.

Internal Hesitation 2: Haunted by Romantic Failures

As you can now guess, if our men seem thoughtless or unromantic, they may simply be taking a safe course after what was (in their minds) a painful romantic failure in the past.

Because men often feel like romantic klutzes, they are incredibly sensitive to criticism or teasing. One man said flatly, "You tease me about not quite getting the candlelight dinner right, that's it—it'll be five years before I try it again."

"You tease me about not quite getting the candlelight dinner right, it'll be five years before I try it again."

Another man relayed this story. "I spent a ton of time finding this special present for her birthday, and I was really jazzed about it. When she opened it, she smiled and said, 'Thanks, sweetheart,' kissed me on the cheek, and started talking about going out to dinner. I felt like, after all that time and effort, I didn't quite get it right. Next time I think it will be better just to aim low and be safe."

Some men have the opposite problem—scoring a romantic success only to be paralyzed by the idea of having to top it. With my husband's blessing, I share an example.

For years I was puzzled by a feast-or-famine trend where Jeff would sometimes go all out to craft a romantic gift but would other times sheepishly give me a gift card. When we lived in Manhattan, he surprised me one Valentine's Day with a children's book about a little girl who longed for ice-skating lessons—just as I always had.

On the page where the girl finally got her dream, he had taped a brochure for a month of private ice-skating lessons with Olympian JoJo Starbuck at Rockefeller Center. I would also meet gold medalists Katarina Witt and Scott Hamilton. I was thrilled and told everyone I knew!

But then I didn't get a romantic gift for the next three years. I was puzzled until Jeff confessed. He was sure that he would never be able to top that Valentine's Day reaction, so he just shut down. "Guys are so competitive, and I'm even competitive with myself. I was sure that the next one wouldn't be as good, so there was no way to win."

Thankfully, I was able to convince him that anything he put thought into made me feel special, which made it safe for him to try.

Internal Hesitation 3: It's Difficult to Change Gears

Even working women may not appreciate how tough it is for a man to switch from the fast-paced, highly practical attitude of work to the tenderness of romance. And my male interviewees have assured me that we shouldn't take this phenomenon personally—they just need space to relax and refresh for a while.

> The men assured me that we shouldn't take personally their need to decompress after work.

And everyone transitions differently. We've already seen how men need time to let go of so much of the workday stuff in their minds, through something like crashing on the couch or mowing the lawn. But for some men, their means of transitioning is totally different. One high-energy friend, who travels with a stressful job, told me he used to arrive home and "bulldoze the house." Then he realized he wasn't leaving his work attitudes at the door and that "it was hurting my wife's feelings," he said. "Now she recognizes that I need help to transition, so she asks me questions, and I babble for about forty-five minutes. Before I know it, I am moving into 'home mode' because I have been able to unload my work issues in a safe environment. Plus I build greater rapport with my wife at the same time."

Almost every man I talked to said he needs to decompress somehow before he can think about being a romantic, loving husband. And if his wife can understand and give him that time, he'll be happier and more available the rest of the evening.

BRIDGING THE DEFINITION GAP

One of my test surveys was of fifty men on a retreat. When I asked the question, "Do you, yourself, desire romance?" one of the men answered, "Yes, very much," but added in the margin, "But we have different definitions." That led me to want to find out what definitions of romance women may have missed.

Redefinition 1: Playing Together Is Very Romantic

Men want to go out and do things together with their wives, and they view that as incredibly romantic. Playing with their wives makes them feel close and loving and intimate; it offers an escape from the ordinary, a time to focus on each other—all things that women also want from romance.

Men want to go out and do things together with their wives, and they view that as incredibly romantic.

Here's a great insight from one husband:

> Most married men don't want to abandon their wife to do guy things. They want to do "guy things" with their wife. They want her to be their playmate. It's no different from when they were dating. For a guy, a big part of the thrill was doing fun things together.
>
> The woman who is having fun with her husband is incredibly attractive. If you see a woman out playing golf with her husband, I guarantee that all the other guys are jealous. Getting out and having fun together falls off in marriage because of various responsibilities, but men still want to *play* with their wives.

Once I heard this—over and over, I might add—I was able to see certain things in a new light. My husband is actually relatively interested in traditional candlelight-and-flowers-type romance—but perhaps more for my sake than his.

Talking to all these men opened my eyes to all the times I didn't fully realize that some activity Jeff suggested would have been romantic for him. In his mind, the activity wasn't just a fun day of hiking or a chance to relax and walk around a quaint little town nearby—it was his version of a candlelight dinner. Recognizing that made it much more fun to jump on the opportunity and appreciate all that it meant.

Men sometimes have different notions of what is romantic. If you take sex out of the equation, which of the following do you find more romantic for yourself? (Choose one answer.)

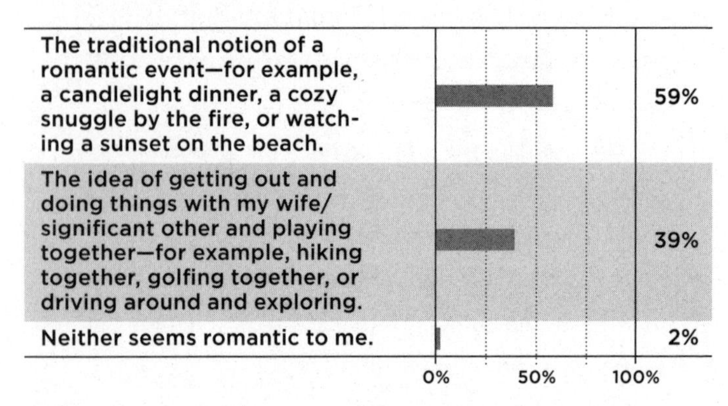

While almost 60 percent of the men on the follow-up survey desired the traditional definition of romance, almost 40 percent said they preferred a more active approach. Perhaps you, like me, have been missing opportunities to enjoy a romantic time with your mate just because you didn't realize it *was* romantic!

Redefinition 2: Romance Without Sex May Not Feel Complete

You can guess from the sex chapter that men consider sex a part of romance. It doesn't always have to be connected, and it doesn't have to happen at the same time, but trust me: when he's romancing you, sex is in the back of his mind.

To make a giant generalization, women can often experience emotional closeness and feel that an evening is romantically complete without sex, but men often can't. Consider these representative comments:

- "It is hard for men to delineate romance without sex. It's all part of it. If men are romantic, they want sex. If there were no moral or societal constraints, romance would always lead to sex."
- "I love setting up a romantic evening, but it is a lot of work for me. And I don't think my wife realizes that, when I am being romantic, I've got a very specific end point in mind. So sometimes there's intense disappointment after all that work!"
- "The guy is thinking, *If romance is about feeling emotionally connected, and sex is my way of being emotionally connected, and we're* already *being romantic, then why not now? If we're going to have sex sometime in the next month, wouldn't now be a good time?*"

Another man brought up the unfortunate dynamic where a husband uses romance to get sex or a wife uses sex to get romance. But he provided an alternative view:

> If a wife only "gives" sex to get something she wants, that is so hurtful to a guy. Sex should not be made a payout after a guy works to earn his wife's favor. A guy wants romance not to somehow manipulate sex but to reexperience the spark of dating, to reconnect after days of draining work at the office, to feel love and intimacy, to know he is wanted and enjoyed, and to utterly escape the crushing nonstop pressure of life. And sex can be a wonderful part of all that. Romance is all about escaping—escaping with the person you love and discovering to one's monumental delight that she, too, wants to escape—with me!

Clearly, just as we want our husbands to love us in the way we need to be loved, our men want the same. And sex is a huge part of making them feel loved.

THE POWER OF A WOMAN IN LOVE

Is it dawning on you just how much power we women have to change the whole romance picture? More than likely, we each live with a motivated man who wants more romantic closeness but who is holding back or frustrated. Which means we often hold the key to the quality of romance.

If you've been disappointed with your romantic relationship and have pushed and prodded to no effect, you've probably realized that nagging doesn't work. So how do we start?

Encourage Him

Although a man always needs his wife's appreciation, it is especially critical when he is outside his comfort zone—which, when it comes to romance, is probably the case for half the male population.

One man was blunt: "Encourage me and affirm my efforts, and I'll run through a brick wall to please you. But don't just assume that I know you're pleased. I'm way outside my comfort zone. I'm willing to be a fool for you, but just tell me that I did good. And give me sex. That helps too."

Remember that many men view taking romantic initiative as a huge risk—a risk of being humiliated or feeling inadequate. So prove to your man that it's not a risk! When he makes an effort, it's your responsibility—and your joy—to demonstrate that it was worth it.

Even when your man isn't outside his comfort zone, he can become frustrated when you don't want to "go outside and play" when the opportunity arises. So next time he suggests something, don't tell him you really need to vacuum the house. Give him his version of a candlelight dinner, and enjoy your romantic time together!

Entice Him

Just as men want to be encouraged, they want to be enticed. One married man relayed this interchange with a female friend who was wondering why romance sometimes dies off in marriage.

> *Her:* Romance is the sense that you're still being pursued.
> *Him:* But we caught you. Hand me the remote.

Many men have told me that, whether in work or in romance, they are always looking for something to conquer—something to "catch." A key element in keeping romance alive is to keep giving that to our husbands.

Keep it fresh—give him something new to pursue. Go hiking with him. Play golf with him. Give him space when he needs it, and intimate attention when he needs that. Make yourself the kind of friend and lover he constantly wants to pursue.

> Make yourself the kind of friend and lover that your man constantly wants to pursue.

Tell Harry What Sally Needs

Several men suggested that, since they can't read our minds, it's fine for us to drop hints about those romantic things we'd like to do...as long as they truly are hints, not directives. Take that classic Harry-and-Sally issue: cuddling. Because cuddling tends to be more important to us than to guys, a little patient reeducation may be in order. And this applies to anything you find particularly romantic that he doesn't get. "Help me understand why it's so important to you," one man suggested. "Help me see that, as I romance you in *your* way, you'll be more motivated to romance me in *my* way."

This approach isn't a damaging, withholding-based model. It is learning to give what the other person needs and enjoying the resulting God-ordained fruits of that selflessness. One man's response to the cuddling example was, "Men can learn to enjoy a time of closeness after sex. And in this case, it is definitely in our best interest to understand why it matters so much to you!"

Keep Him Number One

If we let too many other priorities interfere with romance, it puts a damper on the man's enthusiasm. One of the most common concerns I heard is that we may unconsciously prioritize our kids over our husbands. On the survey, several men expressed concern that "she spends too much time doting on the children" and not enough time doting on the relationship.

A man with three active children commented, "It's considered a Christian thing to do, to be with the kids all the time. But for me as a man, there is a sense of 'I've lost my wife.' It could sound selfish, but it's not. And it's not too healthy for the kids either."

One man said, "It's not just kids that steal a wife. It's the whole to-do list. Even helping others can get in the way."

We have a tremendous opportunity to start over with our men.

That is the cry of a man who just wants to spend more quality, romantic time with his wife. What an irony, considering that most women pine for the same thing! We have a tremendous opportunity to start over with our men...and in the process rediscover the delight of the mutual pursuit.

THE TRUTH ABOUT TAKING CARE OF YOURSELF

Why What's on the Outside Matters to Him on the Inside

You don't need to be a size 3, but your man does need to see you making the effort to take care of yourself—and he'll willingly help you.

Warning! Before you read any further, pray first! I'm not kidding. We're going to navigate some tricky waters here, and to get the most out of this, you'll need to be open to something you may not have heard before, while being protected from hurt. So take a moment now, and ask the Lord to shepherd your process of reading and absorbing this material.

• • •

Okay, ready? This chapter is about something our men desperately want us to know but feel absolutely unable to tell us: The effort you put into your appearance is extremely high on his priority list. Yet the chances that you know his true feelings are extremely low.

What I've learned about men's needs in this area—including my husband's—has been life changing. It has jarred me out of a dangerous complacency. Perhaps it will jar you out of yours.

OUT, BLIND SPOT

Call me naive, but I just didn't realize that a wife's or girlfriend's appearance was such a big deal—such an *imperative* deal—for the guy. Important, yes. Imperative, no. Of course, having learned just how visual men are, I should have gotten a clue. But somehow I assumed that if I was out of shape, I was the only person who was negatively affected.

Then one day, after speaking to a mixed group about the other topics in this book, I was approached by a man I've known professionally for several years. I'll call him Ted. He asked if we could talk privately, and we found some chairs away from everyone else.

"There's something I need to mention to you," Ted said, looking uncomfortable. "I think women have a blind spot in an area that they really need to understand." Taking a deep breath, he spilled the beans. "I don't think women know how important it is to take care of themselves and not to look like slouches around their husbands."

"You mean, not to be overweight...?" I ventured.

"That's part of it, but that's not really *it,*" Ted continued. "It doesn't mean you have to be a size 3. The bigger issue is that your husband sees that you are putting forth the effort to take care of yourself...for him. See, my wife is 115 pounds, but her weight isn't really the issue. It's not about being tiny. If she doesn't take care of herself, dresses sloppily around me all the time, never exercises, and has no energy to go out and do things together, I feel like she's choosing not to do something that she should know is important to me. And then it becomes a real issue because it affects her ability to do things and her self-worth and desire—and then it affects me."

"I just want to see that my wife cares enough about me to make an effort."

That burden off his chest, Ted relaxed. "You may not believe this," he said with a chuckle, "but it's not about whether we want our wives to prance around the house in a Little Bo Peep outfit—although that would be great too. I mean, who are we kidding! But really, I just want to see that my wife cares enough about me to make an effort."

Ever since I decided to add a chapter about this issue, the male response has been astonishing. In fact, when I describe all the topics of the book to a guy, do you know which one he is most likely to seize on as something he wished his wife understood? You got it—*this one* (sex and respect were close seconds). Most of the men who hear about this subject thank me: "Thank you for saying what we are thinking but could never, ever say." "Thank you for taking on a subject that is so taboo, especially in Christian circles."

A FEW THINGS I'M NOT SAYING

Now, nearly all women have some form of body insecurity that we already worry about too much, and I'm not trying to add fuel to that fire! We're hammered relentlessly by media messages that we should all be perfectly shaped and eternally young. But God didn't create us to be Barbie dolls, and those fake and impossible ideals only drive women into eating disorders and other miserable, unhealthy obsessions. This chapter is *only* dealing with weight, fitness, and appearance issues that we can healthfully do something about.

So first, let's celebrate our God-given individuality—sturdy thighs, small boobs, and all—and make the best of them. Men don't mind less-than-ideal proportions. In fact, most men I spoke with wished their partners weren't so sensitive about their bodies.

Second, if you're one of those rare women who is a size 2 and convinced you're fat, be careful. You're probably delusional. This chapter is not trying to get you to lose weight. If what you read here puts you in a panic, please talk to a trusted friend or a medical advisor.

Third, we need to accept how complicated and hypersensitive the appearance issue is for both partners. Many men, for example, feel that they shouldn't care about appearance, but they do. Many women, on the other hand, feel that true love should come with no strings attached. Still, we want to be attractive. And while we were delighted that he liked our looks during courtship, we can find ourselves feeling outright resentful that our appearance still matters so much to him now. (Do you see what I mean when I say *complicated*?)

Finally, please understand that this entire subject isn't ultimately about being tiny or any other current ideal of attractiveness. Primarily, it is about showing our men that we're willing to make the effort to address something that is very important to them.

This subject isn't about being tiny. It is about showing our men that we're willing to make the effort on something important to them.

So, with grace and good intentions firmly in hand, let's take a hard look at what men really think.

EVERY MAN CARES

Almost every man cares if his wife is out of shape and doesn't make a true effort to change. For some it's merely a wistful "Oh, for the good old days" sigh, while for others it's a relationship wrecker. Here's what I asked on the survey:

Imagine your wife/significant other is overweight, wears baggy sweats when you are home, and only does her hair and makeup to go out. She hates being overweight, but nothing much changes and lately you've seen her eating more sweets. What goes through your mind? (Choose all correct answers.)

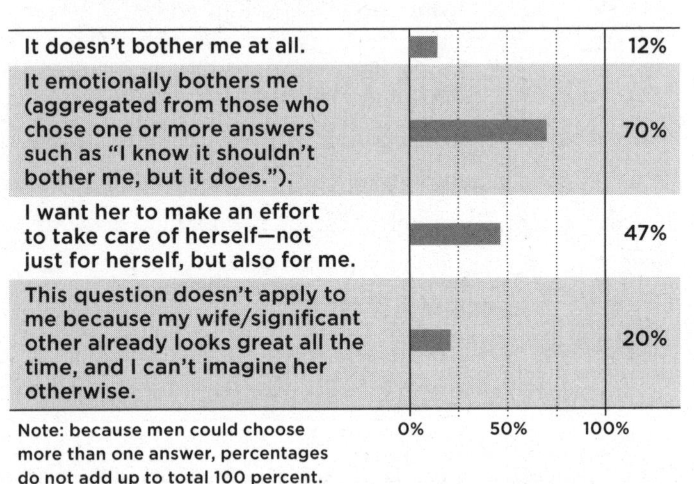

Seven out of ten men indicated that they would be emotionally bothered if the woman in their lives let herself go *and didn't seem to want to make the effort to do something about it.* Only 12 percent said it didn't bother them—and even fewer happily married, younger, churchgoing men weren't bothered.

Once I understood this—and started making the effort myself—my husband felt safe to confirm that most guys do indeed struggle with this issue. With some trepidation, he gently reminded me of when, after our son was born, I used to eat a chocolate doughnut every morning. He said, "I know it's awful, but every morning when I saw those doughnuts on the counter, my heart would just sink. I'd think, *It's never going to change.* We guys keep our spirits up with the thought that some hope is out there—that things will change. For me, those chocolate doughnuts weren't the issue; it was that they said something about you making a choice not to get back in shape, for me."

Your Effort Is What Matters

Most of us can get paralyzed into inaction by the thought of having to look like the impossibly thin twenty-year-olds on television. But over and over again, I heard each man say that what mattered most to him was not that his wife shrank down to her honeymoon bikini but that she was willing to make the effort to take care of herself for him.

What mattered most to him was not that his wife shrunk down to her honeymoon bikini but that she made an effort for him.

So I gathered my courage and asked the question directly:

Is this statement true or false? "I want my wife/significant other to look good and feel energetic. It is not as important that she look just like she did the day we met. It is more important that she make the effort to take care of herself for me now." (Choose one answer.)

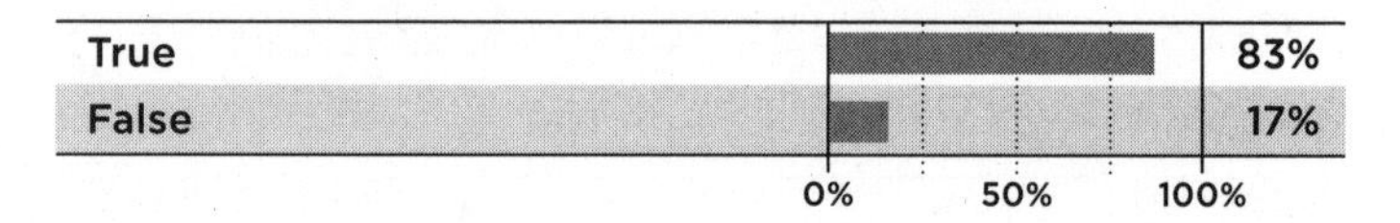

Look at the encouraging response: Five out of six men agreed—with regular churchgoers agreeing even more strongly. It's not that results don't matter; of course they do. But they will be a by-product of our efforts to take care of ourselves.

"For Better or For Worse"

Before we look further, those of us who don't believe in divorce may need to own up to creeping complacency. Think how off-limits it is in a church setting to emphasize the importance of a woman's physical appeal. "God looks not on the outward appearance but on the heart," we say, and expect our husbands to do the same. Our husbands have pledged their faithfulness for better or for worse, and we know "it's what's inside that counts."

Trouble is, we can easily migrate to the idea that what's outside doesn't matter.

But it *does.* And when we seem to be willfully ignoring that truth, our men—even godly men who are devoted to us—end up feeling disregarded, disrespected, and hurt. So let's try to understand why his feelings about your appearance can run so high, even if they're out of sight to you.

WHY DOES YOUR EFFORT IN APPEARANCE MATTER?

One man reading a draft of this chapter looked at this subject heading and exclaimed, "What do you mean, '*Why* does it matter?'!" Men really don't understand why a woman would have to ask the question. So why is it so essential? Here's what men said—when they felt safe enough to tell the truth.

"When You Take Care of Yourself, I Feel Like You Care About Me"

Since men are so visual, seeing us make the effort to look good makes them feel loved and cared for. It matters to them in the same way it matters to us when we notice our husbands making an effort to do things that make us feel loved—especially when they are things that are difficult or don't come naturally.

Consider one husband's honest comment: "My wife is trying to slim down right now, and it makes me feel like a million bucks. I know she's also doing it for herself, but the fact that she cares about how she looks is a total turnon, if you want to know the truth. I tell her all the time how much I appreciate the work she's putting into this."

If you have a hard time believing that your man really cares about your efforts as much as your results, here's a helpful romance-related parallel: If your husband truly puts effort and thought into a romantic event, do you really mind if it's not perfect? If it's your birthday and you come home from work to find that he has gotten friends to watch the kids, the house has been cleaned, and he has slaved over a meal, are you really going to care if the veal piccata is overdone? Of course not. You'll feel loved and cared for.

"When You Don't Take Care of Yourself, I Feel Unvalued and Unhappy"

How does a man feel when the woman he is married to looks significantly different than the one he courted? After I tackled this subject in one of my newspaper columns, a twenty-seven-year-old man wrote to tell me he knew many men whose wives had gained a lot of weight since their wedding days:

> Shaunti, those women need to realize that their doubling in size is like a man going from being a corporate executive to a minimum-wage slacker—and assuming it has no effect on his spouse. A woman's appearance is a simple yet important part of happiness in a marriage. A number of my friends love their spouses, but are not happy, mainly for that reason.

And being out of shape affects more than just appearance. Remember how much a man wants to go out and do things with his wife—and how close that makes him feel to you? One survey taker wrote, "She is a very pretty woman, but she is not taking care of herself, so she feels bad about her looks, she has little energy, and we are limiting our opportunities, such as going to a pool party or the lake or beach."

In a way, this issue for men is like the romance issue for us. Maybe it shouldn't matter whether our husbands ever put one jot of effort into romancing us. But it does. We love them regardless, but it doesn't remove the empty wistfulness we feel or the pain we may suffer wondering why on earth our men don't see that this is so important to us.

In a way, this issue for men is like the romance issue for us.

Guys feel the same way on the issue of how we take care of ourselves. It is critical that we acknowledge that their desire is both real and legitimate.

"When You Take Care of Yourself, Your Expectation That 'I Only Have Eyes for You' Feels Fairer (and Easier to Accomplish)"

As we struggle with this hard truth, it might be helpful to remember that we're not alone. We're also asking our men to do something that is hard and goes against their natural instinct. The man who originally opened my eyes to this issue explained it this way:

> We need to see that you care about keeping our attention on you—and off of other women. Sometimes it is so hard for us to look away. It takes a lot of work and a lot of effort. But it helps me so much if I see that my wife is willing to do her part and purposefully work toward staying in shape and looking good.

"I Want (and Need) to Be Proud of You"

Several men told me something like this: "I want to be proud of my wife. Every man has this innate competition with other men, and our wives are a part of that. Every man wants other men to think that he did well in his choice of a wife."

Now, I'm going to share something that will be difficult to hear. This two-part comment is from a close friend whose heart I trust completely. I'm including it because I've found that it is truly how men think and because I believe it helps to make a critical distinction:

> Sometimes I'll meet a guy who looks just like an average guy. But then, if I meet his wife and she is huge and very out of shape and just sloppy, I feel so sorry for him. It sounds terrible, but my gut just churns for him. It's this "Oh, I'm so sorry" sort of compassion. That sounds absolutely terrible to say out loud, but it is what every man is thinking.
>
> But then sometimes I'll meet a man whose wife is overweight—but she takes care of herself. She puts some effort into her appearance. She dresses neatly or does her makeup and hair. If she is comfortable in her own skin and is confident, you don't notice the extra pounds. I look at that husband and think, *He did well.*

"If she puts some effort into her appearance and is comfortable in her own skin, you don't notice the extra pounds. I look at that husband and think, *He did well.*"

WHERE DO I START?

If you're pretty sure this chapter was meant for you, but you want to run it by your husband first, my recommendation is simple and heartfelt:

Don't.

Most men are wincingly sensitive about this subject, mostly because they remember how wincingly sensitive *we've* been on it in the past. Think about it—if your husband approached you about this, no matter how gently, what would you do? Probably the same as I have done in similar circumstances: burst into tears. That is enough to make most men so distressed and uncomfortable that they will never bring it up again. One man who had dipped his toe in those waters before said, "I know that if I bring it up, it will just hurt her feelings too much. So I'm going to preserve her feelings at the expense of my happiness, or satisfaction, or whatever you want to call it."

Your man is not likely to be completely truthful, even if you—in all earnestness—want the truth.

Your man is not likely to be completely truthful, even if you—in all earnestness—want the truth. Consider, instead, applying Jeff's rule (my own husband to the rescue again). It's a self-inventory that's been confirmed by pretty much every other guy I've spoken with. Jeff's rule is this: if you are not realistically happy with your overall appearance and fitness level, assume he's not either.

Don't make him tell you that—both for your sake and the sake of your future together. (And for the sake of your sanity, note the important words *realistically* and *overall.* We're not talking about someone who is fit and trim but thinks she needs to lose five pounds or is dissatisfied with a certain feature. And we're *certainly* not talking about someone who takes care of herself and eats right but just has a body type that is completely different from the ballet dancer next door.)

A man gets very frustrated when the woman in his life endlessly anguishes about her appearance but takes little or no meaningful action. Many of the comments on the survey echoed what one man wrote: "If she wants to look better, she needs to do something about it, not just complain about it all the time."

At this point, some of you may be throwing your hands up in despair. Even if effort is really what matters, how, you wonder, are you supposed to add this effort to your many others?

Well, once you decide to take action, some very good news opens up to you. As it turns out, the person who cares so deeply about you taking care of yourself is, in almost every case, ready to be part of the solution.

Good News, Part 1: Your Man Wants to Help You

Almost every man I talked with said he would do whatever it takes to help his partner make this particular effort. And that was overwhelmingly confirmed by the follow-up survey.

Imagine your wife/significant other is overweight and really wants to make the effort to get in shape, for you. But her slate is already full; she has no time during the day, and in the evening she has to watch the kids or drive them to their activities. How much effort, financial expense, or additional responsibility would you be willing to take on so she can do what's necessary to get in shape? (Choose one answer.)

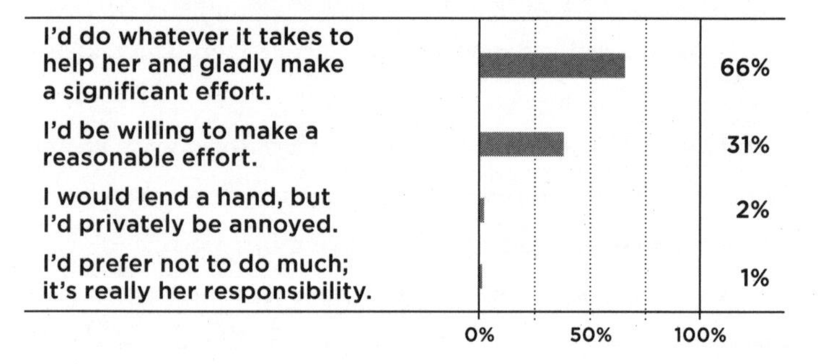

Only four men out of four hundred said they'd be unwilling to help, and it's highly unlikely that your man is one of those cads—er, unaccommodating husbands. Almost everyone else (97 percent) said they would help willingly. One interviewee told me, "If a guy's wife suddenly verbalizes that she's determined to drop some weight and needs his help, any guy is going to jump to it! 'What can I do? Here's a credit card!' "

My husband drew a youthful comparison. "Look," he said, "when we were teenagers, the guys were always busy playing football or whatever. But if our girlfriends needed a ride to the tanning salon, we'd drop everything and drive them in a heartbeat. We'd even give them money to go! It was in our best interest! And that feeling doesn't change as we get older—we're willing to help our wives."

Maybe he watches the kids in the evening or drives the soccer carpool so you have time to work out. Maybe he stops bringing a particularly dangerous food into the house. Maybe he cooks dinner so you don't have to prepare foods you're trying to avoid. Or maybe he agrees to go on the diet with you. (Jeff has sheepishly admitted that several diets he has tried were—at their core—veiled attempts to get me to join him!)

And remember, since it's your sincere concern and effort that matters most, you can expect to see relationship benefits coming your way very soon.

Good News, Part 2: There's a Revolution in the Resources to Help You

Over the years I've tried almost every diet under the sun, only to watch helplessly as the weight crept back. (Can you relate?) But now I've learned that almost everything I had known about healthful eating was wrong. No wonder nothing worked long term! But there has now been a revolution in our scientific understanding of what eating well actually means (for example, eating good carbs and good fats and avoiding bad ones).

Without that knowledge, it is likely that we will keep sabotaging our efforts over the long term. Thankfully, several well-respected books are now available on what it really means to eat well and thus maintain a lifelong healthy weight. (On a personal note, I feel like I can stick with my new eating habits for the rest of my life because of the education I gained from *The South Beach Diet* by cardiologist Dr. Arthur Agatston.)

Good News, Part 3: God Will Help You

You probably feel battered by all of this information, so let me encourage you: God will help you address this health and fitness issue in amazing ways once you realize you need to.

Now that my eyes have been opened to the fact that my efforts are actually so important to my husband (and, conversely, that my lack of effort is so hurtful), you wouldn't believe the difference it has made in my motivation. I feel like the Lord has blessed my desire to serve my husband and our marriage by giving me a permanent internal motivation to have a healthy "temple." And I know He will do the same for you.

> God will help you address this health and fitness issue in amazing ways once you realize you need to.

I hope you have read this chapter prayerfully, allowing God to give you peace rather than a knot in your stomach. God is a God of peace, after all. And He—like our husbands—loves us no matter what our imperfections are.

WORDS FOR YOUR HEART

What Your Man Most Wishes You Knew About Him

The one thing men most wish they could tell us. . .

We've come almost to the end of our journey together. But before I get to the final, most important revelation about the inner lives of men, I want to offer something from my heart as I walk this path with you.

Some of us may be challenged by what we have learned in these pages. These realities may not fit our idealistic or politically correct views of men. But just as we have discussed the difficult choices we expect our men to make, we must make our own. We can remain behind our safe, carefully constructed viewpoints about our men, or we can step out in courage to face the truth—and all that it means for what we must become.

Let us accept this call to maturity.

Let us accept this call to maturity and receive this invitation for our generation to become the strong, gentle, godly women our men need. If we are willing to be molded by His hands, the Lord will shower us, our men, and our relationships with abundance. That is the way He works. He made us for each other. He is the Author of love.

And that brings me to the conclusion of our journey—the single most important thing you need to know about the inner lives of men. The response that surprised me the most from the survey.

THE NUMBER-ONE SURVEY RESPONSE

As you now know, I asked the survey respondents one open-ended question that they could answer however they wanted:

> What is the one thing that you wish your wife/significant other knew, but you feel you can't explain to her or tell her?

Hundreds of responses rolled in, and far and away the top response was this:

How much I love her.

I was stunned. Here was a perfect opportunity for men to vent, if they wanted to, or to share those things they wished their mates would work on. And yet, by far, the largest number of those responding—almost twice as many as the next highest response—chose to use the space to say that they wished their wives knew how much they loved them (or the cousin statement, that there was nothing they couldn't share because they had a great relationship).

After I shared this truth at a large community group, a man came down front after the talk and told me, "That is so true. And it's not that I don't tell my wife that I love her! I tell her that all the time. It's that I never seem to be able to tell her in a way that she'll believe me."

One man surveyed seemed to perfectly capture the way many men feel about the women in their lives, even if there are things in the relationship that need work. He answered that he wished his wife knew, "How important some things are to me that I won't mention because she's more important to me than all those other things."

Men want to show us how much they love us, and they also

long for their women to understand what is going on inside even though they sometimes can't explain it well. In the years since the original edition of this book came out, one of the most powerful things I have seen is the men whose eyes tear up as they listen to me explain these truths, moved by the thought that their wives might be able to—or want to—truly understand them.

So in the Interest of Understanding... the Top Five

In earlier pages, you saw the responses to each of the multiple-choice survey questions. But when the men wrote in what was most important to them, out of all the primary topics, the top five responses looked like this. In reverse order:

10% "I need her to understand my burden to provide / how draining my job is."

10% "I need more sex."

15% "I need more respect, in private and public."

18% "I wish she'd make more of an effort to take care of herself."

And number one...

32% "I want her to know how much I love her" / "There's nothing I can't tell her."

Out of the infinite number of topics a man could mention, to have so many men say that one same thing is astounding...and wonderful.

"HOW MUCH I LOVE HER"

I'll close by reprinting here a sample of the loving comments from the survey. We've talked a lot in this book about all those things your man may need but intentionally haven't dealt with what you and I need. What we need, of course, is to feel our men's love. And if your man is like most men, he really does long to show it to you.

"The One Thing I Most Wish My Wife Knew..." (in Alphabetical Order)

- "After so many years, I hope my wife knows that she is the best hope in my life. We don't have everything that we desire material-wise, but there is so much more to life than that. I hope my wife knows that I love her and cherish our friendship, forever."
- "How great of a person I think she is."
- "How happy she makes me even when I am stressed or down about something else."
- "How much I love and appreciate her."
- "How much I love her."
- "How much I really care."
- "How much I truly do care for and love her and the kids."
- "How much she means to me."

- "I am very happy with my wife.... She may not be the perfect woman, but she is the perfect woman for me."
- "I have a perfect wife and marriage!"
- "I have a wonderful relationship with my wife and we communicate well. I wouldn't change a thing."
- "I love her and only her. It doesn't matter that our relationship isn't perfect—my love for her is so deep that nothing could break it."
- "I love my wife and want to be with her."
- "I love you. Please understand me. Make the leap to try."
- "I love you with all my heart."

"I love her with all my heart and would do anything it took to keep that love alive."

- "I wish that she knew how much I look up to her for *all* she is—intelligent, beautiful, capable, sexy, creative, generous, and kind. It seems that not a day passes when she doesn't feel insecure in one of these categories (or sometimes more than one). I wish that she had the confidence in herself that I have in her."

- "I would like her to know every day that I love her with all my heart and would do anything it took to keep that love alive."
- "That I am a sensitive man who loves deeply and wants to be loved deeply. And that I want to serve her if she would just let me."
- "That I love her more than she thinks I do."
- "That I will love her no matter what."
- "That she is the most important thing in life."
- "That she truly is the light of my life."
- "We have been together a long time, and I hope she knows I will always love her."

THE HOPE OF ORDINARY MEN

As you have read these insights into the inner lives of men, I hope you walk away with two main realizations: How much our men love us. And how much power God has given us to either tear them down or build them up to be the men He created them to be.

One Sunday morning, as we were concluding a pastoral interview in front of his congregation, a well-known pastor said something that perfectly captured this—and took my breath away. He stood up from where we had been sitting, walked to the front of the stage, and gazed out upon a vast auditorium of thousands. His voice was quiet with emotion: "I know you all think you have a good pastor. You don't. *You have a great pastor's wife.*" He knew what all men know, and what we now have the opportunity to do something about, every day, from now on.

Let me close with this great encouragement one man provided for every woman out there who wants to support her man in becoming all God intends him to be.

> It is so true that behind every great man is a great woman. There are a lot of men out there who are mediocre simply because their wives will not support them and bring them to greatness. And there are a lot of mediocre men who are destined to become great men—who *are becoming* great men—because their wives love and support them.
>
> My wife expects great things from me, even though I'm a pretty ordinary guy, really. She looks at me like I'm a genius in my field. She respects me in public and affirms me in private. I love her. And like all men, I want to live up to her expectations.

May the truths you've encountered here and in the preceding chapters encourage you to go forward in your new understanding of your man with hope, in confidence, and in peace.

Acknowledgments

Both editions of this book required the help and input of hundreds of people, and although I cannot list them all here, they have my deepest thanks. A few, however, *must* be mentioned.

The professional surveys that form the backbone of this book were guided and directed by Chuck Cowan of Analytic Focus (analyticfocus.com) and performed by the excellent team at Decision Analyst (decisionanalyst.com).

I am so grateful for the honesty and vulnerability of the many men who were willing to be interviewed, and to protect their privacy, I will not list them here. But I would like to thank Dr. Emerson Eggerichs of Love and Respect Ministries (loveandrespect.com), Daniel Weiss of Focus on the Family, Ken Ruettgers, and the other men listed by name in the book for their willingness to share their insight.

If this book is anointed by the Father in any way, it is because a dedicated team prayed for it every day—in fact, two different teams for the two different editions. They know that they did the real work of prayer, and I am so very, very grateful.

Most important, God used a small team of people—mostly men—to actively shape this book. My eternal gratitude goes to these core advisors: my husband, Jeff (I'll get back to him in a minute); my book agent, Calvin Edwards; and my world-class editors, Dave and Heather Kopp, as well as Bill Jensen and Don Jacobson at the original Multnomah. I'm so very grateful for my continuing partnership with Dave and the rest of the team at WaterBrook Multnomah, including Steve Cobb, Ken Petersen, Carie Freimuth, and Alison O'Hara, as well as for the editing aid of Amy McDonell, Eric Stanford, and Laura Wright on this revision.

Also important were my parents, Dick and Judy Reidinger, my brother, Rick, and my team of male and female readers, including Lisa and Eric Rice, D. J. Snell, Nancy French, Dan Maljanian, Jim Sharp, Roger Scarlett, Ann Browne, Katie Gates, Alison Darrell, Julie Anne Fidler, Bruce and Sue Osterink, and many others. Jenny Reynolds was deeply important as my research assistant on every aspect of the brain science, for this book and others.

Starting when *For Women Only* was first published in 2004, God used the explosion of interest in this book to raise up a whole ministry dedicated to equipping people to thrive in life and relationships through research and eyeopening truths. And in the last eight years, I could not have done *any* of it—or written this new edition—without the incredible support of my staff team, especially Linda Crews, my amazing director of operations who has built the ministry with me, and the outreach support of my wonderful speaking agent, Naomi Duncan. Throughout 2012, Linda and my staff members, Cathy Kidd, Karen Newby, Sally Hendry, and Theresa Colquitt, helped to take everything else off my plate so I could write this new edition and work on other books.

Finally, there is no way to adequately express my love and respect to my husband, Jeff. Bud, there is no other person as responsible for the content of *any* of my books as you. God has given you a special gift of insight and the ability to put into words so many things you would otherwise have found difficult to articulate. Your partnership on these projects has been one of the great joys of my life, and your wisdom, prayer, encouragement, and steadfast support have meant more than I can ever say. You are an example of what a husband should be, which is why my greatest gratitude goes to the Author of love, who gave us to each other.

Notes

1. *The Natural,* directed by Barry Levinson, TriStar Pictures, 1984.
2. "Attached," episode 160 of *Star Trek: The Next Generation,* originally aired November 8, 1993.
3. Francis X. Maguire, *You're the Greatest! How Validated Employees Can Impact Your Bottom Line,* ed. Steve Williford (Germantown, TN: Saltillo, 2001), 210–11.
4. Jack Welch and John A. Byrne, *Jack: Straight from the Gut* (New York: Warner, 2001), 5.
5. Many of the brain-science details in this chapter are drawn from Michael Gurian, *What Could He Be Thinking? How a Man's Mind Really Works* (New York: Macmillan, 2004).
6. Gurian, *What Could He Be Thinking?* 86, emphasis mine.
7. *The Lord of the Rings: The Return of the King,* directed by Peter Jackson, New Line Cinema, 2003.
8. Charlie Rich, "Behind Closed Doors," *Behind Closed Doors,* copyright © 1973, Epic Records.
9. Jill Eggleton Brett, "Not Tonight, Dear…," *Today's Christian Woman,* March/April 2002, 68.
10. Beyond the information in this chapter, further details and detailed citations on the male visual brain wiring can be found on pages 250–53 and 320 of my book *The Male Factor.* But here are a few starting points. One good study about the visual

brain wiring and the action of the nucleus accumbens was conducted by a group of scientists from Massachusetts General Hospital, Harvard Medical School, and Massachusetts Institute of Technology using functional MRI scans. Itzhak Aharon et al., "Beautiful Faces Have Variable Reward Value: fMRI and Behavioral Evidence," *Neuron* 32, no. 3 (November 2001): 537–51. Another study, by Emory University researchers, shows that when men and women see stimuli they perceive as sexual, most men have stronger biological responses than most women. Stephan Hamann et al., "Men and Women Differ in Amygdala Response to Visual Sexual Stimuli," *Nature Neuroscience* 7, no. 4 (April 2004): 411–16. And Joseph LeDoux, a neuroscientist at the Center for Neural Science at New York University, was the first to identify the "shortcut" for gut-level memories that can bypass the thinking centers of the brain and pop up again. Joseph LeDoux, "Emotional Memory Systems in the Brain," *Behavioural Brain Research* 58, nos. 1–2 (December 20, 1993): 69–79; "Emotion, Memory, and the Brain," *Scientific American* 270 (June 1994): 50–57; "Emotion and the Limbic System Concept," *Concepts in Neuroscience* 2 (1991): 169–99.

11. Stephen Arterburn and Fred Stoeker, *Every Man's Battle: Winning the War on Sexual Temptation One Victory at a Time* (Colorado Springs: WaterBrook, 2009).
12. *When Harry Met Sally,* directed by Rob Reiner, MGM Studios, 1989.

Dig deeper!

Ideal for individuals or small groups, the *For Women Only, For Men Only and For Couples Only Video Study Pack* offers materials for women, for men, and for couples. This resource with DVDs and a participant's guide, fosters thoughtful interaction, enabling couples to communicate better and embrace each other's differences.

Also available from Shaunti!

Praise for
For Men Only

"Once again, Shaunti and Jeff Feldhahn have unearthed a treasure chest of insights that are not only eyeopening but life-changing."

—Andy Stanley, senior pastor of North Point, Alpharetta, Georgia; best-selling author

"In our weekly couples' study, we read and discussed both *For Women Only* and *For Men Only* over the course of several months. They were fascinating and very helpful. The findings in *For Men Only* about how women think are so enlightening. My wife and I think these books should be required premarital reading!"

—Comedian Jeff Foxworthy

"When we featured Shaunti's books on *FamilyLife Today,* the phone rang off the hook! When Shaunti and Jeff come back on our broadcast, I'm buying some more phones. *For Men Only* is fresh and relevant—good stuff for every marriage. Read it!"

—Dennis Rainey, president of FamilyLife Today

"Most of my work helping passive Christian men become more like Jesus involves how best to relate to women. I'm going to make sure to keep a case of the Feldhahns' excellent book handy at all times."

—Paul Coughlin, author of *No More Christian Nice Guy*

"If you've ever asked, 'Why does she do, think, or say that?' then you've got to read this book. Shaunti and Jeff not only answer this question, they eliminate the confusion that has kept far too many men from bridging the gender gap."

—Drs. Les and Leslie Parrott, best-selling authors of *Love Talk*

"Men, we're supposed to love our wives and live with them in an understanding way. That's the clear assignment God gives each of us in the Scriptures. So buy this book, read it a couple of times, underline a few key ideas, and then keep it where you can review it regularly. It will help you be the husband God wants you to be."

—Bob Lepine, cohost of *FamilyLife Today*

Praise for *For Men Only* and *For Women Only*

"Whenever Shaunti Feldhahn appears as a guest on the *Focus on the Family* radio program, we know that listener response will be enthusiastic. She has a way of connecting with the audience that is unique and compelling. We're thankful for the unique perspective she provides not only to the Christian community but to the culture at large."

—Jim Daly, president of Focus on the Family

"These are the books I pass out to people as the best on the subject. Shaunti Feldhahn has the rare ability to do impeccable research and then make her findings incredibly practical. There is something to learn on every page."

—Jim Burns, PhD, president of HomeWord; author of *Creating an Intimate Marriage*

"Whatever Shaunti Feldhahn researches, read. Actually, do more than read...study! Shaunti's ability to ask the right questions, find the right answers, and communicate the results clearly and practically sets her apart as a gifted researcher. Her content guides and changes lives."

—Emerson Eggerichs, PhD, best-selling author of *Love and Respect*

"Shaunti Feldhahn has a unique gift for helping men understand women, and women, men. Her books, *For Women Only* and *For Men Only,* are the best I know at providing rich and practical gender understanding that can be used immediately. I highly recommend both all the time!"

—Robert Lewis, author of *Raising a Modern-Day Knight;* founder of Men's Fraternity

for
men
only

OTHER BOOKS BY SHAUNTI AND JEFF FELDHAHN

For Women Only
by Shaunti Feldhahn

For Young Men Only
by Jeff Feldhahn and Eric Rice
with Shaunti Feldhahn

For Young Women Only
by Shaunti Feldhahn and Lisa Rice

For Parents Only
by Shaunti Feldhahn and Lisa Rice

Made to Crave for Young Women
by Lysa TerKeurst and Shaunti Feldhahn

For Women Only in the Workplace
by Shaunti Feldhahn

The Male Factor
by Shaunti Feldhahn

The Life Ready Woman
by Shaunti Feldhahn and Robert Lewis

Shaunti and Jeff Feldhahn

for

A Straightforward Guide to the Inner Lives of Women

REVISED AND UPDATED EDITION

MULTNOMAH
BOOKS

For Men Only

Details in some anecdotes and stories have been changed to protect the identities of the persons involved.

Hardcover ISBN 978-1-60142-445-7
eBook ISBN 978-1-60142-209-5

Cover design by Mark D. Ford

Published in association with the literary agency of Calvin W. Edwards, 1220 Austin Glen Drive, Atlanta, GA 30338.

Published in the United States by Multnomah, an imprint of the Crown Publishing Group, a division of Penguin Random House LLC, New York.

Library of Congress Cataloging-in-Publication Data
Feldhahn, Shaunti Christine.
For men only : a straightforward guide to the inner lives of women / Shaunti and Jeff Feldhahn. — Revised Edition.
pages cm
Includes bibliographical references.
ISBN 978-1-60142-445-7 — ISBN 978-1-60142-209-5 (electronic)
1. Men (Christian theology) 2. Christian men—Conduct of life. I. Feldhahn, Jeff. II. Title.
BT703.5.F45 2013
248.8'42—dc23

2012044585

Printed in the United States of America
2018—Revised Edition

12

Special Sales

To our parents,
who taught us through their
example that working to
understand each other
is worth it.

Contents

RETHINKING RANDOM

Why you need a new map of the female universe

Like some guys I know, you might be tempted to skip this introduction and jump right to the sex chapter. And if you're chuckling right now, it probably means you already did. Or were about to. It's not a bad choice, actually. Just a little self-defeating. If you've been in a committed relationship with a woman for more than, say, a day, you know that going just for what you want isn't actually going to get you what you want for very long.

A week, maybe?

But let's be honest—one of the main reasons you're looking at this book is because you are trying to get something you want. Not sex (well, not just sex), but a more fulfilling, harmonious relationship with your wife, one that isn't quite so hard or confusing. And the back cover gave you the wild idea that understanding her might actually be possible.

Either that or for some reason the woman in question just handed you this book.

Hmm.

Well, either way, take a look at the revelations we've uncovered. We think you'll be convinced. Each chapter explains things about the woman you love that may have often left you feeling helpless, confused, or just plain angry. Each chapter points out simple, doable solutions. The only genius required is that you make a decision up-front that you're willing to think differently. This is a short book, but if you read it cover to cover, you'll walk away with your eyes opened to things you may have never before understood about your wife or girlfriend.

Each chapter points out simple, doable solutions.

That's what happened with me—Jeff. And I'm just your average, semi-confused guy. (Actually, sometimes *totally confused* is more accurate.) And since we average, semi-confused guys have to stick together, that's why, even though Shaunti and I are both authoring this book, I'll be the one doing the talking.

FIRST, SOME BACKGROUND

In 2004 Shaunti published *For Women Only: What You Need to Know About the Inner Lives of Men,* which quickly became a best-seller. Based on nationally representative surveys, focus groups, personal interviews, and other research with thousands of men, it opened women's eyes to things that most of us guys had always wished our wife or girlfriend knew. Things like, most of us need to feel *respected* even more than loved. Or that besides just getting enough sex, we also have a huge need to feel sexually *desired* by our wives.

I'm not sure exactly why, but women everywhere were shocked. And by the flood of letters from around the country—from both women *and* their grateful husbands—Shaunti and I have seen how much good can come when the opposite sex finally has their eyes opened to things they simply didn't understand before.

In this book, the shock is on the other foot. Now it's their turn to exclaim to us, "I can't believe you didn't already know that!"

When Shaunti's publisher first approached us about doing a companion book to *For Women Only* to help men understand women, I had two major concerns. First, I didn't think guys would read a "relationship" book. For most of us, the last relationship book we read was in premarital counseling—and then only because we were forced to. But more to the point, I doubted that women could ever be understood. Compared to other complex matters—like the tides, say, or how to figure a baseball pitcher's ERA—women seemed unknowable. Random even.

> I'm not sure exactly why, but women everywhere were shocked by how men thought.

I explained my skepticism to one early focus group of women:

JEFF: Guys tend to think that women are random. We think, *I pulled this lever last week and got a certain reaction. But when I pulled that same lever this week, I got a totally different reaction.* That's random!

WOMAN IN GROUP: But we aren't random! If you pull the lever and get a different reaction, either you're pulling a different lever or you're pulling it in a different way.

SHAUNTI: What men need is a sort of map to their wives or girlfriends. Because we *can* be mapped. We can be known and understood—firm ground.

JEFF: Uh, no. See, guys think of a woman as a swamp. You can't see where you're stepping, and sooner or later you just know you're going to get stuck in quicksand. And the more you struggle to get free, the deeper you get sucked in. So every guy on the planet knows that the best thing to do is just shut down and not struggle and hope somebody comes along to rescue you.

When I came to, Shaunti and the other women in the focus group assured me—and I have since seen for myself—that guys don't have to live in a swamp. That realization led us to the eventual subtitle of this book: *A Straightforward Guide to the Inner Lives of Women.*

> "Guys think of a woman as a swamp. You can't see where you're stepping, and sooner or later you just know you're going to get stuck in quicksand."

We have been astounded and humbled at the reaction to these simple, eyeopening truths. In fact, the book you are holding is actually the second edition of this book—which was needed because there was clearly a desire for this ongoing research.

Both *For Women Only* and *For Men Only* sparked a huge wave of encouragement and hope among ordinary men and women just like me and Shaunti, selling two million copies in twenty-two languages. We were flooded with e-mails and comments from men and women at our marriage conferences, saying things like "This saved my marriage" and "After ten years together, I finally know how to make my wife happy" and even "Jeff, I owe you one, buddy."

But since we've continued to learn new things, we also wanted to keep the book current. For this new edition, we have included some fascinating new findings, including the brain science behind *why* women sometimes think as they do. Plus we've added a new chapter—"The Reason Hiding in Her 'Unreasonable' Reaction"—that decodes those unpredictable reactions that she thinks of as, uh, normal.

After seeing the impact of this research, I realize that we really did uncover life-changing insights. Surprising truths that average guys like me *need* to hear from an average guy and be encouraged that if someone like me can learn it and do it, they can too.

THE SEVEN REVELATIONS

So let's go back to that swamp—the one we think is there but doesn't really exist. The most important key to "de-swamping" the woman in your life is to realize that some of your basic assumptions about her may be either too simplistic or flat wrong. By simplistic, I mean that we tend to operate with a partial or surface understanding of our wife or girlfriend. And to make matters worse, most guys have no idea how to make their limited understanding work in actual practice.

For example, most guys have heard that women want security. Okay. But what does that mean, exactly? A regular paycheck? A big house? It's a huge shocker to talk to hundreds of women and find that while financial security is nice, it isn't nearly as important to them as feeling emotionally secure—feeling close and confident that you will be there for her no matter what. And believe it or not, ensuring emotional security turns out to be a lot easier than ensuring the financial security you are probably busting your tail to provide.

For Men Only will help you move from surface understandings to the all-important recognition of what those things mean in everyday life with your woman. Once you start testing out these findings, you'll be amazed at the difference it makes for both of you. Because—brace yourself—you will realize that you *can* understand your wife and make her happy.

You will realize that you *can* understand your wife and make her happy.

Sound wildly impossible? I'll go one better. You'll see that this huge shift can happen for you and the woman you love *even if it starts out as a totally one-sided effort on your part.*

The second edition of *For Men Only* is organized around seven major findings outlined on the facing page. Some of these will be surprises to you. Some won't, at least to begin with. (But that's the thing about swamps—what you see is rarely what is really there.)

HOW WE FOUND OUT: OUR METHODOLOGY

In our initial research for this book, Shaunti and I worked for a year to identify inner "map terrain" areas that are common to most women but that most guys tend not to understand. Besides conducting hundreds of in-person interviews, we gathered huge amounts of anecdotal information at dozens of women's events where Shaunti was presenting materials from *For Women Only.* I spoke with stay-at-home moms, business owners, and secretaries; and on airplanes, in focus groups, and over Shaunti's book table while she was being mobbed at women's conferences. I sifted through hundreds of e-mails and forum postings from Shaunti's forwomenonlybook.com website.

In all these venues, I was really just the "embedded male." Like the reporters who rode with the armored cavalry divisions at the opening of the Iraq War, I kept my helmet on, my head down, and my notebook handy.

After all that research, we did a scientific, nationally representative survey. As Shaunti had done for her previous book, we

Our Surface Understanding	What That Means in Practice
She needs to feel loved.	Even if your relationship is great, your mate likely has a fundamental insecurity about your love—and when that insecurity is triggered, she may respond in ways that confuse or upset you until she feels reassured.
Women are emotional.	Women deal with multiple thoughts and emotions from their past and present all the time, at the same time—and these can't be easily dismissed.
She's impossible to figure out.	There is usually a logical reason behind her baffling words or actions—and behavior that confuses or frustrates you often signals a need she is asking you to meet.
Women want security—in other words, financial security.	Your woman needs emotional security and closeness with you so much that she will endure financial insecurity to get it.
She doesn't want you to fix it; she just wants you to listen.	When she is sharing an emotional problem, her feelings and her desire to be heard are much more important than the problem itself.
She doesn't want sex much—which means she must not want me.	Physically, women tend to crave sex less often than men do—and it is usually not related to your desirability.
She wants to look attractive.	Inside your smart, secure wife lives a little girl who deeply needs to know that you find her beautiful—and that you only have eyes for her.

worked with survey-design expert Chuck Cowan, former chief of census design for the U.S. Census Bureau, and the well-respected survey company Decision Analyst. They came together to help us design and conduct a groundbreaking survey of four hundred women from all over the country. Since then, we've done other surveys. Adding it all up, well over six thousand women provided input for this book.

> I was really just the "embedded male." I kept my helmet on, my head down, and my notebook handy.

I know you'll be fascinated by the results. While some of the findings may be challenging or difficult to accept, most men have been surprised by how helpful many of these truths are and how *simple* they are to implement for a better, easier relationship, a happy wife (or girlfriend), and more peace in their home.

THE MAP KEY

Before we tackle the findings, here are some pointers on reading the map:

- **This book holds to a biblical worldview.** Our aim is to be relevant and revealing, no matter what your worldview is, and we surveyed women regardless of cultural background or religious beliefs. But thousands of churches now require our books before a couple gets married. And because Shaunti and I view life through our Christian faith, we have seen that these findings are consistent with biblical principles. We believe that relationships are most fulfilling when both people have a common commitment to serving Jesus. Since our focus is on what we learned through research, we do not quote heavily from Scripture, but we draw from and reference it as the only dependable guidebook for relationships.

- **This is not a comprehensive marriage book.** Since there are already many great marriage books on the market, there's no need to cover topics that other experts can tackle far better than we can or that guys already have a good handle on. (We list several recommended resources at our website, formenonlybook.com.) Instead, we focus specifically on high-leverage surprises—truths that we don't tend to get, where small, simple changes can have huge impacts. Also, while our content is probably a bit more targeted toward married men, these insights will be helpful for any male-female relationship. That said, if your relationship is seriously on the rocks, this little book will probably open your eyes in some important areas, but it is not designed to cover a crisis situation. We encourage you to get the kind of counsel and support your marriage deserves.

- **This is not an equal treatment.** Just as *For Women Only* was intentionally one-sided (and if your wife read it, you may have benefited from that fact), so is this book. Yes, you have needs too, and there certainly may be relationship issues arising because *she* doesn't understand *you.* But *For Women Only* addresses many of those, and this book is not about them. This is only about the inner lives of women, and we're focusing entirely on how men relate to women, not the other way around. (That is also why the survey polled only heterosexual women.)
- **There are exceptions to every rule.** Recognize that when I say "most women" appear to think a certain way, *most* does not mean *all.* We make generalizations out of necessity to be helpful in the widest number of circumstances. Inevitably there will be exceptions. Statistically, in fact, it is likely that some male readers will think in a way similar to their wives in one area or another. Everyone is an individual, so the goal is to have your eyes open for what is most important in *your* situation.

- **Our findings may not be politically correct, but we try to be true to the evidence.** For six years, Shaunti was a newspaper columnist on women's issues, and she sometimes received e-mails from women complaining that she was doing exactly what we intend to do in this book—making generalizations about women. Add the fact that I, as a *guy,* am daring to make those generalizations, and we recognize the potential for controversy. We don't quite know how to get around that, so we decided to just report what we learned.

We decided to just report what we learned.

THE THING TO DO NEXT

We think that in the pages ahead you're going to receive a lot of promising invitations to try some new things. Most are incredibly simple, but they may not come naturally. At least at first. Of course, if all this were already instinctive to you, then you wouldn't be troubled by randomness, confusion, or frustration... and did I mention swamps?

My encouragement to you: Give the process time as you retrain years of incorrect assumptions and counterproductive reactions. Bring a humble attitude. Be willing to practice. Believe it can be done.

Because I've learned that it can be.

After several months as an embedded male, I was watching a movie with Shaunti one night. Halfway through, I casually mentioned that I didn't like the way one of the female characters was treating another. Shaunti sat up on the couch, grinned, and said, "You're thinking like a girl!"

Now, she meant it as high praise, but in the small midwestern town where I grew up, that kind of talk could get a guy slugged. But then I realized: maybe I *had* learned a valuable thing or two about the female universe just by listening in.

Here's hoping that you do too.

THE DEAL IS NEVER CLOSED

Why her "I do" will always mean "Do you?"—and what to do about it

Even if your relationship is great, your mate likely has a fundamental insecurity about your love—and when that insecurity is triggered, she may respond in ways that confuse or upset you until she feels reassured.

Reassurance

Think of the deals you've struck in your life. Your first car. Your first real job. Your first house. You saw what you wanted, did what you had to do to get it—and you came home with a done deal.

No deal compares to winning a wife, though. You pursued

her with all the courage, creativity, and resources you could muster. Then, one day, you closed the deal. Your wedding day was the day you proved your love to the world and to her.

Divorce stats to the contrary, I'd bet that—since you're reading this book—your marriage feels like the most obviously *closed deal* in your whole life. Right?

Well, not exactly. As we'll explain in this chapter, it just feels closed for you.

No, your wife isn't still out looking for suitors. But in an unusual and powerful way that married men don't really understand, your wife doesn't feel permanently loved once the marriage papers are signed. She may have a subconscious question about your love. She may *know* you love her, but there will be times when her *feelings* will need to be convinced and reassured. Sometimes over and over again.

THE TRUTH ABOUT "I DO"

It's no surprise that a woman needs to feel loved. What is a surprise is how easy it is for her to *not* feel loved. It turns out that buried inside most women—even those in great relationships—is a latent insecurity about whether their man *really* loves them and even whether they are truly lovable. In our research, women described it as a subconscious question: *Would he choose me all over again?* This sense of vulnerability may usually be under the surface of their minds, but when it is triggered, most women start worrying about whether the relationship is okay and show signs of distress until the concern is resolved.

You can read "show signs of distress" as "drive their man nuts" if you want.

> Buried inside most women—even those in great relationships—is a latent insecurity about whether their man really loves them.

Fact is, you're going to see (as I did) that many of the things that perplex and even anger us about our wife or girlfriend are *signals that she is feeling insecure about our love or the relationship.* Have you ever wondered why she:

- asks, "Do you love me?" even though you've done nothing to indicate you've changed your mind about loving her? (In fact, you said "I love you" this morning on your way out the door!)
- takes your need for space or "cave" time as an indication that you're upset with her and trying to get away from her?
- wants to talk, talk, talk about your relationship—especially at the times you least want to?

- seems to turn critical or angry with you for no reason you can figure?
- gets crabby or emotional and seems to push you away—but then gets even more unhappy when you *stay* away?
- gets upset or wants to punish you for spending time with the guys or doing other things away from her?

If you're like me, you react to these seemingly unrelated behaviors with confusion and frustration—or worse. If it happens a lot, you may get angry back or you may withdraw and just try to endure, hoping things will someday change. Or you may become convinced that you'll never know what she wants and could never please her if you did.

You'll see those "drive you nuts" behaviors as red warning lights signaling a breach in your wife's confidence about whether you really love her.

But our research for *For Men Only* persuaded me that all of those behaviors are related and many are easy to resolve. Once you're clued in, you'll see those "drive you nuts" behaviors as red warning lights signaling a breach in your wife's confidence about whether you really love her. In fact, the more extreme the behavior, the more serious her doubt.

I know it sounds crazy that your wife might ever wonder whether you love her, especially when things are going fine. But as it turns out, your "I do" actually *didn't* bring permanent emotional closure, forever putting her mind to rest about your feelings for her. It doesn't erase the insecurity about your love that lives under the surface in even the most happily married woman—an insecurity that, when triggered, becomes a deeply felt uncertainty: "Do you *still* love me? Are we okay?"

Now, you might be thinking, *Surely this doesn't apply to* my *wife! She* knows *I love her!*

Yes, she probably does. But we're not talking about what she *knows logically* but rather about the *feeling* that rises up when something triggers it. And it turns out that understanding and knowing how to address *this one thing* functions as a kind of "open sesame" that brings a man a lot more peace and pleasure at home.

THREE SURPRISES (WHAT "NEVER A DONE DEAL" FEELS LIKE TO HER)

As the token embedded male for our surveys and focus groups, I was in for a number of big surprises on the subject of women's relational, triggered insecurity.

My First Surprise: How Frequently These Feelings Appear

Whereas most guys coast along, rarely thinking about the health of their relationship, it is on a woman's mind whether she wants it to be or not. Seven out of every ten women said that their relationship and how their man felt about them was anywhere from occasionally to nearly always on their minds. Fewer than 20 percent said that they wondered about it only when things were difficult. (Just 12 percent never thought about it at all.)

Under what circumstances do you think about your relationship, whether it is going well, or how your husband/significant other feels about you? (Choose one answer.)

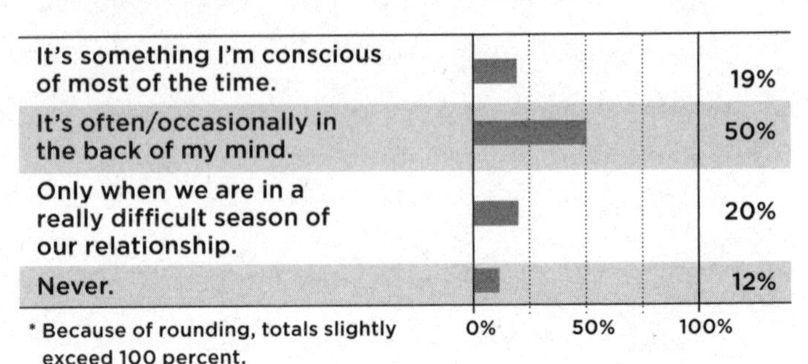

I'm guessing that, for most guys, "occasional" thoughts about the closeness of their relationship might boil down to birthdays, anniversaries, and when something goes drastically, obviously haywire. But when we asked women what they meant by "occasional" concern about how their man felt about them, I often heard that it meant several times a week or *whenever it was triggered* (such as by what we might consider a relatively minor spat).

We checked these results by asking the question another way and got an even stronger response. Four out of five women acknowledged sometimes feeling insecure about their man's love and the relationship. Among women under forty-five, the percentage jumped to 91 percent, and among those with children in middle school or younger, it was almost universal.

I found that we guys can understand this foreign-seeming insecurity if we compare it to one of our own. As one woman put it, "You know that record that's always running in a guy's head about providing? Well, *we* have the same fundamental concern about our relationship all the time. And if it's not going well, it can mess up everything else in our lives."

My Second Surprise: How Intensely Painful These Feelings Are

Almost every woman I asked said that she cared about her man so much that when this relational insecurity was triggered, it was very painful—sometimes almost debilitating—and it became difficult, if not impossible, for her to get it off her mind. As several women put it, "When we're at odds, nothing is right with the world until it is resolved."

On the survey, eight out of ten women agreed, saying that this "Does he really love me?" concern left them feeling anxious, preoccupied, emotionally withdrawn, unvalued, or depressed—and most of these were affected in visible ways. Look at the data:

When you are feeling insecure about his love or the relationship, which of the following are true about your feelings? (Choose all correct answers.)*

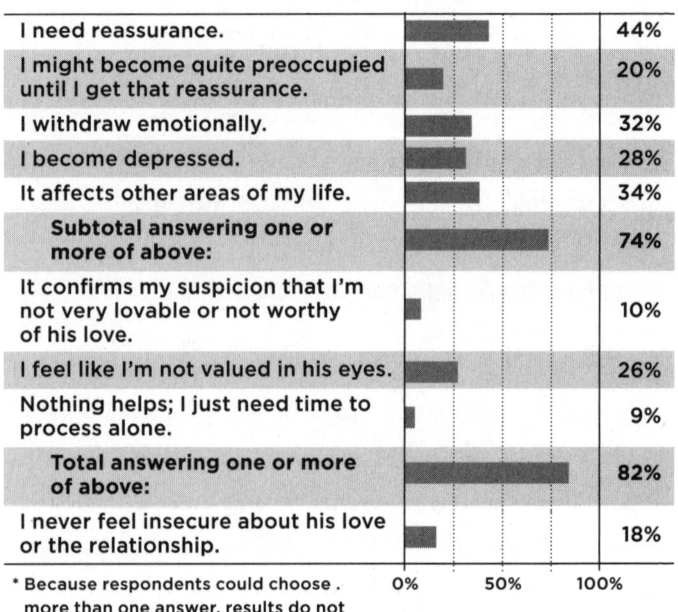

* Because respondents could choose more than one answer, results do not add up to 100%

You and I have every right to think the woman we love *shouldn't* feel insecure. We're faithful, we go to work, we *do* love her...and we're still here. But just because we think our wife *should* feel secure doesn't mean that she always *does.* Which leads to my third realization.

My Third Surprise: How Resistant to Logic (That Is, My Logic) Her Feelings Remain

Shaunti points out, "It's irrelevant whether she should know logically that she's loved. If she doesn't *feel* loved, it's the same for her as if she *isn't* loved." One survey taker put it this way:

> I wish he realized that, where he processes everything based just on logic, I process information based also on emotion. He says that I know logically that he loves me, and that should be enough. But the fact is, emotionally, I don't *feel* loved.

Think about one of our own concerns that's often resistant to logic—our success at work. Even secure, competent men who are good at their jobs inwardly feel—all logic to the contrary—that they still could be just a few mistakes or industry hiccups away from everything going south, even losing their job. When things are tough at work and the economy is shaky, it makes a huge difference when our boss makes a point of reassuring us that our job is secure.

In the same way, even women in good relationships feel they could be just a few bad blowups away from things going south, even losing their man's love. As one woman said, "I don't think we ever take his love for granted." So when there is any sort of trouble between you, she needs you to reassure her of your love and that the relationship is secure.

> Even women in good relationships feel they could be just a few bad blowups away from things going south.

HIDDEN TRIGGERS

In the course of everyday life in a reasonably healthy relationship, what is most likely to drive her to wonder, *Does he still love me?* Here are a few triggers:

- **Conflict.** For us, as guys, conflict is just conflict—it's not a signal or a start of something bigger. But as one woman explained, "A lot of desperate feelings surface for me when I feel like my husband is displeased with me. I know it sounds old-fashioned, and I'm a pretty independent person, but it still really affects me."

- **Withdrawal.** When we're faced with conflict, men tend to retreat into silence to escape unwanted feelings. Often we can't fully articulate something yet or we want to avoid saying something hurtful. Unfortunately, seeing her man withdraw or become moody usually generates *more* unwanted feelings for a woman. Several women described what crossed their mind this way: *What happens if he doesn't snap out of it this time?*
- **Silence.** Because women have a radar for unspoken conflict, it's pretty easy for women to jump to conclusions when their man is more withdrawn or quieter than usual. As one woman put it, "If you're quiet, it must be me." The women told me it makes a big difference when a guy sees the misunderstanding for what it is and uses it as an opportunity to reassure her. ("I'm not mad, don't worry. Just concerned about work.")
- **Her emotional bank account is depleted.** Perhaps she's exhausted, or you've been absent a lot (even necessary absences can be draining). Maybe the two of you have unresolved issues and conflicts. Regardless of the reason, even if it has nothing to do with you, her insecurity will be more easily triggered if her emotional reserves are low.

Once we recognize these triggers and see the red warning light for what it is—a signal that she needs to be reassured of our love—we can take some incredibly simple steps toward being part of the answer for her rather than part of the problem.

A PRACTICAL GUIDE TO TURNING OFF THE WARNING LIGHT

I hope you're seeing by now that a woman is likely to experience an undercurrent of relationship insecurity *even if* you and I are totally innocent of intent, injury, or error. (Not that we always *are,* but work with me here.) Since every day she subconsciously wonders *Does he love me?* she will be looking for clues to the answer every day.

Maybe this is what the apostle Paul had in mind when he wrote the simple admonition "Husbands, love your wives" in his letter to the church at Ephesus. I don't hear any echoes of "The deal is sealed" in his words. Or "Once you've won a wife, Bubba, you're off the hook." What I hear is much more dynamic: *Love, go on loving, continue to prove your love, keep on winning her heart with your love...*

I don't hear any echoes of "Once you've won a wife, Bubba, you're off the hook."

So how do you and I address the fact that our wives carry around this fundamental insecurity about our love? Based on our research, we see two key solutions. The first addresses her insecurity when it is triggered. The second prevents her insecurity from being triggered in the first place:

1. In the face of insecurity, reassure her.
2. Even after you've caught her, continue to pursue her.

Thankfully, both of these are completely doable for ordinary guys like you and me.

Part 1: Regular Reassurance

Once her insecurity has been triggered and her heart is anxiously wondering, *Does he really love me?* the solution is simple: reassure her that you do. Here are four ways to do that.

1. During Conflict, Reassure Her of Your Love

If you're like most guys, when you're in the middle of a conflict, you need time alone to process things. Most women we heard from react exactly the opposite—only 9 percent wanted to handle their feelings of insecurity alone.

The problem, of course, is that your pulling away to get space pushes her "Does he love me?" turmoil through the roof. If you need to get space, reassure her of your love first.

This is the magic bullet that almost every woman told us would make all the difference: if their man would say something like "I'm angry right now, and I need some space, but I want you to know: we're okay." On the survey, a whopping 95 percent of women said that this one step on our part would diminish or even eliminate the emotional turmoil on their part!

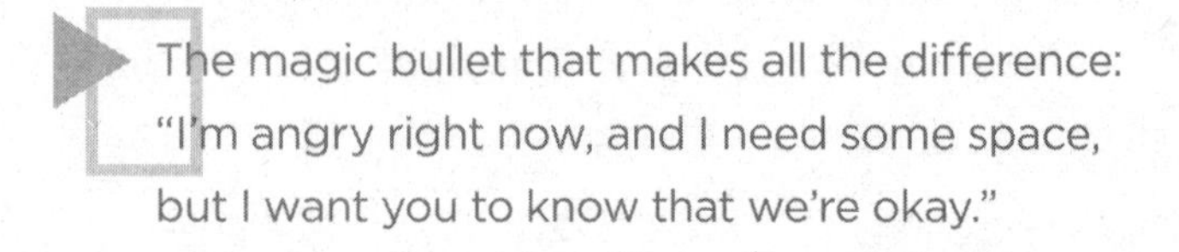

The magic bullet that makes all the difference: "I'm angry right now, and I need some space, but I want you to know that we're okay."

In an emotional conflict, if your husband/significant other initiates a step to reassure you of his love, how much does it help diminish any turmoil you are feeling? (Choose one answer.)

Answer	%
Not at all.	5%
Some.	34%
Quite a lot.	54%
It solves it.	8%

* Because of rounding, results slightly exceed 100 percent.

Chances are, in the midst of conflict, your woman is feeling unloved (even unlovable) and needs you to look her in the eye and tell her that you love her and you're not going anywhere.

Yes, this can be difficult. It's one thing for us to give reassurances when things are peachy, but it's quite another when we're at odds with each other and we'd rather stomp out to the garage and split a block of wood with our bare hands.

But the survey also showed that 86 percent of women said that, bolstered by our "I want you to know that we're okay" reassurance, they'd be better able to give us the space we need. (Do you see the possibilities? Reassure her of your love, *then* stomp out to the garage!) Why? Because we've reassured them on the original question: "Does he still love me?"

Suppose you and your husband/significant other are in the middle of an emotional conflict, and he eventually says, "I don't want to talk about this right now." If he were to add a reassurance, such as, "I want you to know that we're okay," would that make you more or less likely to be able to give him space? (Choose one answer.)

Answer	Percent
Much more likely.	43%
More likely.	43%
Less likely.	2%
It would have no relevance.	12%

0% 50% 100%

There is one final step to making this magic bullet really work. After you've had your space for a while, you have to come back and be willing to address the original issue without making her bring it up.

Easy? No. Effective? You bet. Because, as one woman said, "The fact that he comes back often matters more than the reason for the conflict in the first place."

"The fact that he comes back often matters more than the reason for the conflict in the first place."

2. If She's Upset, Realize That She Doesn't Need Space—She Needs a Hug

When our wife or girlfriend is upset, we do what we would do with other guys: we give her space to work things out. But with few exceptions, when women are upset, they don't want space; they want a hug. I think this next comment is one of the most valuable "just do this" quotes in the book:

> All I want is him to know that half the time I'm just as confused as he is. Instead of getting upset and leaving me alone to "calm down," I just want him to come close and give me a huge hug and let me know he loves me and he wants me to feel better again.

When I shared this comment at a marriage conference, one man shouted out in a joking way (sort of), "You mean hug the porcupine?!" All the men laughed and then looked astonished when all the women shouted "Yes!" and started clapping.

Here's how one woman tried to explain it to the men: "We don't see ourselves as being that intimidating or 'prickly' when we are upset, but I guess we are. If he would just move toward me rather than away—if he would just take a deep breath and hug me instead of retreating—he'd see those porcupine quills melt."

3. If She Needs to Talk About the Relationship, Do Your Best to Listen Without Becoming Defensive

The next step is more intimidating but essential. If she *does* need to talk, try to see it as she does: a joint problem-solving session instead of an attack on *you.*

"When I tell him how I feel about something concerning our relationship, I am just trying to share my feelings so we can discuss it," one woman said. "But he takes it as criticism, and then I feel like the bad guy for bringing it up. I wish he could understand that it's important for me to be able to talk about these things and understand that I'm not just being critical."

All this research has convinced me that when most women bring up a problem, they are *not* thinking that we've failed. We need to push through our natural tendency to view what they are saying as criticism.

4. If She Is Being Difficult, Don't Stop—Keep Reassuring Her of Your Love

Finally, let's address a dynamic that confuses and even aggravates us: the importance of reassuring and showing love to our wife *even when* she's difficult, critical, resistant, or pushing us away. As you can probably guess, that is the ultimate sign of the "Do you really love me?" question.

It seems crazy to us, but it turns out that for many women, the more unloved she feels, the more likely she is to push her husband away or to make it hard for him to love her. She's hoping he will prove that he *really does* love her by staying put and reassuring her of his love instead. One woman provided this explanation:

> You have to realize, if a woman says, "I need to hear that you love me," and the guy dutifully says, "I love you," well, that's essentially meaningless: like she made him say something he didn't feel. So if she's feeling confused and neglected and really does want to be assured of his feelings, she can't just ask.
>
> And if they are at odds, she's maybe a little mad at him, so when he approaches her, she pushes him away *even though closeness is what she most wants!* But if he'll put aside his pride and try again, if he'll risk grabbing her hand and saying something like, "Don't go away. I

want to know what's wrong," that will break through her defenses. It tells her that no matter how she's feeling right then—*whew*—he really loves her.

Notice that this type of reassurance doesn't mean "nobly enduring her mood(s) in silence" but rather doing the intensely difficult but courageous work of not just *hugging* the porcupine but *pursuing* the porcupine. Fair warning: this will include times when we've sensed insecurity and are trying to reassure her and still get pushed away. Few things drive a guy more crazy than the sense of being tested or manipulated, and most of us soon give up in disgust. I can't tell you how many times when facing resistance, I've thought, *Fine, suit yourself. I've got to cut the lawn anyway.* And then I pretty much put the incident out of my mind.

This type of reassurance doesn't mean "nobly enduring her mood(s) in silence."

Unfortunately a woman can't. She's still seeking the answer to the original question: "Do you still love me?" If the contentious, aggravating, push-you-away behavior is recurring, it is *because your wife truly is feeling that you don't love her—and has probably been feeling that way for some time.*

You may be trying your utmost to be a loving husband, but

clearly something is not getting through. She may need to feel loved in an entirely different way than you ever realized. So as you learn what that looks like, even if you're speechless with frustration, you're still in the game. Forget giving speeches and simply reach for her. We'll explain more in chapter 4.

Part 2: Persistent Pursuit

Now to an even more valuable tool for a man who wants to show his wife that he'd choose her all over again *today:* pursuit. Where reassurance *heals* insecurity, pursuit *prevents* a lot of insecurity. Pursuit actively makes her feel loved. In other words, it is likely to be the thing that makes you a great husband in her eyes.

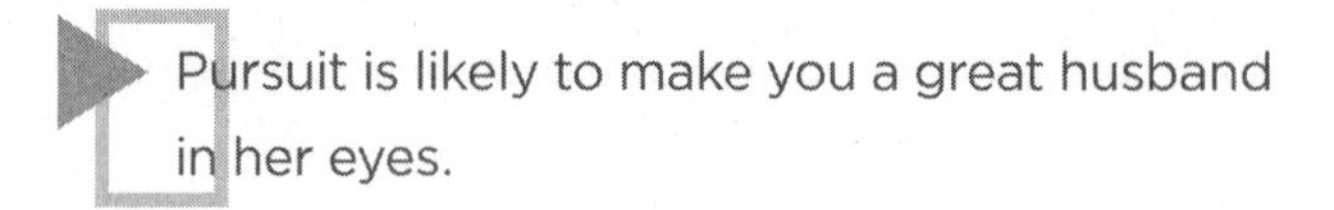

Pursuit is action. It's what you did when you first wanted to make her yours. It fills up her emotional bank account. And pursuit is what she still deeply needs in her marriage, even if we "close the deal" kind of guys are already on to the next big deal—completing our education, launching a career, raising kids, perfecting our golf swing…

All worthy goals, mind you. But they tend to make us forget that the pursuit of her that we thought was completed, really isn't.

One woman we interviewed recounted a common story line that captures the dilemma perfectly:

> I know a woman who was divorced for quite a few years, but then this new guy started pursuing her. At first she was cautious—she was fine on her own and didn't think he was her type. But he just *wooed* her—there's no other way of putting it. He was very attentive and made it clear that he thought she was something special and that he wouldn't be dissuaded easily. He sent her flowers all the time, which is one of her "things," and dropped her little notes, and it just made her feel so special.
>
> As he pursued her steadily like that for several years, she saw all his terrific qualities and fell hard in love. They got married—and almost immediately she began to think that something was wrong. All those little things that said "I love you" to her, well, he stopped doing them! No more flowers or notes or pursuing. It seemed to her like, once they got married, he suddenly stopped caring about her.
>
> And now he doesn't understand why she's upset. He just says, "Of *course* I love you, honey!" and then goes on about his day. Meantime, he doesn't realize that his wife is getting seriously, seriously depressed.

Of course, you and I can identify with this story from the guy's side. It's common for men to think that pursuing goes with dating, not with marriage. But remember: for women, there is never a magic moment of closure when they feel permanently, fully, deeply loved. *They think that's what the rest of married life is for!* In fact, several women compared the need to feel pursued by their husbands with the need that a man has to feel sexually desired by his wife! If it's that important, what is a smart married man to do?

Big-screen answer: Give chase.

Pixil answer: Ask yourself, *What did I do when we were dating that made me so pickin' irresistible?*

Ask yourself, *What did I do when we were dating that made me so pickin' irresistible?*

Probably you spent hours just hanging out together. You listened. You flirted. You sent e-mails or texts during the day just to say hi. You shared dreams. You said things like "I can't imagine life without you" and "I'm so glad God brought us together."

In other words, you proved to her that you were smitten.

Want a portrait of pursuit in marriage? You and I should consider that we might already be masters of it. Now that we know the chase isn't over, we just need to remember to do what came so naturally before.

Before you groan and say, "But that was exhausting. I got married so I could *stop* doing that stuff!" let me put in a reassurance of my own. I'm not talking about the big-deal events you planned to impress your bride-to-be, like the picnics in the park or the months you spent secretly getting tickets to her dream concert. I'm talking about the *little* things that speak love to her. Every. Single. Day. Like putting your arm around her in church. Or the text message that says, "I was just thinking about what a great mom you are." Or reaching to take her hand when you're walking across a parking lot.

No matter what you do, those little things say one thing: I *would* choose you all over again. Today. That reassurance—every day—goes so deep into her heart that all those buried doubts are laid to rest.

"YOU DIDN'T COME AFTER ME"

Maybe you remember the 1998 remake of the old Disney movie *The Parent Trap,* starring Dennis Quaid, Natasha Richardson, and a twelve-year-old Lindsay Lohan.[1] Our kids love this movie, and we were watching it for the twentieth time one night when Shaunti pointed out a perfect illustration for this book.

In the movie, two preteen girls realize they are twins who were separated at birth when their parents divorced. So they plot to get Mom and Dad back together by switching places. The British mom and American dad still care about each other, and when they finally meet again, Nick asks his ex-wife, Elizabeth, about what happened between them.

> NICK: It ended so fast.... So about that day you packed... why'd you do it?
>
> ELIZABETH: Oh, Nick. We were so young. We both had tempers, we said stupid things, and so I packed. Got on my very first 747, and...you didn't come after me.
>
> (Dead silence.)
>
> NICK: I didn't know that you wanted me to.
>
> ELIZABETH (smiling bravely): Well, it really doesn't matter anymore. So, let's just put a good face on for the girls and get the show on the road, huh?

Shaunti said this was an example of where the woman really *wanted* the man to come after her.

I asked, "But why didn't she just *tell* him that she wanted him to stop her from leaving? Why play games and make him read her mind?"

She looked at me, totally astonished. "Because if she said 'Come after me,' it wouldn't *mean* anything! It would be her decision, not his. She'd always doubt whether he did it on his own or because she asked him and guilted him into it."

Oh. Now I get it.

The movie, by the way, ends well. Nick finally realizes that, in spite of Elizabeth's seeming to push him away, she still wanted him to follow. And so he does. Because he learns to pursue, learns to reassure, the family is reunited.

Chances are, your wife or girlfriend is carrying around an unseen uncertainty about your love and needs you to come after her, look her in the eye, and tell her that you love her...and you're not going to let her get away.

WINDOWS...OPEN!

What you should know about the fabulous female brain (a guide for lower life forms)

> *Women deal with multiple thoughts and emotions from their past and present all the time, at the same time—and these can't be easily dismissed.*

One day early in our research, my kids and I dropped by the home of some close friends, Alec and Susie. While our children played outside, Alec asked me what I'd been learning about the mysterious other gender. I tried to describe a growing realization:

The female brain is not a normal instrument.

Normal, Alec and I agreed, would mean *male.*

Instead, I described what many women had told me: that their thought lives were like busy computers with multiple windows open and running all at once, unwanted pop-ups intruding all the time, and little ability to close out or ignore any of that mental or emotional activity until a more convenient time.

My friend shook his head in amazement. Strange, we both agreed. Very strange.

Women's thought lives are like busy computers with multiple windows open and running all at once.

Susie, sitting at a nearby computer, had been listening, much amused, to the male sleuths at work in her kitchen. So my friend and I decided to test my working conclusions on the spot.

"Okay, hon," said Alec, "what is in your brain *right now*?"

She looked up. "Right now? Well, let's see." She started ticking things off on her fingers. "I'm thinking about all the points I want to make in this article I'm writing. I'm thinking I need to check the pizza in the oven pretty soon. I'm hoping the kids are doing okay out on the trampoline and that I should check on them. I'm wondering whether we're going to hear back tonight on this business deal we're waiting on. And I'm thinking about what I can say to move things forward."

She hesitated a moment, then looked back up at Alec. "And if you really want to know, I keep worrying about the argument you and I had this morning, and whether you're still upset."

He and I looked at each other, stunned.

"There's probably more," she said. "You want me to keep going?"

Alec said what any guy would be wondering: "How do you get anything done with all that stuff in your head?" And more to the point, "Why don't you just turn off all the other thoughts so you can concentrate?"

Susie looked perplexed. "Because I can't," she said. "And even if I did, they'd come back."

This female multitasking of thoughts and feelings impacts how your wife or girlfriend relates to you every single day.

After hearing this sort of thing dozens of times, I realized that how a woman multitasks her thoughts and feelings isn't just an interesting academic difference between the sexes. It probably impacts how your wife or girlfriend relates to you every single day. That means a closer look at this mysterious mental difference is definitely in order.

HER MYSTERIOUS MATRIX

Picture this: you're at your computer, moving among six or seven windows. Perhaps you're juggling three or four Word documents, an Excel spreadsheet or two, and your home budgeting program. Your e-mail program and Internet browser are running in the background, and your computer is playing your favorite webcast radio program. It's a digital Grand Central Station.

Now imagine that some of the files and programs have been open and running in the background for weeks. Even worse, your computer is infected with spyware that causes annoying advertisements to pop up. You've tried to close these unwanted files and pop-ups many times, but they just keep coming back. The best you can do is to minimize or ignore them so you can focus on the other half-dozen tasks you're actively juggling at any one time…

Welcome to a woman's mental and emotional world—a world that has probably affected yours more than you realize. Here's what our surveys found:

1. Most women juggle multiple thoughts and feelings at the same time.
2. About half of all women have stored thoughts or feelings from the past that regularly pop up into active mode *whether they want them to or not.*

3. Women seem consistently unable to close these windows and "just not think about it" as easily as men can.

Let's look more carefully at what each of these statements means, how this affects you, and how to make the most of the mysterious but wonderful way your wife or girlfriend is wired.

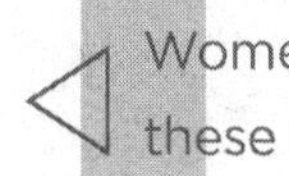

Women seem consistently unable to close these windows as easily as men can.

THERE'S A LOT GOIN' ON IN THERE

Take multitasking. I've suggested that, like a computer running multiple programs, my wife tends to have many different thoughts and feelings running in her brain all at the same time. Where I would tend to process thoughts and feelings sequentially—working on one window at a time, closing it, and moving to the next—Shaunti is likely to have many windows open simultaneously and is able to jump back and forth among them at will. Or against her will.

In fact, on our survey, nearly eight out of ten women described themselves in similar ways. Agreement became almost universal (in the 90–95 percent range) for women under forty-five and those with middle-school or younger children at home.

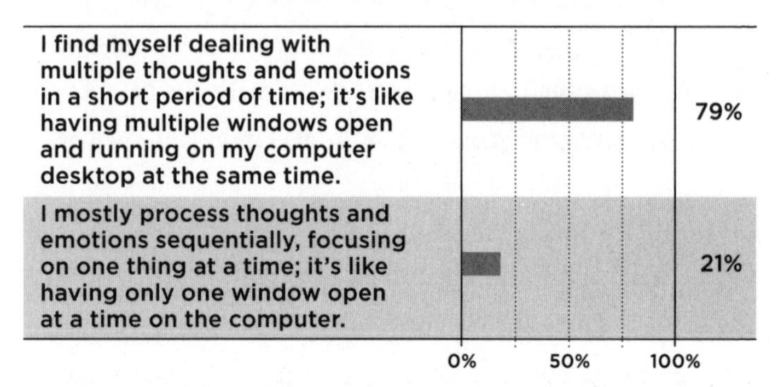

To be honest, most guys I know would be tempted to conclude that women clearly have major processor problems (to stick with the computer analogy). To our way of thinking, *their* way of thinking needs a fix!

But that's not the case. Interestingly, new research continues to show that a woman's brain is fundamentally different from a man's brain, and it doesn't need fixing—we just need to understand how it works. The fact is, every behavior I've described so far in this chapter can be traced in large part to the unique way her brain is wired.

Peeking into Her Brain

We've learned about some pretty interesting brain science since we published the original edition of this book—brain science that shows that women aren't *trying* to have all these open windows any more than we're trying to have just one open at a time. Women are simply designed this way.

Here's the main thing you need to know: a key reason for all these female windows is the ratio of gray matter to white matter in the corpus callosum superhighway between the hemispheres of a woman's brain.[2] Essentially, gray matter is like the computing power of the brain (where the actual processing and functioning is done) while white matter is like the network cables that connect the computers for speed, allow them to work together, and send signals from one computer to the next. Well, women have more white matter in their brain's superhighway than we do; while men have more gray matter. Neither is better or worse, but each leads to different ways of working through thoughts and emotions.

In practical terms, what does this mean?

Women's brains are designed specifically to process a lot of different things quickly, all at the same time—to be working on all those windows simultaneously—while men's brains are designed specifically to process deeply one thing (one window) at a time without being distracted.

What It Looks Like on the Outside

Although a woman's wiring may seem foreign to us, think how the unique properties of the female brain prepare her in so many ways for success. Think, for example, of how you've watched in amazement as your wife or mom managed an onslaught of cranky kids, made dinner, talked on the phone to a colleague, and let the cat out...all at the same time. Think of how her brain has nurtured countless relationships, done the advance work to arrange play dates, activities, birthday parties, and summer camps, or deftly managed the web of commitments in an extended family while holding down a job outside of the house. You get the idea.

Because of our brain's wiring, of course, most men are different. I have compared notes with a lot of guys, and to a man, we all get a charge out of the feeling of going into "the zone" and thinking deeply about one thing with absolutely no mental distractions—a sensation that perplexes most women when I describe it.

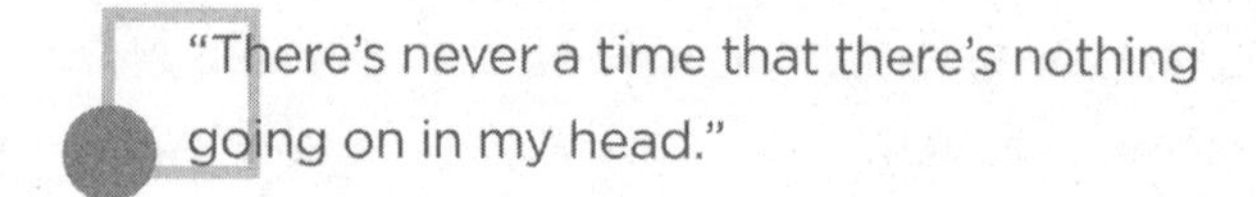

Of course, we men love having no windows open at all. Early in our marriage, if Shaunti found me sitting by myself, she'd ask me what I was thinking. When I answered, "Nothing," she'd get irritated and press me to *please* tell her what I was thinking. She didn't understand that I really was thinking about nothing! My desktop was empty, a screen saver was up, and no one was home.

Do you relate? Women don't. As one woman emphasized,

"There's never a time that there's nothing going on in my head. If I answer 'nothing,' it's because I'm mad at him!"

INVASION OF THE POP-UPS

Not only do women have multiple thoughts running all at once, about half of all women regularly experience uninvited thoughts, worries, or feelings—from the present or the past—that pop up and interrupt their day. For the men who live with them, that means they often interrupt ours too!

With their particular brain wiring, a woman is more likely than a man to be hit with unresolved concerns from something that happened last night, last month, or ten years ago. It might seem that she's choosing to dwell on something that's better left alone—even choosing to irrationally rehash or return to a matter that he thought was closed. But for her it's not irrational. In fact, since this is the way she's wired, it would be irrational for her *not* to address something that has circled back around.

According to our national survey, about half of all women are interrupted by these pop-up thoughts or feelings multiple times a week, even multiple times a day. Among younger women and those with children at home, the proportion was higher: 55–60 percent of survey takers. Perhaps not surprisingly, the percentage rose as high as 80 percent among women who described their relationship as shaky and those in difficult financial straits.

Some women say that emotions from experiences in the recent or even distant past (particularly negative ones) sometimes rise up in their minds. These may be triggered, or may seem to arise from nowhere. How often do you experience this? (Choose one answer.)

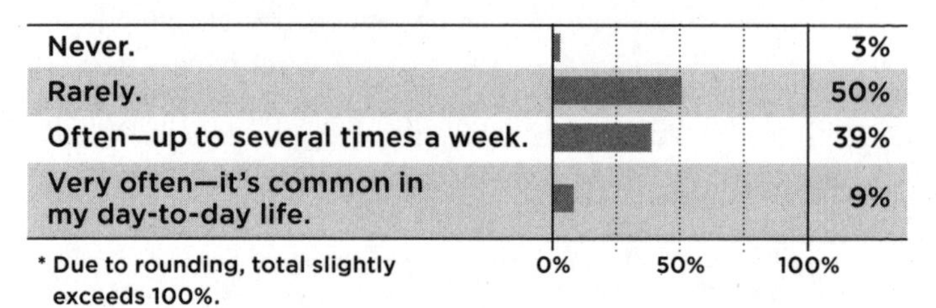

Answer	%
Never.	3%
Rarely.	50%
Often—up to several times a week.	39%
Very often—it's common in my day-to-day life.	9%

* Due to rounding, total slightly exceeds 100%.

It's not that women are helpless victims of these mental and emotional intruders. They're just more likely than men to experience them and to have difficulty getting rid of them. One woman in a focus group put it this way: "A lot of women will say, 'Don't play that tape in your head. You have to stop. Stop, don't go there with that thought.' It's easier said than done, but at least we try."

Actually, We Do This Too...

Does that comment sound startlingly familiar to you? I realized that we men can understand this struggle intimately because we have a visual parallel. Every man knows what it is like to have tempting, unwanted images pop up in his mind. In fact, this also is due to our different brain wiring. Our memory circuits as men are more tied to the things we see—so we're far more likely to have pop-up visuals. A woman's memory circuitry is more tied to language and emotions, so she is more likely to have pop-ups about her feelings and what has transpired in a relationship. As one woman wrote,

> If all men are truly visual and can't help it, then I think they should please understand that women are truly verbal and can't help it. For example, the things men say to us are in mental tape archives and are as real today as they were the moment they were spoken.

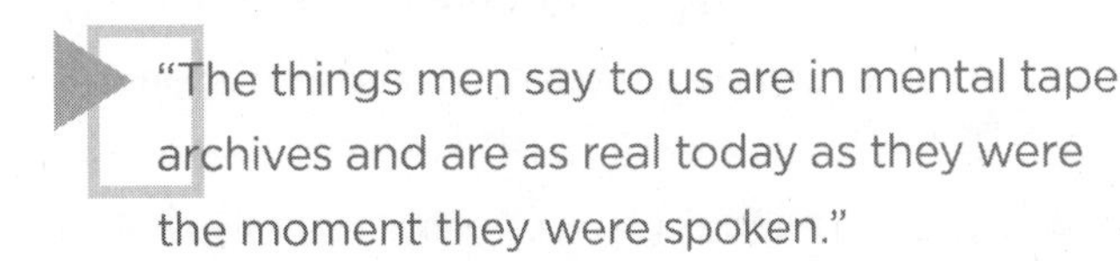

So That's Why...

The involuntary, long-term nature of this can help explain why more than one husband has felt:

- blindsided when his wife brings up something that happened two years ago.
- surprised by a sudden flareup of emotion attached to a memory.
- stung by unexpected heat that turns a conversation into an argument.

- annoyed when a woman jumps topics in a conversation.
- dismayed that his wife got hurt by something seemingly outside the moment's mood or context.

If you're like me, you might think that she is unwilling to let go of something—an old offense or memory or grudge. Or that she's choosing an emotional response instead of a rational one—as if the two were mutually exclusive. (Hint: for women, they're not.) What's more likely is that some unwanted concern is invading her mind—an old problem that has never really been resolved or healed. Or some current trouble keeps invading her awareness—an open, running window that keeps painfully popping to the fore even if she doesn't want it there. If an unwanted concern is invading her mind, her emotional reaction is a reasonable response.

If an unwanted concern is invading her mind, her emotional reaction is a reasonable response.

WHERE'S THE CLOSE BUTTON?

And that brings us back to the most important insight for this chapter: because of her brain wiring, the woman in your life finds it difficult or impossible to close out and ignore unwanted thoughts and feelings. These unwanted intruders are simply there until whatever is causing them is resolved in some way.

We've all heard that women don't compartmentalize like we do, but I never before understood what that meant. To illustrate, let's go back to the conversation in Alec and Susie's kitchen. I, too, had several things on my mind, including that I should check on the kids in the backyard. But when I compared notes with Shaunti, we realized that I handled those thoughts much differently than she could have in the same situation.

JEFF: I'm talking with Alec and thinking, *Should I check on the kids? Yeah, I'll do that in about five minutes.* Then I simply put it out of my mind—like on a five-minute mental timer. I don't give it another thought until the timer goes off.

SHAUNTI: How do you *do* that? I would love to put a thought on a timer and not think about it, but it's impossible. I simply have to function around that awareness that the kids need to be checked on or my friend is having a hard time with her marriage and needs me to call her or whatever. It never really goes away until the issue is resolved.

Of course, when I told Shaunti my timer function could actually put an issue that I didn't want to deal with on hold and out of mind for *weeks,* her interest in my brain turned to alarm.

> The vast majority of women just aren't wired to easily ignore unwanted thoughts.

Our survey shows that the vast majority of women just aren't wired to easily ignore unwanted thoughts. As one woman said, "The best I can do is to 'minimize' the other windows, not close them. I'm not actively thinking about those things every minute, but they aren't gone either. And they often pop back up and become active when I don't want them to."

On those occasions when you have multiple emotional "windows" open, how readily can you usually dismiss negative thoughts and emotions that are bothering you? (Choose one answer.)

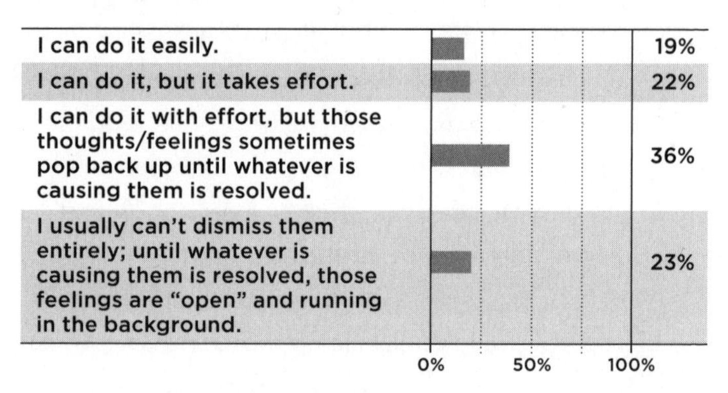

For more than four out of five women, closing out their unwanted thoughts either required effort or was impossible. The vast majority indicated that those thoughts would never really go away, or would at least keep returning, until whatever was causing them was resolved.

Which means our usual manly advice "Just don't think about it" is about as helpful as another shovelful of sand in the Sahara.

WE CAN RELATE

Here's a way that you can almost certainly relate to what this feels like. Imagine that your company just lost its biggest client, and at 5:00 p.m. on Friday your boss says, "I need to see you in my office first thing Monday morning." If you're like me, your weekend is ruined and anxious thoughts wreak havoc until Monday arrives. Your normal ability to compartmentalize is compromised by the magnitude of the concern.

Women aren't that dissimilar; it's just that their magnitude threshold is far lower than ours. Just as you couldn't close out anxious thoughts about what might happen on Monday morning, she can't close out all sorts of open windows.

That gives you a glimpse into how your wife feels when you have a bad argument in the morning and are at odds with each other. You can usually go off to work and put it out of your mind, but she may be completely unable to do that. The awareness that something is wrong stalks her thoughts all day—until you reassure her, "We're okay." Once you do that, even if the argument itself isn't resolved, she can usually take a deep breath of relief. (See chapter 2 for why.)

> You can usually go off to work and put an argument out of your mind, but she may be completely unable to do that.

DINNER WITH BOB AND DONNA

I think we men need to have our eyes opened to the real-life examples all around us so we can see how this actually works and know what to *do* about it. So let me pick an example that happened while Shaunti and I were in the middle of writing this chapter.

Shaunti was out of town with the kids, and a colleague invited me over for dinner with him and his wife, Donna, and their two small children. When I arrived, Bob was working in another room with one of those fire-starter devices that you click to get a flame. The following conversation occurred as the adults sat down for dinner a few minutes later.

Donna: Honey, what did you do with the fire starter?
Bob: I left it in the other room.
Donna: But…the kids are in there.

Bob: It's okay. It would be impossible for them to figure out how to get a flame—it's pretty difficult to use.

Donna: But what if—

Bob: Really, hon, there's no way they would be strong enough to click the flame on.

Donna: Okay... That's true...

Previously, I wouldn't have thought a thing about this conversation. But now, as I watched Donna across the table, I could tell—with my newly acquired supersensitive male radar—that a window had popped open and was not going to close until something set her mind at ease. So I mentioned to Bob and Donna what I'd been learning about how women couldn't usually just *decide* to close a window and not think about something that was bothering them.

Donna sat bolt upright. "That's it!" she said. "That's exactly what I'm feeling." She pushed away from the table, moved the fire starter out of the kids' reach, and came back.

"Now," she said, "I can enjoy dinner."

Bob and I realized that if she hadn't been encouraged to take that ten-second action, she would have been distracted and unable to truly relax and enjoy the next hour of dinner. Even though she acknowledged that Bob was almost certainly correct that the kids couldn't ignite the fire starter, the window would have been open and bugging her.

> If she hadn't been encouraged to close that window, she would have been unable to relax and enjoy dinner.

I hope you see all sorts of ramifications of this female wiring. It explains:

- *why she seems preoccupied by "little things"*—even if you tell her to just ignore them.
- *why she seems to have been stewing over an argument*—or seems (to your male mind) to feel overly insecure about a disagreement you'd already dismissed or forgotten.
- *why she seems not to trust your decision*—or seems not to respect that you thought something through (for example, that the kids were too little to get past the child safety design of the fire starter).
- *why she might be too tired or upset for sex*—one woman put it this way, "Try to understand, we're carrying around *a lot* that we need to get out of our heads before we can really even feel like sex."

I don't know about you, but I don't even *need* my head to feel like sex.

SEQUENTIAL STRATEGIES FOR SEQUENTIAL MINDS

What's the average taken-aback man to do?

The good news of this chapter and this book is that a little understanding can go a very long way. It turns out that when you are confused by a concern that is bugging the woman in your life, taking a few ultrasimple action steps will usually bring immediate benefits to you both.

Remind Yourself: She Can't "Just Not Think About It," and That Fact Is Painful to Her

Let's say a pop-up of an old hurt from something you said has arisen involuntarily in your wife's mind, and she's having trouble closing it. Or maybe it's more recent: the two of you had words this morning, she knows you are angry, and her "Are we okay?" insecurity has been triggered.

Perhaps, though, it has nothing to do with you. Maybe she's unable to get a conflict with her boss off her mind. Or she's simply bugged by the thought, *Did I close the garage door when we left?*

Remember that because it's hard for her to just push something out of her mind, there's a risk she'll live in a marginally unhappy state for hours or, for the big concerns, days until her concern is addressed and hopefully resolved. Thankfully, you can play an important part in resolving it!

Use Her Pop-Ups as Your Trigger to Help Her Close Those Windows

Here's what most men don't see as an opportunity—and where you now move from Average Joe to GI Joe. The next time you want to say "Just don't think about it" or "Don't worry about it, honey," stop yourself and realize, *This is my chance to earn major points.* Do as follows:

> *If the concern involves you and the relationship, listen and reassure.*

Now's the time to step up and help her close that window by giving her a listening ear, a hug, or the reassurance she needs so she can let go of any insecurity and resolve it in her mind. In particular, remember that if she brings up old wounds, she may not be holding on to a grudge but actually trying to process it so she can resolve it, close the window, and let it go.

> She may not be holding on to a grudge but actually trying to process it so she can let it go.

In any of these cases, you can help by letting her—actually encouraging her to—process these things the way she probably needs to: by talking it through and having you listen. (Note to self: *If I'm smart, I'll ask if she's okay well before bedtime.*)

> *If it doesn't involve you, listen and encourage her to take some action—or take it for her.*

It is astounding how loved it makes your wife or girlfriend feel when you encourage her if she needs to take some action to close her open window so it doesn't keep coming back. For example, "Would it help to call the Fosters across the street so they could check if our garage door is down?"

If it's an emotional problem (she's at odds with her boss or a close friend), part of helping her close the window means listening for a few minutes. But if your wife then keeps worrying out loud, "I'll bet my friend misunderstood me and is really upset with me right now. Maybe I should call her tonight." She will feel loved if you avoid the usual male line—"Ah, I'm sure it's fine. You can talk about it with her in the morning." Instead, simply say, "You know, honey, it sounds like calling her might make you feel better. Do you want to do that?"

Even better, take some action yourself. Get up from the dinner table, get her the fire starter, and say, "I wanted to be sure you could enjoy dinner without worrying."

Try it. Be one of the few, the proud, the in-the-know heroes.

4

THE REASON HIDING IN HER "UNREASONABLE" REACTION

How you can actually break the code of baffling female behavior

> *There is usually a logical reason behind her baffling words or actions—and behavior that confuses or frustrates you often signals a need she is asking you to meet.*

You sit at the computer keyboard and hit the *q* key, and it works. The letter *q* appears on your screen. Hit the same key again, and there it is again. The same *q*. Every time. No fuss. No variation.

Hit *q*, get *q*. Hit *q*, get *q*. Input equals output. *Ahhh!* In that predictability and order, a man finds comfort. And thankfully, this is how business, technology, barbecues, and the television remote work. Pretty much, anyway.

And then there's the woman you love.

Your experience with her, we're guessing, looks more like this: Hit *q*, get *q*. Hit *q* again, get…*4*?

You're thinking, *This worked, this worked… What happened here?* Ever since Cro-Magnon days, men have been sure of just one thing about women: on a regular basis—and usually when you least expect it—women will stop making sense.

You think you're talking about changing the oil in the car. Out of nowhere, she wants to know if you think her sister is still mad at her. As you pull into Oil Changes to Go, she's now mad at *you* for forgetting to tell her that her sister called.

You think the restaurant is fine. Out of nowhere, she says you just don't care anymore.

You thought you had a great evening together. Out of nowhere—or so it seems to you—she puts on flannel pajamas and turns in for the night.

All too often, we think, there's no rhyme or reason behind her reactions. Or if there is a reason, we're sure we'll never be able to understand it. Clearly, the only sensible thing is to throw up our hands and try to ignore the problem. We leave her alone until she calms down, hoping it will get better on its own.

Here's the thing, though. With a computer you'd never do that. You would reboot, try to figure it out, call a help desk. You'd never just ignore it.

Why the difference? It's not because you really love the computer and don't care as much about the woman in your life. It's always the other way around. (And if it's not, you've got bigger problems than are covered in this book, my friend.)

No, the reason for the difference is that with the computer *you know there's a reason things aren't working.* And you assume it can be fixed, so you take a crack at it.

Imagine my shock when I discovered that the same thing holds true for women.

CLUES TO THE CODE

I'm not a literature guy, but I once saw a quote by Oscar Wilde: "Women are meant to be loved, not to be understood."

That pretty much sums up our mental default setting ever since Cro-Magnon man proudly brought home a giant sloth for dinner, only to be met with a cold female stare because his hunting party got home two days late. Grunting whatever sounds meant "Fine!" he took refuge with the other bewildered hunters who had been tossed out by the communal fire for the night.

That also sums up the mental default setting most of us learned as teenagers. Nothing prepares you for that moment when you are thirteen—thrilled to be standing in the hallway with the cute girl you're crazy about—and suddenly something awful happens. Whereas yesterday she smiled at you like you were the middle school's Big Man on Campus, today she won't. She's upset. She's cold. She won't even look at you!

You're desperate to know what happened, what went wrong, but you don't have a clue. So you retreat to the locker room, lick your wounds, and joke that girls are impossible to understand.

We have to sweep up the little pieces of our ego somehow, right? As the years pass, a teen guy's feeling of cluelessness about girls morphs into a generally acceptable view among men that women are impossible. "Good luck trying to figure *her* out!" we say to each other in those moments of frustration.

Trouble is, we're setting ourselves up for one of the most damaging assumptions to a relationship we can make. Especially because it is totally wrong.

It turns out, a huge percentage of men have to unlearn what we think we know about the reasonableness of women. Because in our research, when a woman seems inscrutable or her attitudes, actions, feelings, or words change in confusing ways, there is almost always a specific, discernible reason—a reason that men would usually see as legitimate if we understood it.

And the truth is, we can—if we pay attention.

Believe it or not, even among those teenage girls who crushed our hearts with their unpredictable behavior, there are actual, board-certified reasons for what baffled us. Look how even the most hormone-riddled adolescent girls answered on their survey:

Many guys believe that there aren't really rational reasons when a girl's attitudes, actions, or words change from day to day. Which of the following is true of you? (Choose one.)

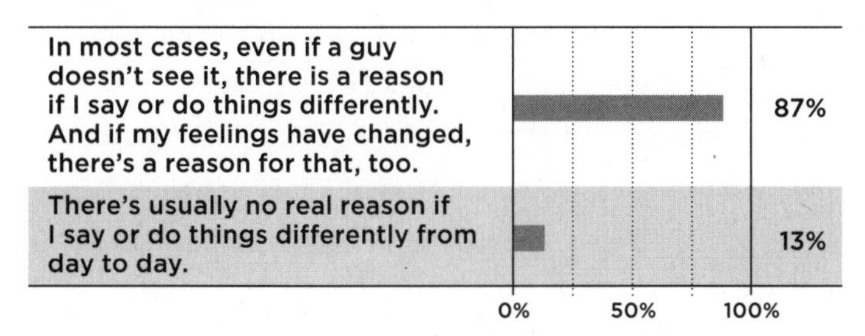

Almost nine out of ten girls emphasized that there is a reason for everything they do and say. Among the adult women we interviewed, the number was nearly 100 percent. Lest you think they are simply delusional, this was verified, in personal interviews and focus groups, by asking each time, "What was the reason?" and getting a well-thought-out answer that left the previously skeptical men in the room stunned.

In the last chapter we saw an example of this. We saw that even some of the weirdest displays of supposed randomness—such as when a female worry resurfaces "out of nowhere"—actually stem from the brain wiring of multiple mental windows running in the background.

In this chapter we take things further. We show that "female" and "illogical" don't actually go together as much as we thought, if at all. Perplexing behaviors aren't coming out of nowhere. Further, we'll show that once husbands and boyfriends decide to proceed on the assumption that (1) good reasons exist for her actions and (2) that we can discover and act on those reasons, our relationships will dramatically improve.

That's because those convenient (and centuries old) assumptions of randomness can actually prevent us from finding happiness with a wife or girlfriend—and from making her happy as well.

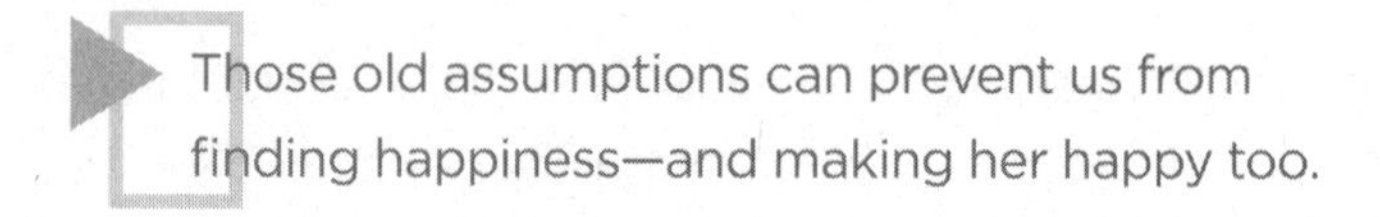

Those old assumptions can prevent us from finding happiness—and making her happy too.

You see, when a confused husband frequently resorts to the "throw up his hands, retreat, and hope it gets better on its own" routine, real trouble can develop in his relationship, and he risks not seeing it coming. We have seen some heartbreaking survey responses where a man described his marriage as being at the happiest mark on the scale while the woman in the same relationship described the marriage as being "very unhappy." Ouch!

To be clear, we're not trying to put doubts in your head about your relationship. We just want you to know that the advice in this chapter is both important and full of promise. Because once you assume she can be understood, a good outcome is not only possible but likely.

Which beats being totally confused and ending up out by the fire with the other Cro-Magnons.

BREAKING THE CODE

As a starting point, when we see something that seems confusing, random, out of proportion, or completely nonsensical, we have to believe there's a reason for it—probably a legitimate reason. Work with me here, okay? I know that may seem as unlikely as the Detroit Lions making it to the Super Bowl (yes, it's been a long few decades for us Michiganders), but proactively choosing to trust that fact is essential. Once we do, we're ready to discover the reasons behind baffling female behavior. The women in our surveys offered four possible code breakers that can help us understand even their most "irrational" words, feelings, and actions.

Possible Reason 1: It's Something You've Done, Even If You Don't Realize You Did It

This troubling insight won't surprise you. Most of us learned it in the throes of our first white-hot, kindergarten romance. Out of nowhere (there's that phrase again), guys are to blame. Since then, when anything seems suddenly awry, we have learned to wonder, *What did I do?*

Of course, moments later we have moved on to the only possible conclusion. *Nothing. I did absolutely nothing wrong.* Or we do a quick gallop around the options and conclude that it is absolutely ridiculous for her to be upset. She's being irrational. Obviously. Time to throw up our hands!

Not so fast, hunter-gatherer.

The following is a real-life example that may help us see how something we do can cause the woman in our life to behave in confusing and "unreasonable" ways.

It's a Date

Marco and his wife, Krissy, decide to have a long-awaited date night. He's been traveling, and she's been working long hours, helping Marco's brother, John, and his wife in their family business. After weeks of not seeing each other much, the two agree it's time for some romance.

So they make a plan for Friday. She will arrange a baby-sitter for the kids, and they'll each get off work early so they can catch an early movie. Then they'll go to dinner, come back home, get the baby-sitter returned safely by 10:00 p.m. (as promised), and—Marco hopes—enjoy the fact that the kids are asleep.

Marco gets home from work a bit later than he hoped, so they have to rush to make the movie. Fortunately, Krissy is generally pretty easygoing, so she doesn't seem to mind.

The movie is great, and they both laugh a lot. After too many weeks of distance, they're really enjoying being with each other. They hold hands and share popcorn.

Then on the way to dinner, Marco remembers something. He needs to stop by his brother's house.

"Why?" Krissy asks. She looks startled.

"Well, John told me there's something he needs to show me. Something exciting for his business. It'll just take a minute." He looks over at his wife. "Uh, is that okay?"

"Sure. Okay. If you need to," she says.

They drive to his brother's house, which is a bit out of the way, where John shows Marco something he's excited about that is getting rave reviews. It dawns on Marco that his wife must already know all this, since she has been working on the project intensively with his brother. Still, he lets John know how pleased he is for him (and Krissy) and spends about twenty minutes talking before he sees it is 8:30 and says they need to get going.

As they drive away, Marco is in cheerful spirits,

excited for his brother, and glad to be having such an enjoyable evening out with his wife.

"So where do you want to go to dinner?" he asks.

"I don't care," Krissy answers. "You pick."

Those words don't sound quite right.

"No, really," he says, trying to be thoughtful. "Let's pick a place you've been thinking about. This evening is for you."

"Oh, really?" she replies.

Okay, now, he's *sure* those words don't sound right. "Yes, of course!" he insists. But he suddenly feels like he's in deep weeds.

Silence.

He presses ahead. "Uh...is something wrong?"

"No, it's fine."

But he can tell it's not fine. What to do but onward into the weeds. "Go ahead and pick a place, sweetie," he says, reassuring her, and then adds a helpful detail. "I guess it should be closer to home, though, since Jessie has to leave at ten."

"Yep."

Marco and Krissy drive to a restaurant near their house, a place they've been to before and know is nice.

Silence all the way.

By now Marco's male brain is spinning. *What happened to my sweet, affectionate wife? What's she doing to our enjoyable evening?*

Then he starts to get angry. If she's upset because he took twenty minutes out of the evening to talk about work with his brother—work she's been a part of—that's completely unreasonable!

After a fifteen-minute wait, they're seated at the restaurant, and out of nowhere—really—an argument starts over something stupid. By now it's after nine, and the two of them are seriously irritated with each other. They both try to smile and make small talk, but the evening is ruined. As Marco hurriedly asks the waiter for the check so they can get home by ten, he's pretty sure that the evening won't be ending the way he had hoped.

Sure enough, his wife returns from taking the baby-sitter home, climbs into bed in her flannel night-gown—the one that might as well say "Keep Your Hairy Paws Off" in big letters—and settles down to go to sleep.

Talk about unreasonable, confusing, and random! Marco gets up and trundles downstairs to watch late-night TV. With every step, he's wondering, *What on earth happened?*

If you and I put ourselves in this story, we can easily empathize with the unlucky husband. Obviously, his wife got upset because she was looking forward to time together, and the little side trip to his brother's house took time away from that. Too much time, as it turns out.

Really, we're thinking. *Ruin an evening over a silly twenty minutes?*

But let's look at the story—and our reaction—in a fresh light. If women do have logical reasons for their reactions, then we need to be open to the possibility that the unlucky husband in the story did something—more than one thing, actually—that legitimately upset his wife. He could have done something truly hurtful, even if he didn't intend to, and, while he's sitting alone in front of the television, still doesn't know what it was.

Krissy told us it would have made all the difference if her husband would have indicated that he realized he may have done something insensitive and then done something more: taken the steps to pursue her further rather than accepting her "fine" as the last word and driving in silence to the restaurant.

Although we see "Is anything wrong?" as a thoughtful—and sufficient—way of finding out if there's a problem, many women don't see it that way.

Although we see the "Is anything wrong?" question as a thoughtful—and sufficient—way of finding out if there's a problem, many women don't see it that way. We'll explain why in a moment. But for a woman, the necessary (read that, "reasonable and logical") steps instead often look like this:

1. If she's upset, always assume that it could have been something you did (not that it always *is,* but assume it could have been).
2. Ask her to tell you if you did something to mess things up.
3. Assume that "I'm fine" is not her final answer, *unless she specifically seems happy again and isn't upset like you suspected.*
4. Pursue her—gently and persistently—until she lets you in and reveals what she's really feeling. For example, "I know you say things are fine, but I think maybe I hurt your feelings just now. Can you help me understand what I did?"

Don't believe me? Here's what Krissy told us her husband would have heard if he'd assumed her confusing behavior was because of something he did *and then* pursued her further to discover the reason behind the behavior. Now, pay attention, cave mates, because—as you're about to find out—Marco's wife had a *lot* more on her mind than he ever realized:

Really, all I wanted from the date night was two good hours over dinner to catch up. We hadn't really seen each other in weeks. The movie was nice, but that wasn't the point. What I was most looking forward to was finally having a couple of good hours over dinner.

And it wasn't just to reconnect. I had been managing this big project for my brother-in-law and was so nervous about it, since I'd only been back in the workforce a short time. But when it started to get all these clients and such good reviews, I was so thrilled. I couldn't wait to surprise my husband with it. I had purposely not told him on the phone. I wanted to see his reaction and wanted to see that excitement on his face and see him be proud of me.

I know it's probably stupid to be upset, but when he drove all the way across town to see John, I knew that not only had we lost any chance of a good, long conversation over dinner, but I had lost my big surprise announcement. I'm probably overreacting because I'm tired, but it was just a double whammy, and I was really wishing he would have picked up on it instead of just charging right ahead.

And then the fact that he *didn't* pick up on it just made it worse. Like, when you realize that it's not really "fine," why wouldn't you just ask another question? We're

> sitting there in frosty silence; clearly it's not fine! If you would just say, "I didn't mean to, but I think I hurt you—what did I do?" it shows me that you care about me, that you're willing to deal with it if you did do something wrong. *That one action* on his part would actually help make it fine!

Truly, I've seen that once we know the real reason behind seemingly random or confusing behavior, we often completely get why our wife was upset.

Possible Reason 2: It's Not Necessarily About You—It's About a Hidden-from-You Emotional Need Inside Her

This reason is closely tied to the first one, but it's so important, I want to dig further.

First, some background. In the reassurance chapter (chapter 2), we talked about the fact that even the most secure women are plagued by insecurity running under the surface. It's a deep personal doubt that makes her question, "Does he really love me?" and "Are we okay?" If that insecurity is triggered by conflict or distance between you, she needs reassurance of your love. Unfortunately for us take-things-at-face-value males—and this is where we get the most frustrated—in this situation your wife or girlfriend is likely to subconsciously pull back. Not because she needs space but because she is *desperately hoping you will follow.*

> She subconsciously pulls back, not because she needs space, but because she is desperately hoping you will follow.

We showed in chapter 2 that, rather than get frustrated that she's playing games or testing us or even being manipulative, we need to see her actions for what they are: a plea for reassurance.

One key type of reassurance is to pursue her when you think you might have done something wrong (Possible Reason 1, above), even if she isn't owning up to it yet. Go with your gut. If she's saying "fine," but you think it's not, or if she's insisting nothing's wrong, but you suspect something is, don't drop it just yet. As Marco and Krissy's story illustrates, be willing to ask another question.

You may think the whole thing is illogical, unreasonable, foolish (or less polite words to that effect). Join the club. When Shaunti did this kind of thing, I used to think, *No way I'm playing her games.* Eventually, though, I realized that to Shaunti, it wasn't a game. Her inner doubt was very real. I didn't realize it, hadn't intended it, but her behaviors were explained by a deep and very understandable emotional need: she was feeling distant or insecure about my love.

After I finally got it, what I had thought of as a test became my visible signal of her invisible need. My next move wasn't always easy, but it is simple: don't withdraw but ask more questions. Do so without defensiveness, so you prove to her you truly *want* to know the answer. I don't always do this right, but I try to say something like, "I feel like I screwed up. I'm sorry. Help me understand." Your willingness to own the problem releases her ability to get her hidden-from-you emotional need out where you can both deal with it.

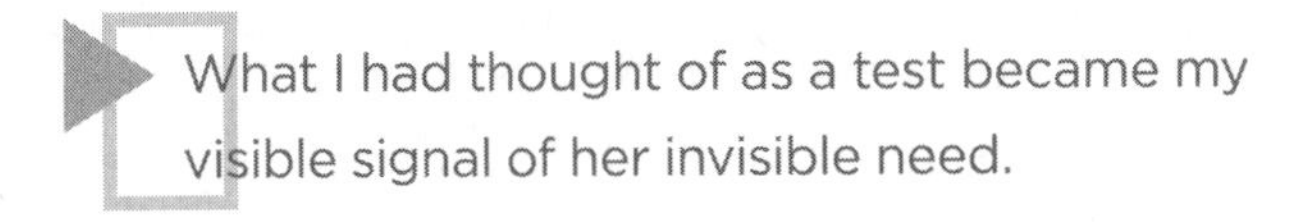

Well, why don't they just tell us?!

Ever wonder why women don't just tell us they are feeling insecure? Or why they don't just tell us the real deal the first time we ask? Here's why. According to the vast majority of the women in our research, we've trained them not to. And we've done that by consistently getting defensive and angry when they tell us what they're feeling or when they answer our questions honestly the first time.

If you doubt that, ask yourself how you would react if you had been Marco and your wife answered your "Is something wrong?" with what she was *really* feeling? Think about it. She says, "I feel bad that you didn't think through the fact that this 'short' trip to see John would take at least forty-five minutes or an hour away from our dinner. I'm upset that it didn't occur to you that I might know *exactly* what John wanted to tell you, and you didn't seem to care that I was really looking forward to a long dinner to catch up with you!"

Honestly, how would you respond? I'm guessing that most guys would feel surprised and stung by such criticism. Then we'd feel dumb. Then we'd get angry.

So, then, as the women in the focus groups put it, "Is it any wonder that we subconsciously hold back, to make sure that you *really* want to know before we give you the real answer?"

Oh. Yeah. That makes sense.

Possible Reason 3: It's Not About You—It's About Her Circumstances

Just like you have bad days, so does she. You get short with your wife or kids because you're just on edge, and it has nothing to do with them.

What do you need at those times? Well, you hope your wife won't react in kind, that's for sure. You need her to give you a little space to get your bearings. Or maybe you need her to let you take your Craftsman cordless and drill holes all over your boss's face. (Okay, drill holes all over some plywood scrap in the garage and just kinda *pretend* it's your boss.)

What you don't need is her taking it personally. You certainly don't need an escalation, getting all upset that you're all upset.

Ditto for her. Sometimes it's not us. First, as mentioned earlier, ask if you did something wrong. (You're a man. You would jump in front of a speeding eighteen-wheeler to rescue her. I *know* you can ask her if you did something wrong.) And if she sincerely reassures you that it's not about you, bring out the listening ear or a shoulder for her to cry on.

Possible Reason 4: It's Not About You—It's Hormones

Okay, I have to be delicate about this, but let's all acknowledge the obvious: for some women, there are a few days each month when the reason behind the supposed randomness is simply chemical and biological, not something she's trying to do.

One of my buddies (wise man that he is) worked out a great system to handle this with his wife. She suggested that he keep rough track of her, er, situation, and when he's confronted with something seemingly out-of-the-blue irrational, before he answers (or responds in kind), he will gently ask her a question to confirm his suspicion.

Now, this is a jokester couple, so she thinks it's funny when he asks, "Am I talking to my sweet wife Lori or Helga the crazed mutant?" But for you to find out what kind of proactive measures your Lori might suggest for the two of you, we suggest a gentle conversation on a day when Helga is but a distant memory.

YOU CAN UNDERSTAND HER AND MAKE HER HAPPY

We didn't have this subject in the original edition, but once men started reading *For Men Only,* we got e-mails saying, as one put it, "Your research and surveys were helpful—but realizing that there *is* actually a method to her madness, and that I can find it if I look closely enough is, by itself, the single most important thing I learned."

To help you process the insights in the chapter, we've embedded many to-do suggestions in the text. Here's a quick summary:

- Assume there is a legitimate reason behind what looks unreasonable to you.
- Take the time to gently and persistently pursue her to find out what it is. Listen to what she has to say without getting defensive or overreacting.
- Read those "illogical" behavior signals that cue when to step up as the Chosen Dude who can meet an important (previously hidden) need.
- Enjoy newfound bliss with the woman you love.

No matter how logical or linear you think you are, you can make the insights in this chapter work for you.

A friend of mine is an engineer (translation: trained to find solutions based on readily observable facts and formulas). He and his wife have a strong marriage, but he was at times confused and frustrated because he couldn't understand how seemingly small stresses and circumstances could overwhelm her and cause "irrational" anxieties.

On a recent flight, he was rereading *For Men Only* and began to consider what might be going on inside her during those anxious times. He wondered if it was comparable to certain things that had made him anxious.

So he wrote a letter and e-mailed it from the plane, wondering if those situations might be similar to what she regularly goes through. He ended the letter with "Does any of what I said relate to what you experience? Am I gaining an understanding of what you experience? I hope so. Not that any of this helps resolve anything. But at least you and I are closer because I understand what you go through...I hope."

How did she react to his letter? Here's her e-mail back to him:

> As I sit here reading your letter, tears are streaming down my face. Thank you for caring enough to even try to "get" my thought processes. Thank you for never giving up on me as I go through episodes of anxiety. Just the thought of you taking the time to try to understand humbles me beyond words.

As my friend's story shows, once you take the step to trust that the woman in your life is *not* an unreasonable alien that you'll never figure out, you can begin to take seriously the visible signals of her invisible inner life. Then, with a dose of courage and some sincere practice, you can do the seemingly impossible.

You can make her happy.

And—we know this, men!—that will make us happy too.

YOUR REAL JOB IS CLOSER TO HOME

How your provider/protector instinct can leave her feeling more unsafe and less cared for

> *Your woman needs emotional security and closeness with you so much that she will endure financial insecurity to get it.*

It happened the minute I decided that Shaunti was the woman I wanted to marry. As soon as I thought about accelerating our relationship…I stalled.

Most guys I've talked to can relate. All my forward momentum vanished as anxiety stopped me in my tracks. The issue wasn't her or how much I loved her or what I really wanted to happen between us—and soon. The issue was money. It suddenly hit home: how will I take care of a wife and provide for her financially? I didn't know much about relationship stuff, but I knew one thing: women want security.

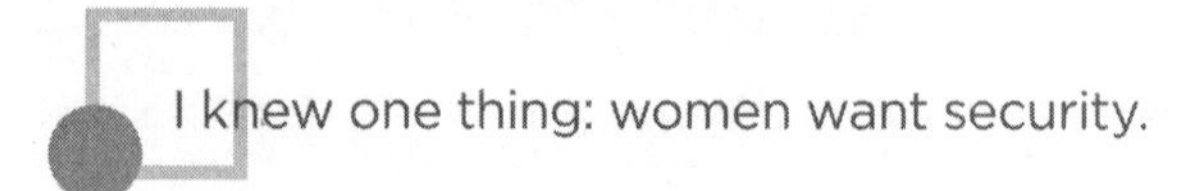

I grew up in a small farming community in Michigan and had known plenty of financial struggles in my life. After high school, I scraped by in the restaurant business for seven years before I went to college. But Shaunti was from the upper-middle-class suburbs of Washington, DC, and hadn't experienced similar struggles. I was concerned about what she would consider a normal standard of living and whether I could provide it. So I waited. With that in mind, when I graduated from law school, I took a job with a big New York law firm that included a very good salary.

Finally, I figured, I could provide. So we got married and moved into a doorman building in the heart of Manhattan. In New York, doorman buildings are common *and* pricey. But Shaunti preferred one because it made her feel more secure, she said.

Aha! I thought, confident in my manly insight into her needs. *Even if I might have preferred a different job, I'm doing what men do. I'm providing security for my wife.*

Then I proceeded to work eighty-hour weeks to pay for it all. During the next five years, whenever Shaunti said that I was choosing work over her or that I didn't care about her, I experienced a strong and predictable reaction—I got upset. *How can she accuse me of not caring about her when I am busting my tail to prove exactly that?!*

Recently, when I asked a friend what he thought "women want security" meant, he described a common male dilemma. "It means I can't ever stop running," he said. "I need to do whatever I have to do to *ensure* that she doesn't feel financially insecure. And if it means that I have to work really long hours or stick with a job that I don't like all that much, so be it."

Perhaps you, too, have felt caught between a rock and a hard place, knowing that your wife wants you to provide a nice life for her and the kids, but she also wants you home by dinner. Impossible financial expectations on her part?

Maybe. But probably not.

As you'll see in this chapter, men may be really frustrated by what they think their wives expect, but their wives may have no such expectations. In our case, it turns out the doorman building in Manhattan wasn't nearly as important as I'd thought.

MONEY TALKS BUT EMOTIONAL SECURITY SINGS

Our research shows that, yes, women want security. But they mean something very different by it than we do. A woman's primary thought is not about a house, a savings account, or tuition for the kids. For her, *emotional* security matters most. As we'll discuss, this means that she feels emotionally connected and close to you and *knows* you will always be there for her, no matter what. Sure, providing financially is appreciated, but for most women it's nowhere near the top of their list.

In fact, as one woman told us, "It's not even on the same list! Feeling secure and close in the relationship is so much more important, it's not even part of the same discussion as work or money."

When a woman thinks of security, her primary thought is not about a house, a savings account, or tuition for the kids.

Forgive my confusion. Yes, I heard Shaunti *say* she wanted more of me. But I also heard her say she wanted the doorman building. I assumed that she was choosing financial security over a saner and more enjoyable career for me. Her insistence that she wanted to make changes so I could be around struck me as appreciative gestures aimed at making me feel less pressured.

But now, I realize (a little late) that she actually *meant* it. And a lot of women feel the same way. On the survey, seven out of ten married women said that, if they had to, they would rather endure financial struggles than distance in the relationship.

Why don't you read that again. I know we find it impossible, but it's true: 70 percent of married women would prefer to be financially *insecure* than endure a lack of closeness with their husbands.

In fact, even single women showed the same preference. And women who described themselves as struggling financially were even *more* likely to prefer emotional security!

If you had to choose between these two bad choices, would you rather endure... (Choose one answer.)

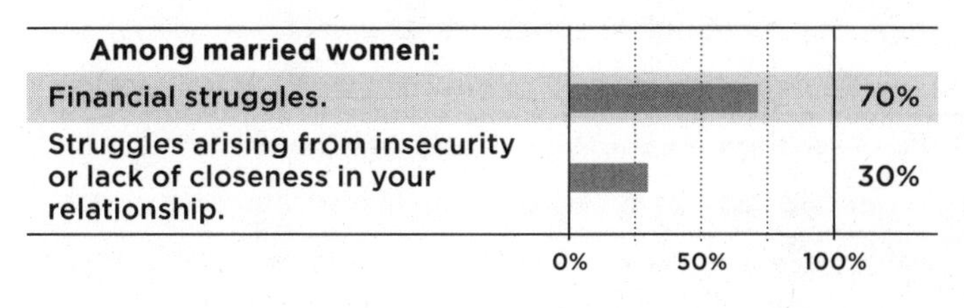

The problem here is that what seems blazingly obvious to women is barely visible for most men—or men simply don't believe it. One time, a male pastor was interviewing Shaunti onstage in front of a large group of twenty-something singles. A few minutes in, Shaunti decided to test our emerging hypothesis on this issue. She turned to the women in the audience and asked our survey question: "If you had to choose, would you rather endure financial struggles or would you rather endure struggles arising from insecurity or a lack of closeness in your relationship?"

Nearly every female hand went up for the "I'd rather endure financial struggles" option.

Shaunti used that demonstration as a launching point and began outlining for the women how men think about providing. After a few moments, the moderator interrupted. "I'm so sorry, Shaunti," he said, clearly flustered. "Could we back up a bit? I'm still so...shocked by what I just witnessed that I'm not hearing a word you're saying!" Much to the women's astonishment, men around the arena were nodding in agreement.

Yet women have an incredibly hard time believing that *we* think that *they* think financial security would ever be so important. As one woman asked in a focus group, "How could any man ever think we'd choose money over him?" Another said, "So in essence you guys are thinking that we are materialistic—really, really materialistic—and that we'd choose *things* over your happiness?!"

Uh...yeah. I guess that is what we're saying. But apparently we're wrong. For once, being wrong is very good news. Not only does the woman in your life care far more about you than about anything you could provide, but she's also willing to sacrifice financially to have more *of you* and more happiness *for you.*

THE INNER LIFE OF MR. PROVIDER

Are you still skeptical? One reason this is so hard to accept may have nothing to do with a woman's wiring but with ours. Shaunti's research for *For Women Only* demonstrated that three-quarters of men are "always" or "often" conscious of their burden to provide—and most of us wouldn't have it any other way.

Guys can't just demote work to some corner of our life. What we do defines us. Most days, it *is* us. That means our sense of self-worth—and a lot of other feelings—are wrapped up in it. For example, working toward our family's financial security is an important way we show our love. It's not a big jump to then think that longer hours = more love. And we assume the woman we love knows it!

The problem, I found, is that she *doesn't* know it.

In fact, since what she wants is your time and attention (which creates emotional security), if you appear to give more time and attention to work, it appears that you are making work your priority. To her, that means she is *not* your priority. That choice leaves her feeling distanced and unloved by you—even if the main reason you're busting your tail is to show her your love.

> Since what she wants is your time and attention, if you appear to give more time and attention to work, it means that she is not your priority.

Thankfully, there's a solution to this dilemma. To begin with, if security doesn't mean what we thought it did, let's redefine what security does mean to our wives.

WHAT SECURITY MEANS TO HER

Since most guys would never think to put *emotional* and *security* together in the same sentence, what does such a foreign concept look like in practical terms? Here's what we learned:

1. She feels that the two of you are close.
2. She sees that you make time together a priority.
3. She sees your commitment to her.
4. She sees that you are active in the life of the home.
5. She sees you making an effort to provide (as long as that doesn't crowd out 1–4).

Let's briefly outline each of these.

1. She Feels Secure When You Feel Close

Creating a sense of closeness between the two of you is more important than anything else—to a woman, it is almost a synonym for emotional security. And I was encouraged to see that it was *so easy.*

For us guys, money in the bank helps us feel safe and successful. But for women, the currency that counts is more likely to be a strong sense of closeness or intimacy with their man. In other words, your wife wants to be your love *and* your best friend—to know that she is yours and you are hers.

Here's the surprise for us guys: living in the same house and even having sex doesn't necessarily mean that she feels close to you. Most married guys I know just assume a level of closeness. We share a house and a bed. How could we *not* be close?

> For women, the currency that counts is a strong sense of closeness or intimacy with their man.

But for our wives, proximity and sex do not equal closeness. Consider the following exchange from one focus group when we asked how women felt when men traveled away from home:

Q: Is the only cure for loneliness for him to be there?
A: Not necessarily. Anyway, it's very easy to be lonely when he is physically there.

So what builds closeness?

Much of what creates a sense of closeness are the little things that come along with being each other's (1) love and (2) best friend.

Closeness means that she feels you belong to and love each other.

Even small gestures convey love and build closeness in a way I never would have thought. And they are so doable. Shaunti puts it this way:

> It's not that the little things somehow make a difference. It's that the little things *are* the difference between feeling secure and loved or not. The big things don't do that as much. The romantic dinner is wonderful once in a while. But that doesn't come close to building the same feeling of being loved that comes when you reach for my hand in a parking lot or leave me a silly voice mail calling me a special nickname that's just between us.

Here's the thing, guys: I didn't used to do those things that much. But once I discovered that the little things were that important… Well, heck, those I can do!

> "The little things *are* the difference between feeling secure and loved or not."

Every woman will be touched by different little things. But thankfully, this isn't rocket science. In one focus group, we were talking about what makes women feel loved, when to my surprise, Shaunti began to describe a recent incident. We had been walking through a parking lot, and I put my hand on the small of her back to steer her through some rows of cars.

Hearing that, every woman in the room put her hand to her heart or clasped her hands together and sighed: "Awwww," "Oh, that's so sweet," "What a good guy." The other men in the room and I looked at each other in shock. Especially because at the time I'd been worried that Shaunti might get mad at me for "telling her what to do"—since that would have been my reaction in a similar situation!

Closeness means that she feels you two are best friends.

Being close doesn't mean that you are her best *girl* friend—expected to talk for hours—but it does mean that you two know each other better than anyone else. As one woman put it, "My sense of security with my husband doesn't just come from expressing my emotions, but from knowing his."

2. She Feels Secure When You Make Time Together a Priority

As you might imagine, another thing that makes her feel secure is knowing that, after God, she's your priority. Knowing that she and the kids come before your job and that *you care for her first,* even if you feel your job is what you do to care for your family. Of the many women who echoed this view, one wife put it like this: "We can have plenty of money stored away and be very secure financially, but if I'm not secure about whether I'm a priority for my husband, all that money doesn't mean much. But on the other hand, if I know that he is there for me, I can face any struggles financially."

For us nuance-challenged men, here's a simplified summary of what "being a priority" usually means to her: it is the amount of time and attention you give her outside of traditional work hours (meaning, outside forty or fifty hours a week) compared to anything else. Since there are only a limited number of possible "together" hours in a day, she views every above-the-norm hour spent on your work or outside interests as coming directly from the few hours she expected to spend with you.

"If I know that he is there for me, I can face any struggles financially."

A wife does *not* expect her husband to spend every off-the-job hour with her. But to feel emotionally secure, she can't feel that he's consistently choosing other time priorities over her. As one woman said:

> My husband is a very good provider, dearly loves his family, and says I complete him in every way. But he rarely seems willing to spend one-on-one time with me or to share my life, yet he always has time for the guys. I know he also needs his friends, but this lack of *me* in his day-to-day life is causing a big drift in our marriage.

3. She Feels Secure When You Demonstrate Your Commitment

Your wife needs to feel, in the core of her being, that nothing will scare you away and that you will do whatever you need to do to ensure that nothing comes between the two of you. One woman put it perfectly: "I need to know that he will be there for me, no matter what. We have a good relationship, but I still need to *know* that he's not going anywhere—physically or emotionally."

One simple way to demonstrate commitment is to reassure her after conflict, as we talked about in chapter 2.

4. She Feels Secure When You Are Active in Parenting and the Life of the Home

Women feel secure when they see their husband choosing to be an active participant in the life of the home, even if it means reworking other priorities. Unfortunately, if a man isn't careful, his laudable drive to provide may prevent him from taking that active role in the life the couple set out to enjoy together.

Some wives we surveyed felt like they started out as a general partner with their husbands, but somewhere along the way they wound up as a sole proprietor. One wife said,

> While we're not wealthy, we have some good funds saved up. But my husband seems to feel like we're always on the

> verge of a problem, so he has to always get that extra client, that extra paycheck, even if it means being locked in his home office all night after dinner, with no time to play with the kids. Will he ever feel that we have enough? I appreciate having that cushion—but not when it hurts *us*.

Another, by contrast, explained why she felt so secure:

> My husband is working hard, but I'm so grateful that he also recognizes that kids need a dad's presence as much as they need a mom's. So many of my friends are frustrated that they have to ask their husband to "baby-sit," as if the kids aren't his kids too. My husband is so wonderful about recognizing that, yes, he's tired, but so am I. And the fact that he'll play with the kids or manage the dishes really gives me the sense that we're all in this together.

Further, quite a few busy moms told us that simply being appreciated by their husbands also helped them feel very secure. Any hardworking guy can understand the security that comes from feeling appreciated.

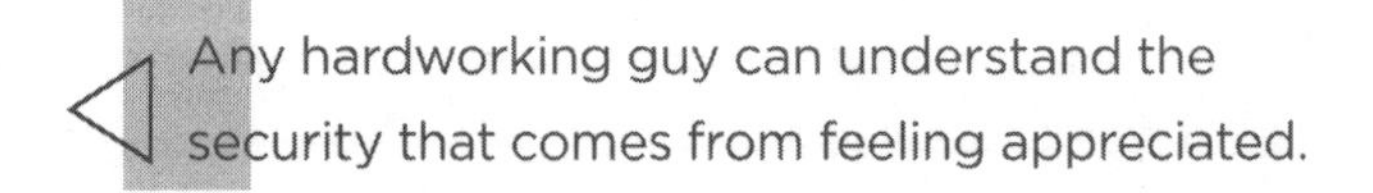

5. She Feels Secure When You Do Make an Effort to Provide

Lastly, after all this discussion of finances not being a woman's top priority, you should know that the effort you make to provide for your family does add to a sense of emotional security, even if the results aren't bringing in the amount of money you assumed she wanted. Where guys focus on the results, our wife focuses on the effort—and the effort does make her feel loved as long as it doesn't crowd out the other elements of emotional security.

The women we talked to agreed that in the choice between financial insecurity and emotional insecurity, it's not that they would *enjoy* financial struggles, but they would prefer to *endure* them if they could get more of you. As one woman said, "Financial struggles, by definition, are difficult. But if I had to, I'd rather have them than lose him."

Security

"Financial struggles, by definition, are difficult. But if I had to, I'd rather have them than lose him."

Obviously, in all of this, we need to find a balance. You are designed to want to provide for your family, and women do appreciate that. None of us would want to use these findings about emotional security as an excuse to quit our jobs, sit on the couch for hours, and eat Cheetos. Not that there's anything wrong with Cheetos, but all things in moderation.

THEY WANT US TO BE HAPPY

One of our most encouraging findings was that, even though women truly wanted their husband to have a job where he worked less in order to have more of his time, they also wanted him to work less so that *he* could enjoy life more. A great deal of a woman's stress and insecurity comes from knowing that her husband is working long hours at a job that causes him stress just to provide a certain level of income. If there were another option, most women would choose a lower-stress, lower-income job that he'd enjoy, even if it meant going through financial insecurity.

On our survey, we asked women to choose between two different job scenarios. Again 70 percent said they'd rather their husband take a lower-paying job that would require financial sacrifices if it allowed more family time. And even more fascinating, the number appears to rise to 89 percent if they felt *he* wanted to make that choice (adding in those women who were neutral)!

And encouragingly, even though women want emotional security and closeness, we could find none who would want their husband to take a family-friendly job that would make him unfulfilled or unhappy in his work life. They knew there was no emotional security in that solution. As one wife put it, "Then I would just have a depressed man on my hands, and that would defeat the purpose!"

Put yourself in this scenario: Your husband/significant other has a very well-paying job that requires a lot of hours and emotional attention away from home. You enjoy a comfortable lifestyle and all the enrichment opportunities for the kids that come with it, but you and the children often do feel distant from your husband/significant other, and when you two are together there is often discord. Now suppose that your husband/significant other was offered a different job that he'd enjoy, that would allow much more time with family—but it would also mean a substantial pay cut and some lifestyle adjustments for your family. Which best describes your likely feelings in this scenario? (Choose one answer.)

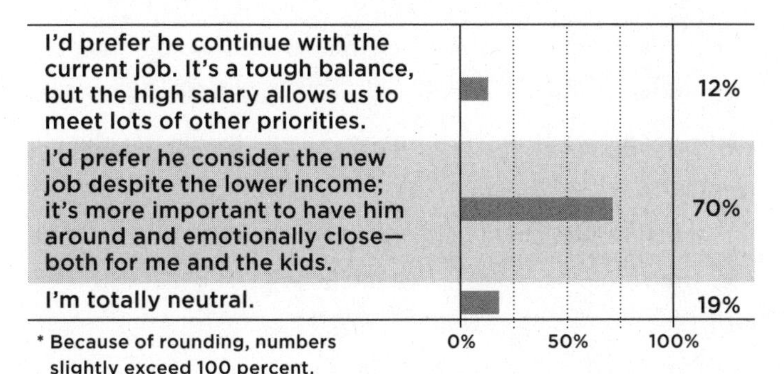

RETHINKING OUR PROVIDER/ PROTECTOR ASSUMPTIONS

This whole topic boils down to asking ourselves—and asking our wives—one question: *Am I providing the type of security she genuinely wants and needs?*

One friend put his finger on the crux of the difficulty for many of us: "Men focus on income and possessions because it is so much easier to measure success in numbers. 'Loving attention' is much more difficult for us to quantify."

I started this chapter with the comment that we men often feel caught between a rock and a hard place. But we've now heard from hundreds of women that while there may be a rock on one side—her absolute need for emotional security—there is no hard place of absolute financial desire on the other. It's more like a *soft* place, since for most women all the money and things aren't nearly the priority that *you* are. Shaunti didn't want more of me *and* the doorman building. She wanted more of me, period. When I finally got that through my head—five years later—we moved from New York to a more family-friendly life in Atlanta.

If you suspect that perhaps your wife has been trying to say the same thing, have a talk. You might be surprised at what you hear.

For most women all the money and things aren't nearly the priority that you are.

WHAT MATTERS: HAPPY DAD

We all instinctively know that as our children grow up and as we and our wives age together, our best memories will not center around the cool things we bought or the size of the house. Invariably, the measure of success will be something much simpler: the life we shared on a daily basis.

A woman who grew up in a large family in Flint, Michigan—one of those gritty industrial cities of the Midwest—described how more "providing" by her father had not turned out to be a better life for any of them:

> When we were little, we lived in a small house right in the city. The neighborhood wasn't great, but I loved my life. And my dad was a happy dad. When he was home from work, we'd all play. He was so much fun to be around.
>
> When I was eleven, my dad wanted to provide a better future for us. So he decided to have a special home built outside of the city. Since we didn't have tons

> of money, he knew he'd have to do a lot of the work himself. He said we were worth it.
>
> Unfortunately, he didn't realize what all the extra stress and pressure would do—not just to him, but to us. The stress of juggling everything began to wear my dad down. We lost happy dad and instead found grumpy dad. He stopped playing with us so much, and he was just on edge a lot, not relaxed and fun.
>
> I now know that he was sacrificing himself to provide a better future for us kids, but we wanted *him* much more than we wanted the new house or better schools. We just wanted happy dad back.

She says that if the kids or her mom had been given the choice of the little home in Flint with happy dad or the bigger country home with grumpy dad, it would have been no contest. They all would have chosen happy dad.

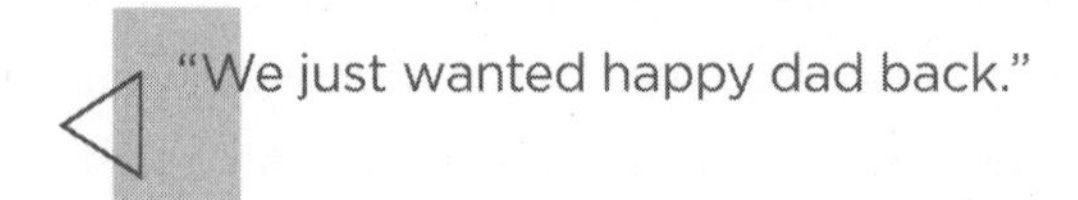

A PERSONAL JOURNEY CLOSER TO HOME

Every guy I know who works hard does it at least in part because he believes he's doing what is best for his family. Providing for our family is commendable and a biblical injunction. But we must be willing to ask ourselves whether we are delivering what our family genuinely needs, or whether we have bought into some internal or cultural assumptions that might actually be sabotaging what matters most. If so, some adjustments are probably in order.

Looking back, I realize that my own dad *did* make those adjustments. My dad worked long hours in the unstable real estate business, but when he came home and there was any daylight left, we always threw the football around. Or he would hit fly balls to my brothers and me in the empty field beside our house. Good times.

Because of my dad's presence in our lives, not a single memory centers on what we lacked. What I remember are the things we did together.

We always had a roof over our heads and three meals a day, but I do remember feeling the stress of belt-tightening measures during times when no commissions came in. But here's the thing: despite the pressures and despite knowing that we didn't have some of the things that other kids had, *because of my dad's presence in our lives* I have only amazing memories of my childhood. Not a single memory centers on what we lacked. What I remember are the things we did together.

Of course, cutting back financially to improve real quality of life does introduce its own stresses. Shaunti and I can attest to that. For several years, I struggled to keep a start-up technology company alive while developing a part-time legal practice. Many months we didn't know how we were going to pay the mortgage until it was due. Yes, that is stressful!

But we have managed, we've seen the truth that God always provides, and our family relationships are stronger than they've ever been. In fact, during one particularly tough financial season, Shaunti actually got *alarmed* when I floated the idea of going back to a big law firm. Honestly, I wouldn't trade the time I've been able to spend with Shaunti and the kids for any high-paying law firm job on the planet.

For men struggling with unemployment, job uncertainty, and tough economic times, it can be extra challenging to feel successful at home. Trust me, I know. You and I are wired to provide. When we can't, we easily fall victim to deep doubts about our worth as husbands and men. If you're facing this challenge today, I hope this chapter has convinced you that while you may sometimes feel like a failure, it does *not* mean your wife feels the same way.

To her, you are more than a paycheck. You mean more than the mortgage. You *do* hold the key to her sense of security, *especially* in hard times. But that security is not all about what you earn. It's about who you are—and how you love her—that counts most of all.

> You *do* hold the key to your wife's sense of security, *especially* in hard times. It's about who you are—and how you love her—that counts most of all.

LISTENING *IS* THE SOLUTION

Why her feeling about the problem is the problem and how to fix your urge to fix

> *When she is sharing an emotional problem, her feelings and desire to be heard are much more important than the problem itself.*

Not long ago, Shaunti and I were cleaning up after dinner when I noticed that she seemed down. She had been working long hours on several projects, so I knew she was tired. She'd also just found out that an expected invitation to talk about *For Women Only* on CNN the next day had fallen through.

Supersensitive guy that I am, I probably would have stayed quiet and given her the space to work through it. But my recent work on mapping the female mind set me up to try something else. *She doesn't need space,* I realized. *She needs to talk.* So I paused, dish in hand, and asked if she was okay.

She sighed. "I'm just a little bummed about CNN," she said. "I know how networks work. I shouldn't have gotten my hopes up."

When I asked if she knew why it fell through, she shook her head. "Not really. They said everyone loved the topic, but when they got to the production meeting, some segments had to be cut. Nothing personal."

Since I really wanted to cheer her up, I decided the time was perfect to give Shaunti one of my best count-your-blessings pep talks.

"But, wow, think about what an amazing opportunity it is to even be in a position to be *considered* by CNN," I said.

"I know, but—"

"And think about what a blessing it is to be on *other* radio and TV all the time, to be able to share this message and save marriages."

"Yeah, but it's not the same as CNN."

"Oh, I don't know. You had five million viewers on that Hollywood talk show last month." I smiled. "That's a lot of people."

To my surprise, my reasonable, well-adjusted wife suddenly got angry. "I'm trying to tell you something, and you're acting like you don't even care!" She stood up from the table and seemed to be fighting back tears.

"Huh?" She'd really caught me off guard.

My mind started whirring. *You gotta be kidding me!* I thought. *You think I don't care? What do you think I've been trying to show you? That's the last time I try to encourage you!* But of course, I didn't say any of that. Instead, I muttered two tried-and-true gems: "Okay, fine." Then I shut down and went to see what was on TV.

Does this little scenario strike you as familiar? Here's the sequence again:

- She seems to need a listening ear.
- You care, so you say, "What's up?"
- She reveals what's bugging her.
- You care, so you try to help.
- She reacts with, "Obviously you don't care!"

Later, Shaunti and I both apologized. And we were able to identify the problem in our scenario: apparently, what I thought was listening and caring, wasn't. Of course, I *was* listening—using my ears, my brains, my stunningly good intentions. Really.

Trouble is, it just wasn't happening in the way that *felt* like listening and caring to my wife.

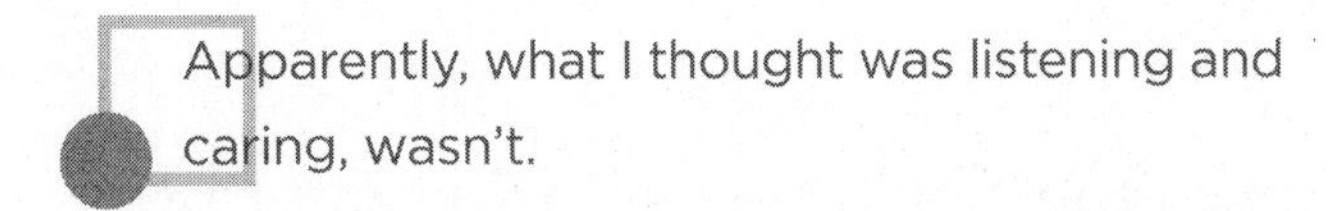

Apparently, what I thought was listening and caring, wasn't.

Now that I've seen the massive response to this issue from women around the country, I believe that learning to listen in the way women need is a huge missing-in-action skill for most guys. If you're at all like me, the issue is complicated by more bad news—you already think you listen well. Heck, you think you're a listening machine—a real superman of sympathy! Most men do. I did.

Chances are, though, we're not.

But there's good news. Men might be broke down on this issue, but we're also just a few steps away from listening habits *that actually work,* which is what this chapter will show you.

Whether it's with your girlfriend or your wife, listening to her so she actually *feels* listened to will pay immediate dividends in a deeper, stronger, more rewarding relationship. Why? Because smart listening tells a woman louder than almost anything else that she is known, cared for, and loved. It's probably not too far off to state that smart listening has more power in her life and heart than—get this—all the things guys do first and best. Like analyzing, rescuing, deciding, doing, helping—or fixing the problem.

Listening to her so she actually *feels* listened to will pay immediate dividends in a deeper, stronger, more rewarding relationship.

"SHE DOESN'T WANT YOU TO FIX IT"

We've all heard, "She doesn't want you to fix it. She just wants you to listen." But even though that phrase is accurate (according to all our interviews), most guys have no idea what it means or how to do it. I'll explain *how* in a minute, but first here's what it means. Three things:

- *She doesn't want you to fix it* = She doesn't actually want or need your solution to the problem—at least at the beginning.
- *She just wants you to listen* = She does want and need you to understand how she's *feeling* about the problem.
- *It* = an emotional problem. This listening rule does not apply to technical conundrums.

Let's take these one at a time.

"She Doesn't Want You to Fix It" = She Doesn't Need You to Fix It

In case you're wondering, this doesn't mean "she needs you to do nothing." Instead, the key is to understand *why* she's sharing something. And it's not—as we think—because she needs our help. In fact, our women usually feel quite capable of solving their problems without any help from manly men like us. That's not what they are looking for—at least at first.

Look at the results from the survey. Even if a man provided a very reasonable solution to the problem under discussion, just 5 percent of women said that would actually solve their problem. Add it up, guys. An enormous 95 percent of women feel that a reasonable solution would *not* solve their problem.

Suppose you had a fairly serious conflict with someone important to you, and have been dealing with strong emotions about it all day. That evening, you start to tell your husband/significant other what happened and how you feel about it. After listening for a little bit, he jumps in with a reasonable suggestion for fixing the problem. How is this most likely to make you feel? (Choose one answer.)

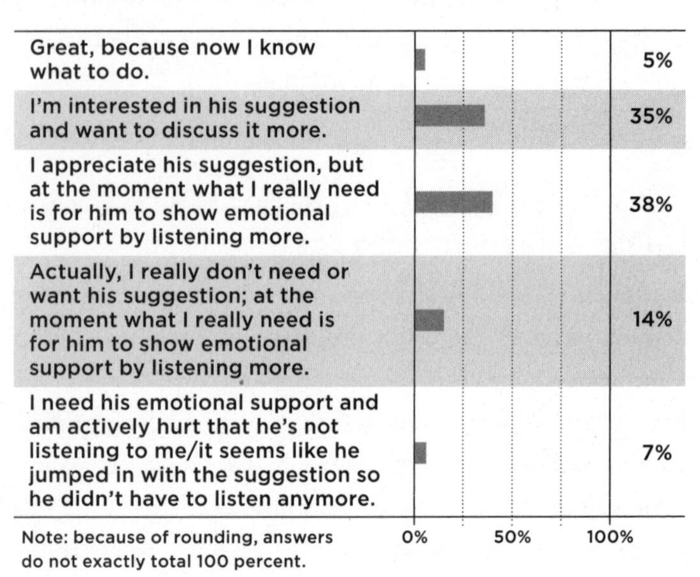

What's more, fully 60 percent of the women felt the offered solution—no matter how reasonable—was a negative. Some appreciated their man's suggestion, some didn't, but the majority felt that it detracted from the sense that he was listening and being supportive.

To see why this is true, we turn to the second and most important principle.

"She Just Wants You to Listen" = She Wants You to Focus on Her Feelings, Not the Problem

She's not sharing something so you can fix it. She's sharing it so you can understand how she *feels* about something that is bothering her.

Here's the thing: for most of our lives, we men have trained ourselves to cut through the clutter of emotion in order to focus on the "real issue." Instead, we need to grasp the single most important key to being a good listener: for a woman, her negative feelings about a problem *are* the real issue. In other words, her *feelings* are what she is trying most to share and have understood, even more than the problem itself.

> We have trained ourselves to cut through the clutter of emotion in order to focus on the "real issue." But for her, those feelings *are* the real issue.

Her need to get her feelings heard explains something that has confused many of us: *If she doesn't want me to fix it,* we wonder, *why does she keep talking about it?* Look at these revealing comments from women:

- "Most men feel they have to fix areas of concern for the wife and family. But when he jumps in before I am finished, he proves he isn't interested in listening to something that is important to me. This leaves me feeling devalued."
- "A few days ago, I was telling my husband about a longstanding relationship tension I have with someone. It was so sweet that he just listened, showed me his concern, and said, 'I don't know if it's going to get better, honey.' I felt so heard."
- "Just being able to share what's going on *actually fixes* something for a woman!"

"Just being able to share what's going on actually fixes something for a woman!"

"It" = An Emotional Problem, Not a Technical One

The "she doesn't want you to fix it" mantra has confused many of us because we know some situations *require* a fix. Here's the difference: If it's an area of emotional concern, apply listening skills. If it's not, apply fixing skills.

Apply listening skills to areas that define a woman's relationships, well-being, and sense of self-worth. Home stresses, for example. Work. Friendships. Conflicts.

You.

This simply doesn't apply to those times when your wife tells you something is starting to howl under the gearshift in her Toyota. In such cases, you can safely forget her feelings—as in, "Honey, how does that make you feel when the transmission does that?" Just go male and fix away to your heart's content—as in, "I'll take it in to the shop tomorrow."

If you are ever confused about what the situation requires, women suggested that a guy just ask, "Sweetheart, do you want my help or do you just want me to listen?"

For any man who wants to be a good listener, the good news is that we don't have to shut off our Mr. Fix-It nature. We just have to apply those skills to the right problem—and in the right order. Let me assure you, this is a skill worth learning!

HOW TO LISTEN

As any guy at his workbench knows, sequence matters. And so it is with listening. Because the key to listening in the way a woman will feel heard is for us Mr. Fix-Its to fix it in the correct two-step order:

Step 1: You ignore the problem and listen to her feelings about it.

Step 2: You sit down together and focus on the problem.

Get them in the right order, and the woman in your life will be beaming. Do them in the wrong order, and—trust me on this—you'll hear, "But, honey, you're not *listening* to me!"

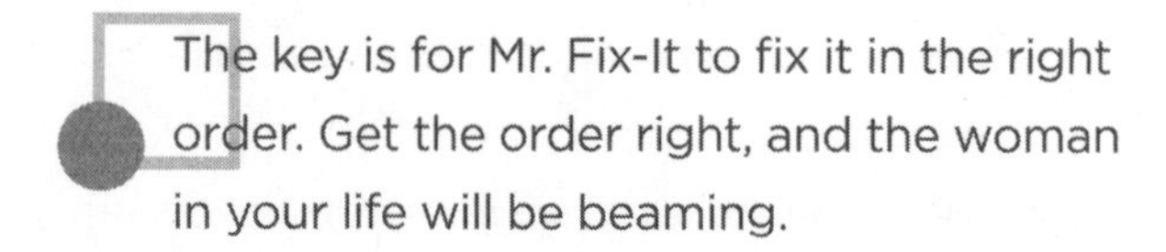

The key is for Mr. Fix-It to fix it in the right order. Get the order right, and the woman in your life will be beaming.

Step 1: Ignore the Problem and Focus on the Feelings

The reason many women think we don't listen is that, when it comes to an emotional issue, we aren't necessarily listening for the right things. Our definition of listening is often a bit more basic. Something like, "She's talking, and *I'm hearing what she's saying*—therefore, I'm listening."

But look at those italicized words and realize something: she does not want you to hear what she's *saying;* she wants you to hear what she's *feeling.* So the first and most important step for Mr.

Fix-It is to listen for the right thing: how she *feels* about the emotional issue she's bringing to you.

Most of us feel like all those jangling emotions will only get in the way of clear thinking and addressing the problem properly. So we try to filter them out. We don't realize that what we are so busy filtering out is what she most wants us to listen to!

In Step 1, we need to retrain ourselves to do something that will feel very weird at first: filter out the problem and instead focus on those jangling feelings about the problem. In fact—and I know this might be a scary thought!—we need to purposefully investigate and pull out those feelings to help her work through them.

> We need to retrain ourselves to filter out the problem and focus on all those jangling feelings about it.

In the CNN example, Shaunti didn't need a pep talk, and she didn't need my stellar business advice about how to approach CNN in a new way. All those things had already occurred to her. What she needed most was for me to share in her disappointment. For example, giving her a big hug and saying, "I'm so sorry. I know you were excited about being on CNN, and you must be really disappointed."

Since filtering out the problem and focusing on the feelings feels weird at first, it can be really easy to slip back into "man mode" and listen the old way, which may result in a bad back. From sleeping on the sofa. I'm just saying.

To save you the Sofa Step, here are a few hard-learned keys to success.

Key to Success 1: When She Wants to Talk, Give Her Your Full Attention

Most of us think, *I can listen well even if I'm doing something else.* Well, you probably can, if she is telling you that the car is making a funny noise. But feelings are a whole different landscape from fan belts. And it's *highly* unlikely that you will be one of the tiny percent of men who can truly grasp, acknowledge, and affirm those feelings while also watching Bear Grylls demonstrate how to skin a rattlesnake.

It makes a great difference when you take your attention *off* every other distraction and put it *on* her. It may also mean running interference when other distractions threaten.

For example, a year later, Shaunti still remembers a simple action I did when she really needed to talk and the kids kept interrupting. I asked the kids to play elsewhere for a minute, pulled her into the living room, sat down with her on the sofa, and asked her to share what was on her mind. Those two or three minutes were an incredibly good investment if they still make her feel loved a year later! And I have to confess that I have absolutely no memory of this event. Not because I do this all the time, but because it took so little time or effort!

Key to Success 2: Acknowledge Her Feelings Out Loud

Remember, she has absolutely no idea whether you understand her feelings unless you *show* it. Acknowledging to her what you're hearing—a simple verbal restatement of her words—is the magic bullet.

Thus, when I say to Shaunti, "I'm so sorry to hear that CNN didn't come through—that must have been so disappointing," she *feels* heard.

Key to Success 3: Affirm and Sympathize

No matter how good you are at acknowledging her feelings, all your brownie points go away if you then say, "But you shouldn't feel that way." Whether or not you think she *should* feel that way, it is vital to realize that she *does.* If acknowledging her feelings comes out as "I'm sorry you felt disappointed," then affirming them means recognizing (and maybe even saying) that it's okay that she felt disappointed.

Affirming her feelings means recognizing (and maybe even saying) that it's okay that she felt disappointed.

If you don't honestly believe that, at least avoid trying to talk her out of feeling that way. The time will come later for philosophical discussions. Right now she needs the most important person in her life to try to share her feelings and, as the Bible puts it, "Rejoice with those who rejoice, weep with those who weep." As two women told us:

- "Trying to talk me out of my feelings doesn't accomplish what he's trying to accomplish. In fact, it makes me feel absolutely terrible, like my husband doesn't care one jot about how I feel."
- "Men don't realize the value of affirming our feelings when they seem irrational or out of proportion to them. If a man could just grasp the value of that, he could cut arguments or long discussion times in half."

Key to Success 4: Realize That She's Probably Not Attacking You

I can't emphasize enough how important this is. When emotions start flying around, especially if the conversation is about our relationship, I can so quickly conclude that Shaunti is attacking *me.* If she feels unhappy, I—like most men—assume she thinks I blew it.

But I'm realizing that often a man's performance isn't even

on his wife's mind. Instead, her brain wiring means she best processes thoughts and feelings by talking about them. And the *only* way she can do that with us is if we don't get defensive and take it personally. Consider what one survey taker said she most wished her husband knew:

> That when I tell him how I feel inside about something concerning our relationship—that I am just trying to share my feeling with him so we can discuss it. He takes it as criticism and turns it around so I feel like the bad guy for bringing it up. He says, "I never do anything right," or "I can never please you," which isn't true. And so the problem never really gets discussed. I wish he could understand that it's important for me to be able to talk about these things and understand that I'm not just being critical.

Key to Success 5: Help Her Understand Your Limits in Advance

Because most women don't have an emotional or even physical limit to their ability to listen and process emotion, they don't understand that most men do. I can be totally *willing* to listen to Shaunti share her feelings about something. But just like my body would shut down if I tried to run too many miles, my brain starts to check out after a while, whether I want it to or not.

So set yourself up for success by mentioning this to your wife or girlfriend at some neutral time, and help her to understand the limits of *your* particular listening capacity.

Be reassured, though, that listening won't usually mean a marathon. As one male marriage counselor told us, "Guys need to know that their wives aren't looking to them to be their best girlfriend and listen for hours. For most women, even taking a fifteen-minute walk with them a few evenings a week would totally fill their need."

If we get the listening sequence right—addressing her feelings first—then the right and healing solutions will follow.

Step 2: Offer Solutions Together

You'll remember that most of the women in the survey found suggestions to be a negative if their husbands weren't listening and being emotionally supportive first. But next we asked, when the women set aside how they felt about their man's emotional support, how would they feel about his actual suggestions? Thankfully, more than two-thirds said they were helpful suggestions—and we can infer that more than 80 percent actually *agreed* with the suggested solution! Just 19 percent said that the solution itself would not be a good one.

Consider times when you have actually been in the type of situation described in the previous question. Setting aside how you feel about your husband/significant other's emotional support, how useful or valuable are his actual suggestions? (Choose one answer.)

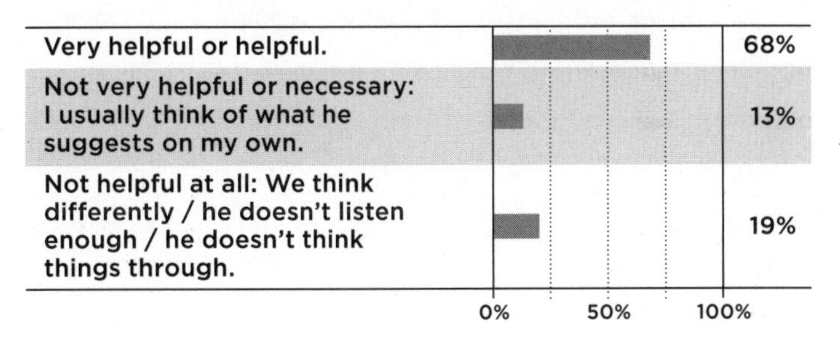

WITH GREAT POWER

When I was a kid, one of my favorite Marvel Comics characters was Spider-Man—the average guy who has great power thrust upon him and has to learn how to use it well. He is challenged with one of my favorite quotes of all time: "With great power comes great responsibility."

Which brings us to more good news for guys on listening.

Virtually all the data in this chapter point to one often-overlooked principle for a man who wants a happy relationship: *the person who listens well holds enormous power.* If we can learn to listen the way our mate needs us to, we have great power to defuse conflicting emotions, power to acknowledge and affirm—and, yes, power to *then* help find solutions.

Most of all, though, when you and I listen, we wield great power to tell the woman we care about most that she is truly loved. As one woman told us, "After a great conversation, I just want to kiss him and tell him how very, very much I appreciate him."

7

WITH SEX, HER "NO" DOESN'T MEAN YOU

How her desires are impacted by her unique wiring and why your ego shouldn't be

> *Physically, women tend to crave sex less often than men do—and it is usually not related to your desirability.*

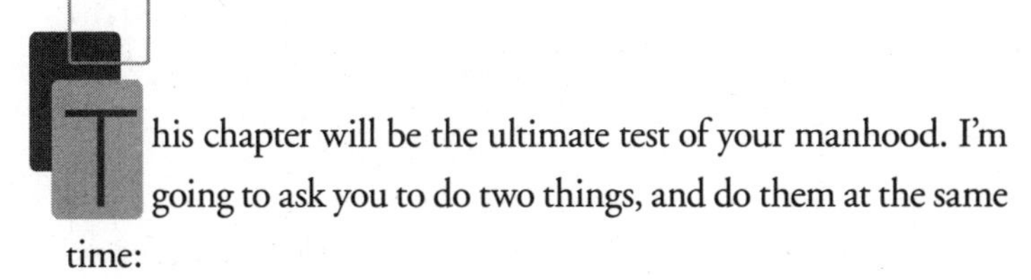

This chapter will be the ultimate test of your manhood. I'm going to ask you to do two things, and do them at the same time:

1. Think clearly.
2. About sex.

I've noticed, and probably so have you, that what we men do so well as separate tasks—clear thinking and sex—we routinely, embarrassingly, miserably fail at doing together.

As I found out after I got a full dose of the honest truth from about 450 women in Colorado.

There I was, the only guy, listening while Shaunti presented what she'd learned about men while writing *For Women Only.* It was a weird and wonderful experience.

And here was the wonderful part—at least at first. During a lively question-and-answer session, almost all the questions focused on sex! I was so amazed at the ladies' one-track minds that I could barely listen to the questions. I knew that my buddies back in Atlanta would be as ecstatic as I was at the idea that women really did want sex more than we'd thought.

Fast-forward to Jeff and Shaunti doing in-depth focus groups of women for this book. I am over the weirdness by now, but unfortunately the wonderful is no longer in sight. Instead, what I'm hearing doesn't jibe at all with the good news I'd heard in the Rockies. Finally, I do my best to describe for these women the absolute obsession with sex among their counterparts at higher elevations.

The women stare at me politely. Then one breaks the news. "Well, um, since Shaunti's book emphasized how central sex is to a man's emotional well-being, the women were probably wondering how to handle their man's requests."

Okay, I think to myself. *Cool. Nothing wrong with that.*

She sees that clear thinking has yet to occur. "And it was *not* because they want sex so much," she continues. "A lot of women don't have that same need to *pursue* sex as much as guys do. So they were simply trying to figure out what on earth to do!"

In desperation I shoot a questioning look at my wife, but Shaunti is already nodding. "I'm afraid so," she says. "That's exactly what was happening."

THE WHOPPING BIG MISS

How could I—a smart, married, and extremely likable man—have completely missed a full dose of the honest truth about sex from 450 women? And I hadn't just missed it. What I thought I heard was almost the direct opposite of what they were actually saying.

After spending hours going over surveys and listening to focus groups, I've come to believe that my whopping big miss is pretty much what men do in their marriages every day. We think male and female humans are the same creatures, only with different and nicely matching body parts. We assume we have the same sexual wiring. So when there seems to be a mismatch, we have no idea why. As one of my puzzled buddies put it, "If sex is free and it's fun, why does she not want *lots* of free fun?"

Now, we do know that in some marriages it's the woman

who is pining for more—one in four, according to our survey. So if you're in that situation, you're not alone.

Of course some wives indicated that they and their husbands were happily on the same page—to the envy of all. But since we have limited space, we're focusing on the apparent majority of husbands who want "more and better" and don't know what to do about it.[3]

"If sex is free and it's fun, why does she not want lots of free fun?"

Thankfully, solutions exist, and our research confirms good news for men who find themselves in that situation. In particular: most women do care about what their man wants. And they *do* care about sex. And they *do* want great sexual relationships with their husbands.

But to get there, we need to do that "thinking clearly" thing.

THE IMPOSSIBLE SURPRISE ABOUT THE SEX GAP: "IT'S NOT YOU"

If you're a typical married male, you probably want more sex with your wife than you get. But that's not the end of the story. I know, because in Shaunti's professional survey for *For Women*

Only, 97 percent of men said "getting enough sex" wasn't, by itself, enough—they wanted to feel genuinely wanted.

Men are powerfully driven by the emotional need to feel *desired* by our wives, and we filter everything through that grid. *Do I feel desired or not desired by my wife?* If we feel our wives truly want us sexually, we feel confident, powerful, alive, and loved. If we don't, we feel depressed, angry, and alone. And this goes way beyond the amount of sex we're having.

But here's where the first breakdown in communication comes between the average husband and wife. Our surveys showed a startling, hard-to-believe, but oddly encouraging truth for men. *While you want to be genuinely desired by your wife, her lower level of desire for sex likely has nothing to do with your desirability.*

You might want to read that again. And if you think about it, that's actually good news for the 99.9 percent of us who don't look like a shirtless Matthew McConaughey.

Here are the facts. Among survey takers who wanted less sex than their husbands, fully 75 percent indicated that it had *nothing* to do with his desirability, sexual prowess, or general studliness. In fact, of the remaining 25 percent, less than 4 percent said their lower interest in sex was specifically because their husband was "not attractive or desirable." (The hesitation of the other 21 percent primarily had to do with not anticipating pleasure, including for physical reasons.)

One survey taker spoke for that astounding 96 percent of women when she said that the one thing she most wished her husband knew was "that just because I do not want sex as often as he does, I still love him deeply and find him very attractive."

> While you want to be genuinely desired by your wife, her lower level of desire for sex likely has nothing to do with your desirability.

Look at the top three reasons (by a wide margin) that women gave for wanting less sex:

Among women who said they wanted less sex than their husbands, the top three reasons why:*

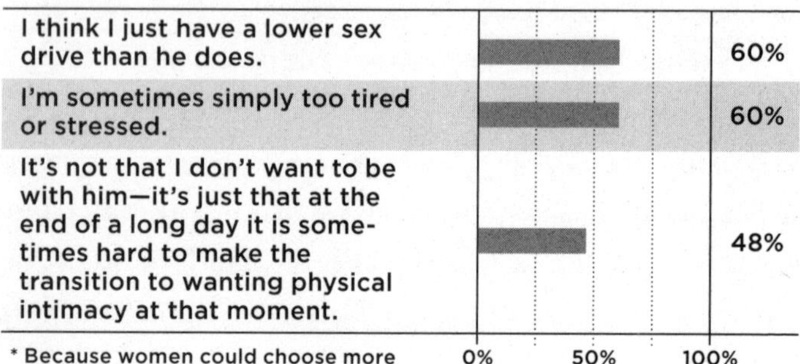

* Because women could choose more than one answer, percentages did not add up to 100%.

Our results show that, although there certainly are issues that can be addressed, the frequency gap is usually *not* because a wife doesn't desire her husband. In fact, usually, she does! Instead, in the great majority of cases where there is a frequency gap, the cliché is actually true: "Look, it's not you. It's me."

> The frequency gap is usually not because a wife doesn't desire her husband.

If you're still thinking clearly, your brain likely has ground to a halt on an apparent impossibility: *I can't imagine finding my wife attractive, being in love with her, and not wanting to have sex with her often! So how can she be that way?*

But remember, that's guy thinking, and we're trying to learn female thinking. For the moment, take a step away from that seeming impossibility and let your driving question instead be, *So if it's not about me, what is it about?*

"SO IF IT'S NOT ABOUT ME...?" FIVE TRUTHS ABOUT WOMEN AND SEX

Shaunti and I want to relay what women around the country told us about their sexual wiring and what they want to give—and get—from their man. These five revelations, should you choose to believe them, have the potential to radically improve this area of your marriage.

Truth 1: She Has a Lower Sex Drive than You, and She'd Change That Fact If She Could

Physiological Fact 1: Brain scientists explain that the average woman simply has less testosterone and other sexually assertive hormones than the average man and therefore has less of an urge to *pursue* sex. This doesn't mean she doesn't want it or won't enjoy it once it's happening, but seeking it out isn't usually on her mind.

This doesn't mean she doesn't want it or won't enjoy it once it's happening, but seeking it out isn't usually on her mind.

Most men know this fact, but—Physiological Fact 2—we forget it on a regular basis. Like, every evening. We forget because we can't really feel the truth of it, especially when she says or implies "no" the minute we show sexual interest. Admit it: an analysis of physiological differences is not where your mind goes following another nonencounter. So let's step back and look at some implications of her physiology:

- *Lower level of sexually assertive hormones = less craving for sex*

Not *no* craving, mind you, just *less.* It's a fact, and we need to stop assuming it has something to do with *us.*

As several experts explained, this is a complex issue, but it boils down to the surprising fact that there are actually two different types of sexual desire: assertive desire and receptive desire. Where men have more testosterone-type hormones linked to assertive desire, women have more estrogen, which is tied to receptive desire. This means that they tend to be *available* but simply don't have as much craving to pursue it.[4] And studies have shown that a common form of birth control (the Pill) can reduce libido even further. It doesn't help that movies, television shows, and advertisements seem to imply that all women would be sexually charged bimbo wannabes if you were just enough of a stud.

On the survey, when we asked women what they most wished their husbands understood, one wife put it this way: "I want him to know I don't love him less just because my sex drive isn't as strong as his."

▶ *Lower level of sexually assertive hormones = less likely to initiate sex*

As one book put it, "Receptive doesn't necessarily mean passive [but] available, and perhaps willing, but without the initiative to pursue sex."[5] Related to this, we received a telling e-mail from a man whose wife had read Shaunti's book *For Women Only.*

> My wife then explained to me that she simply has no physical drive to pursue sex. When we are having sex, she says that she loves it. The problem is that otherwise, sex just never occurs to her, whereas there is never a time when it does *not* occur to me! Thankfully, after reading *For Women Only,* my wife understood how important sex really is to me and has even begun to initiate sex. She does it because she wants to show that she loves me. It works…

In one of our focus groups, a woman said,

> I just don't feel that drive to go after physical pleasure as often. For me, it's about once every ten days that *I'm* the one looking for the physical pleasure. The other times are because he needs it. And from my standpoint, it's time to be together, it's uninterrupted time, it's a way to have his undivided attention. Not that it's not physically great once we get started—it is! It's just that for me, there's usually not the drive to start.

▶ *Lower level of sexually assertive hormones = more susceptibility to nonsexual distractions*

Like a noise from the kid's room. Like a headache. Like stress or leftover thoughts from her day. Like exhaustion.

She's not making it up. In relation to her lower sex drive, she's more sensitive to hindrances and feels them more intensely than you or I would. As one woman said, "For guys, it seems, sex provides relief or escape from exhaustion. For women, we have to pull ourselves out of exhaustion in order to want to have sex."

She's more sensitive to hindrances and feels them more intensely than you or I would.

But there's reassuring news too. Not only is the woman in your life not making up the hindrances to sex she experiences, *she would readily change her sexual responsiveness if she could.* Look at the data:

(Answered by women who said they wanted less sex than their husbands.) If you could magically change your sex drive and/or some of the reasons you don't want sex as much as your husband does, would you? (Choose one answer.)

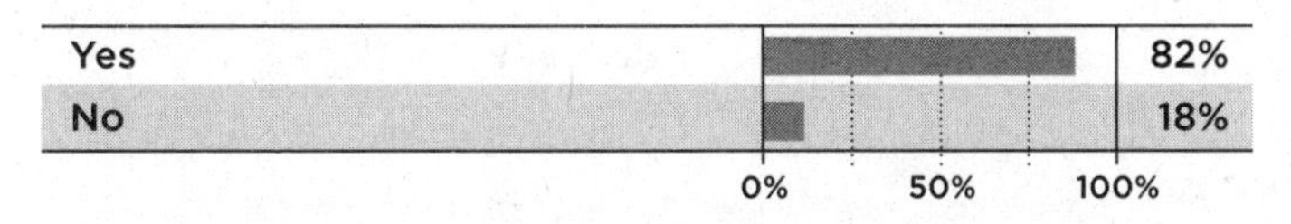

You can see that more than eight out of ten wives would prefer to want sex as much as their husbands...if they could. (And among happily married women, that desire was almost 100 percent.)

Truth 2: She Needs More Warmup Time than You

A guy's sexual motor is pretty much always running. Pop the clutch and go. Not so for a woman. But once her sexual motor is warmed up and running, she is raring to go, just like we are. One respondent told us:

> I wish my husband would understand that as much as I love to be intimate with him, there are times when it takes a long time to "get me there." I have been busy running after kids all day, cleaning, cooking, etc. Sex also helps me to unwind, but I need a little help. He seems to think that just because he is ready and set, I should be too. He gets frustrated because I do not seem like I am enjoying him, but if he would just take his time, we would both enjoy the experience more.

Another woman provided a great word picture:

> It's not that I don't *want* to make love, but at the end of a long day with four kids, my mind is set on a course like a cruise ship headed for port...port being that quiet bit of space a mom anticipates when the kids are asleep, the chores done, and the house quiet. And just as I'm within

> sight of that port, my hubby rolls over and says, "Whatcha doing over there?" It's not that I don't want to be with him, but mentally, it's like trying to stop a cruise ship that's going full steam ahead and making it turn on a dime. I can't quite turn off the day and do an about-face in the blink of an eye like he can.

Many other women echoed what one said she most wished her husband knew: "How much I truly and deeply love him, but my body just doesn't have the same sexual drive as his *until we are engaged in the act* [emphasis added]. Then I'm *very* into it."

The "very into it" part is great news. But to get there, what this means in practice is one of two things: either (1) she needs you to take it slow, to give her brain a chance to catch up, or even better, (2) she needs what we call anticipation time.

> Either she needs you to take it slow, or she needs anticipation time.

Look at the anticipation example one woman shared:

> My husband and I don't get too many nights alone, but we carved out a dinner date one night, and while we were having dinner he whispered in my ear, "I can't wait to get

> home and have my dessert." I knew the dessert was me, and I don't think I've ever eaten so fast in my life. I couldn't wait to get home.

I know we guys think that if we were desirable enough, sex would be spontaneous because our wife couldn't keep her hands off us. No such luck. If she's like most women and wired for receptive desire, even with the wonderful dinner date you planned, the flowers you brought home, or your thoughtfulness in washing the dishes so she could get to bed earlier—all that by itself doesn't mean she's thinking about sex.

Don't despair, though. The key is working with her wiring rather than wishing it were different, and we get to that in the ultra-important "what do we do about it" section coming up.

Truth 3: Your Body (No Matter How Much of a Stud You Are) Does Not by Itself Turn on Her Body

Maybe you should sit down. Take a breath. Clear that head. Because average male assumptions simply will *not* work here.

Let's start with how *you* work. Your eyes see an attractive woman, and generally your body registers attraction. Instantly. If the attractive woman isn't wearing much, your physical reaction is even stronger. It's like metal shavings pulled toward a magnet.

Your wife, though, is not like you. She is not sexually aroused simply by seeing you at your studly best. If you are looking particularly handsome or sexy, she *will* notice and she *will* find you attractive. But—get this—her body is still not lusting over your body. Listen in on an actual conversation relayed to us by one long-married couple:

SHE (delivering the shocking news): "There isn't one thing about your body that makes me sexually attracted to you and want to go to bed with you."

HE (disbelieving): "I thought I was sexy and good looking. You always told me I was!"

SHE (calmly): "You are. But that has nothing to do with why I want to have sex with you. (Noticing his blank look, she continues.) Really. Nothing about your naked body makes me hot—that is, until *after* we're sexually involved."

HE (sputtering): "But…I…how…?"

SHE (reassuring): "Babe, I like you and I like your naked body. It's sweet, actually, and you're mine. But it's not like my body is lusting after yours."

HE (grasping): "What…what about me in my black leather jacket? You always come up to me and growl. Are you saying…?"

SHE: "Nope, even you in that jacket. You look totally hot, mind you, and I do want to be with you. But I'm just telling you, physically my body does not become sexually aroused *one bit*!"

The truth is that our wives can find us desirable and attractive but still not be turned on by that alone. Women get turned on in other, less visible but equally powerful ways. And that leads to another truth about sex that most guys have heard over and over...but have never quite come to terms with.

Truth 4: For Her, Sex Starts in Her Heart

Her body's ability to respond to you sexually is tied to how she feels *emotionally* about you at the moment. If she's not feeling anything in her heart, her body's sex switches are all the way over on Off. Even if you put on your black leather jacket.

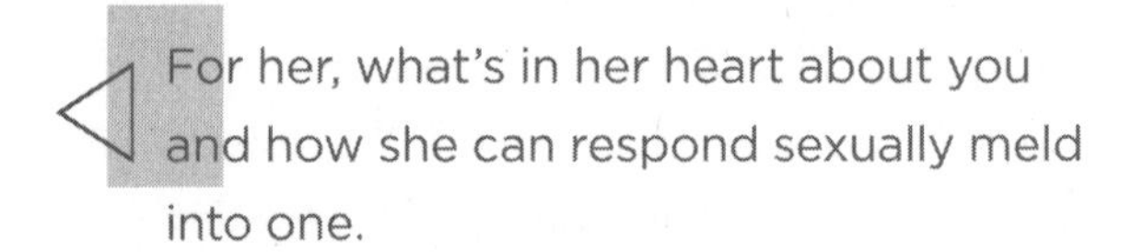

For her, what's in her heart about you and how she can respond sexually meld into one.

One consequence: where you might greatly desire her even though she was rude to you this morning, how *you* treated *her* this morning really matters. She's not keeping score, by the way.

She just can't help it. For her, those two things—what's in her heart about you and how she can respond sexually—meld into one.

One woman explained it to her husband this way: "All my power to turn you on is how I look. But where *you* have power, and where I don't, is how you treated me today. It's all emotional."

We talked a lot about your wife's need for closeness and affirmation—how to treat her today—in chapters 2 and 4. Bet you didn't realize we were talking about sex too!

Of course, there's a reverse consequence of her "start in the heart" need: the potential for hurt feelings. Shaunti's honest thought here is that if a relationship has become strained and a wife says, "The only time you're interested in me is for sex," realize that by definition, she's feeling neglected and perhaps even used.

Now, you may be initiating sex in order to try to make it better and get those feelings of closeness back, but women aren't wired that way. If they are feeling serious emotional distance or hurt, sex does not fix it—and it may exacerbate it.

Truth 5: She Wants Pleasure as Much as You Do, but If It's Not Happening, She May Be Reluctant

Okay. This might be difficult, but face it we must: some wives don't experience pleasure when they are intimate with their husbands. According to our survey, this is an issue for only a relatively small minority—just 16 percent said that was why they desired less sex. But that means it is still an issue in one out of every six or seven marriages. And only if we are willing to bring up this subject with our wife, set aside our defenses, and hear what she has to say are we going to learn if this has been a reason for her lack of interest. One woman wrote to Shaunti,

> Men think women aren't as interested in sex as they are. But some men need to know that their wives are just not experiencing sexual satisfaction. Although they might be enjoying the process, they may not be 'finishing' it. This is a difficult subject, and many women don't want to talk about it because they don't want to depress their husband or make him feel inadequate. So they protect his feelings at the expense of their own. But if a woman isn't crossing the finish line, running the race just isn't going to be as important to her—which only makes it easier to find excuses to sit it out.

I suppose you and I only have to think about what it would be like if we always "went there" sexually only to never "get there" to know how frustrating and demotivating that would be.

Clearly, it's time for you and me to sweep up our rattled egos, maybe throw on our black leather jacket just for luck, and go looking for answers.

A GUIDE FOR ORDINARY HUSBANDS

When one of my friends heard that we were writing this chapter, he chuckled. "If you can get the average husband sex even a dozen more times a year, men will build statues to you in city parks across the country."

So the following is my stab at immortality.

Think of these practical suggestions as directions on a map—directions that apply those little-understood truths we talked about and get the two of you where you both want to be.

> "If you can get the average husband sex even a dozen more times a year, men will build statues to you in city parks across the country."

1. Pay Attention to Her Outside the Bedroom and Help Her Out—it's the Little Things

Great sex starts with helping your wife feel happy and close to you outside the bedroom. On the survey we asked each woman who wanted less or the same amount of sex what their husband could do to increase the chances that they would want to make love more frequently. Look at the top three responses:

Are there things that your husband can do to increase the chances that you will want to make love more frequently? Please rate the helpfulness of each of the following statements: (Choose one answer for each statement.)

	NOT PARTICULARLY HELPFUL	VERY HELPFUL
Maintain or increase his level of emotional attention to me	**27%**	**73%**
Create a context where he often shows me little gestures of love throughout the day	**29%**	**71%**
Engage in caring listening and conversation regularly	**33%**	**67%**

Those helpful things that build closeness are the little things we've mentioned throughout the book, such as:

- putting your hand on the small of her back to guide her through a parking lot.
- reassuring her of your love when you two are at odds.
- getting up from the dinner table to get the fire starter so she can "close the window" and enjoy dinner.
- listening for her feelings and saying, "I'm so sorry you were disappointed, honey."

And it's not just emotional attention that matters. On the survey, up to 70 percent of women said that simple helpfulness around the house would increase their interest—if only because they would have more energy! (The highest agreement came among moms with school-age kids.) A study by famed marriage psychologist John Gottman confirmed that men who do more housework have both happier marriages *and* better sex lives.[6]

Great sex starts with helping your wife feel happy and close to you outside the bedroom.

As one stay-at-home mom said, "My husband and I have a little joke between us. I say, 'Honey, there is nothing more sexy than watching you clean something. And there's *really* nothing more sexy than watching you clean the toilet!' It's all about feeling that he wants to take care of me."

2. Give Chase, Agent 007. The Time for Pursuit Is...Always

I love this comment that came in to Shaunti's website:

> A woman needs to feel sexy to her man. But many men do not spend the time or effort in affirming their spouse sexually *outside* of the bedroom. That means, when we're

in the bedroom, it's difficult for the woman to figure out whether he really wants her or whether he's just trying to satisfy his own need. A woman who knows she is sexy to her husband outside the bedroom will never have an excuse at lovemaking time!

Another married woman told us:

Women want to be romantically pursued. It's as powerful as the man's sex drive. Men think women can't resist James Bond because of his body, his money, or his fast cars. But that stuff is almost irrelevant. James Bond is *romantic.* He pursues a woman, flirts with her, woos her. I think women are a lot more aware of the need to work hard at meeting their man's sex-drive needs than men are aware of the need to work at meeting her romantic-pursuit needs. Guys have to realize that for a woman, they go hand in hand!

"Women want to be romantically pursued. It's as powerful as the man's sex drive."

Whether it's calls, notes, conversations, or simply admiring eye contact, the whole point of pursuit to a woman is that you notice her, you're interested in her, and you belong to her...and she belongs to *you.* Remember chapter 2? There will never be a day when she permanently feels loved. She needs to feel, day to day, that you are choosing her all over again.

Of course, it won't help you at all if your wife feels she's only being pursued *so that* you can get sex! In the busyness of life, we guys sometimes simply forget about doing the loving little things just because we love our wives, so the thought of sex becomes a sort of trigger to remember to be a bit more attentive. But that means we risk training our wives to be cynical and to suspect total self-interest on our part whenever they see our attentive gestures—it looks like we only care about them when we want sex! So there's a need for a little reconditioning. Sometimes we need to hug her just to hug her. Send her a sweet e-mail during the day, rub her back, help her out around the house, cuddle with her in bed...and not ask for sex. At least sometimes.

3. Give Her Anticipation Time

This step is the one most guys miss, yet it may be the most important. We need to think about ways to get her anticipation engine running several hours in advance. That's because you can do everything else we're saying—be kind and thoughtful, share chores around the house, and be the best listener on the planet—but if she has receptive desire, she's *still* not likely to be thinking about sex. So find ways to let her know what you'd love to happen later...and give her time to savor what you have in mind.

One woman showed how simple that can be. "One thing that will help get a wife in the mood is something as small as a flirting call or e-mail. Something like 'I saw you getting dressed this morning and I can't stop thinking about you. I can't wait to see you undress tonight.'"

That's an easy chip shot if I ever saw one.

"One thing that will help get a wife in the mood is something as small as a flirting call or e-mail."

Another woman proposed something that other women agreed might be helpful, as nonspontaneous as it sounds to men:

> With kids and jobs, for me, sex needs to be planned and expected or it just won't happen. He thinks having set days to expect it means that it is just another thing to check off my to-do list. But actually, when I have it in mind to expect it, then it is really a reward at the end of a long day. If I don't know to expect it, then that *is* when it becomes a chore and just another thing that needs to get done. The planning means I am making him a priority, not putting him on a list.

4. When in Doubt, Ask Her

Just like the existence of this whole chapter, this particular to-do runs against the grain of my middle-class, midwestern, don't-talk-about-sex reticence. While it may not be comfortable, you just need to ask your wife what she likes, what she doesn't, and how to improve. If there is an issue, it could be as simple as personal hygiene. (Several women, upon finding out that we were writing this chapter, asked Shaunti privately, "You will tell them to brush their teeth, won't you?") And make sure she knows that you *want* to know whether she's not only enjoying the race but also crossing the finish line.

If the two of you aren't clicking in this area, it's also possible other things could be going on. I'm not an expert, but if your wife seems to love you but avoids sex (or finds it emotionally painful), make sure there aren't any deep-seated issues that need addressing. If there are, be her advocate in getting the help she needs to address them.

And I know we guys pretend it's never an issue, but if by chance *you're* the one experiencing "performance" problems, be brave and seek help from your doctor or counselor. One woman wrote about this, "His unwillingness to seek medical help is breaking my heart."

You have a lot of life ahead, and your wife wants to enjoy it with you. One wife put it well:

I appreciate feeling like we are team players, not just in the bedroom, but in everything. After a long day, I want to feel supported and uplifted, just as he does. And of course, theoretically, a good roll in the hay will do that! But there are times at the end of the day when I feel as if I can't quite get started. I want him to be sensitive to me and minister to me! He is who I am counting on for this. And I know if I can, he'll be able to count on me too.

8 THE GIRL IN THE MIRROR

What the little girl inside your woman is dying to hear from you—and how to guard your answer well

> *Inside your smart, secure wife lives a little girl who deeply needs to know that you find her beautiful—and that you only have eyes for her.*

When we were writing the original edition of this book, our daughter was five years old and definitely at that "Daddy's girl" stage. She could whack a pretty good line drive for her age. But she was happiest, I think, when she was dancing for me in a consignment-store costume dress Shaunti had bought for her. It was pink and had a twirly skirt. Pink and twirly matters a lot when you're five. I can still see her twirling around our living room. Absolutely beaming with delight. Twirl left. Pause. Twirl right.

"Daddy, watch!" she calls as she spins and the skirt does its thing. "Daddy, look at me! Do you think I'm pretty?"

If you've ever had a little girl twirling around your house, you know what I was thinking right then: *Lord, just let me hold on to this moment! Please don't let my little girl grow up.*

That's what this chapter is about. Because you see, in a way, little girls never really do.

THE GIRL INSIDE

Would it surprise you to know that your gifted, hardworking, secure, grown-up wife is still (silently) asking the same question, *Do you think I'm pretty?* Only now it's *you* watching. It's you she's asking, you who will decide her haunting question, *Am I beautiful?* And even more important: *Am I beautiful...to you?*

In a culture where women are bombarded with expectations to lose weight, look younger, look sexy—actually, look perfect—that question has killer consequences. It also gives clued-in men an opportunity that we didn't even know we had to affirm our wives in a very important way.

On our survey most women told us they had a "deep need or desire" to know that their husbands or boyfriends found them beautiful. And younger women were even more likely to have that need. Among women age forty-five and younger, more than three out of four felt this need (77 percent). With women thirty-five and younger the percentage rose to 84 percent.

Regardless of how you think you look, do you have a deep need or desire to know that your husband/significant other finds you beautiful? Which answer most closely describes you? (Choose one answer.)

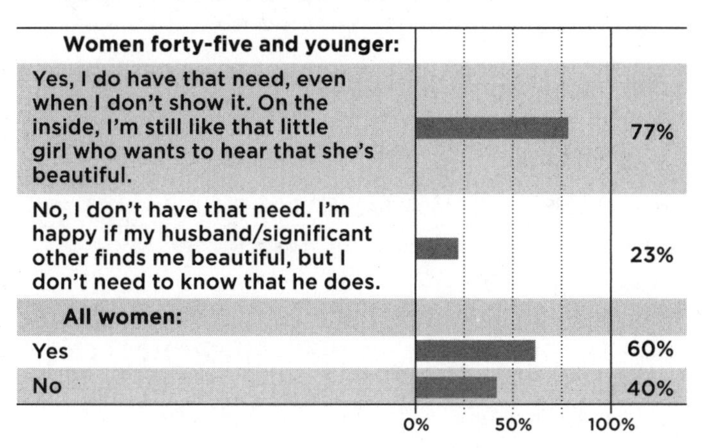

Women with children at home were also much more likely to have a deep desire to hear that their husbands found them beautiful—up to 85 percent of them. One survey taker said the thing she most wished her husband understood was that "women need to be reassured often that they are beautiful and they are loved."

The good news is that when their men *do* tell them they're beautiful, the consequences are...beautiful! Almost 90 percent said it made them feel good or made their day. And that percentage was still huge (77 percent) even among the mostly older women who said they didn't *need* to hear it! Only a tiny number (3 percent) said it made no difference.

How beneficial is it to you when your husband/significant other tells you that he finds you beautiful? (Choose one answer.)

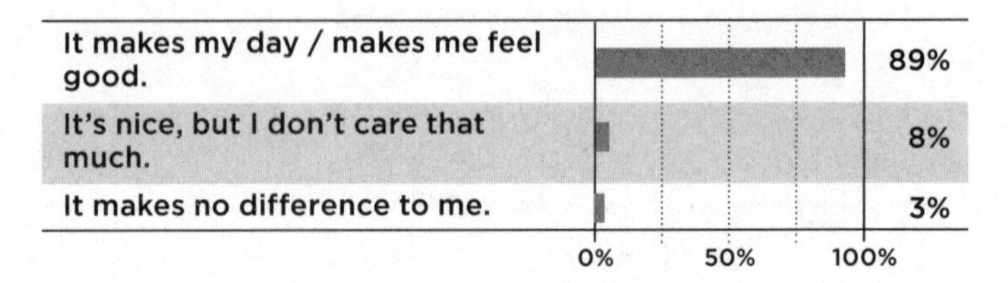

ONE GUY, ONE MIRROR, ONE HAMMER

You might be thinking what Shaunti has already heard from a few skeptical women: *Why is this chapter focusing so much on a woman's looks? Shouldn't we as a society be getting past that?*

Well, here's the thing: This *isn't* really about a woman's looks.

It *is* about what a woman feels about herself and the fact that her man has a great ability to build her up or tear her down in that area.

"Wait a minute!" I can hear you saying. "But she *knows* I think she's beautiful."

Does she? Have you told her recently? More recently than that time last year when you two got all dressed up for that wedding? You *did* tell her she looked beautiful then, didn't you? Sure you did.

Okay, you *probably* did.

I too think my wife is beautiful, but until Shaunti and I talked about this chapter, I realized that I rarely tell her so. It just wasn't something I thought she needed to hear or that I needed to do.

Then we talked. Oh, boy. All has *not* been well in the land of the free and the home of the Braves.

What I've since learned, and what kept surprising me on our surveys, is that even if a woman knows in her head that her husband finds her beautiful, *she still needs to hear it.* And often. Every day is good.

She still needs to hear it:

- no matter how successful, self-assured, or mature she is.
- no matter how long you've been together.
- no matter how gorgeous other people might tell her she is.
- no matter how moved to tears of gratitude you were last time you said it.
- no matter how old or young she is.

> Even if a woman knows in her head that her husband finds her beautiful, she still needs to *hear* it.

As it turns out, your wife's continuing desire to feel beautiful—and to be beautiful *for you*—is a deeply rooted need that explains a lot of other behaviors that have baffled men for centuries. For example, have you ever wondered:

- why, after trying on outfit after outfit, she gets frustrated and declares that she has nothing to wear?
- why she wants to buy new clothes even if she knows you are on a tight budget or even if few of her clothes could possibly be considered old?
- why she's always asking you how she looks when there are mirrors in the bedroom and the bathroom?
- why she asks, "Do these pants make me look fat?" when what she really means is, "Tell me I'm not fat"?
- why it's such a big deal if your eyes linger on another beautiful woman?

Listen, after an inexcusably long learning curve, I've come to realize a few crucial facts about beauty and my wife. These facts are fundamental in every marriage and have the power to radically change your relationship and mine for the better, beginning with the next words we speak to her.

Fact 1. That little dancing girl is still very much alive inside my dear wife. Only now she twirls for me.

Fact 2. In our marriage, whether I find her beautiful may or may not be foremost in my mind, but it is an everyday (even if subconscious) issue for her.

Fact 3. In our house, there's really only one mirror. And that mirror is me.

Fact 4. Every day I can reflect back to her the words she so needs to hear. But if I don't, I leave her vulnerable to both her inner questions and external pressure from an intimidating world.

Fact 5. In my hand I hold a hammer.

I hope you're beginning to see why a clued-in husband or boyfriend can create so much good, and why a clueless one can cause so much damage.

And I haven't even told you what the hammer is yet.

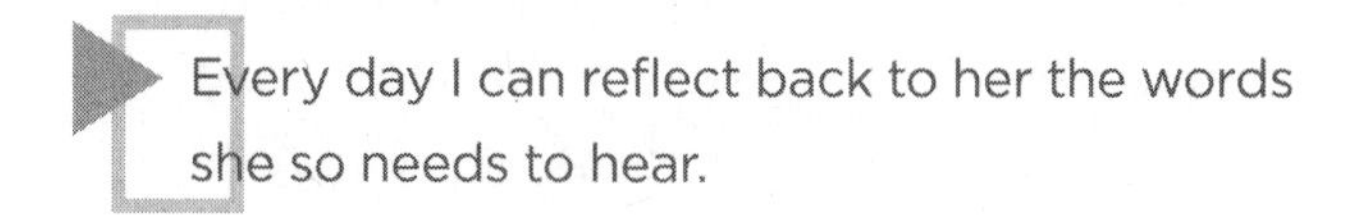

Every day I can reflect back to her the words she so needs to hear.

THE UGLY TRUTH ABOUT FEMALE BEAUTY IN OUR WORLD

Just so you and I know that our wives or girlfriends aren't the only body obsessed or oversensitive women around, let's hear what some women told us about the pressure they feel from our culture and from themselves. It's almost like they must fight their way through a war zone every day—and men don't even realize it. Listen in:

- "I know in my head that I am not unattractive. I wouldn't wear a bikini anymore, but people still tell me I'm pretty or that I look really slim in that outfit or whatever. But in my heart, I don't believe it. Because my head is also very aware of all my flaws, especially since the kids came along. Almost every time I see a picture of myself, I cringe inside. I'm guessing that my husband thinks I'm attractive, but I can't think of the last time he made it a point to tell me so. If he would, it sure would counter that secret negativity about myself that I feel inside."
- "Every day we are bombarded with these images all around us of how we are supposed to look. We have this fear that we feel like we'll always have to live up to our husband's expectation of this perfect Hollywood body image, and we know we can't do that. Somehow we get this idea that if we don't, oh, no, maybe his attention will turn elsewhere. It's a very insecure feeling, even if it's totally ridiculous. We may know in our heads that that's not true, but that head knowledge doesn't do anything to counter our silent insecurity."

And last, here's one that may be hard for any father or married man to hear:

- "In this culture, women are not being protected emotionally. They are being humiliated."

Do you really think it's possible for you and me to understand just how on stage and under review our wife or girlfriend feels every day? I have to admit—until now I haven't given much thought to how demeaning and threatening our world is for Shaunti and other women. Or how demeaning their own thoughts about themselves can be, even if they hide them well.

When I think back on typical male responses to this unseen struggle, I'm not encouraged. For Shaunti, I'm the one man in her life who can really relieve the pressure and make her feel beautiful. But because I haven't known I've needed to, my response on an average day to her unseen need has tended to be...a yawn. Or even irritation at how long she's taking to get dressed.

Or on a good day, maybe, "You look nice."

> I'm the one man in her life who can really relieve the pressure and make her feel beautiful.

Guys, we are divinely positioned to encourage and build up the woman we love. We can't be nodding off in the living room chair while the little girl twirls in front of us.

So now that we're awake to the problem, what can we do?

REFLECT BACK THE TRUTH ABOUT HER

Remember, you're not just the guy who shares her space, you're her most important mirror—the man who can reflect back to her how lovely you think she is. The man whose opinions of her are the best antidote for the damaging internal dialogue and external pressure that stalk her thoughts. So how should and could you respond for the greatest benefit to her—and you?

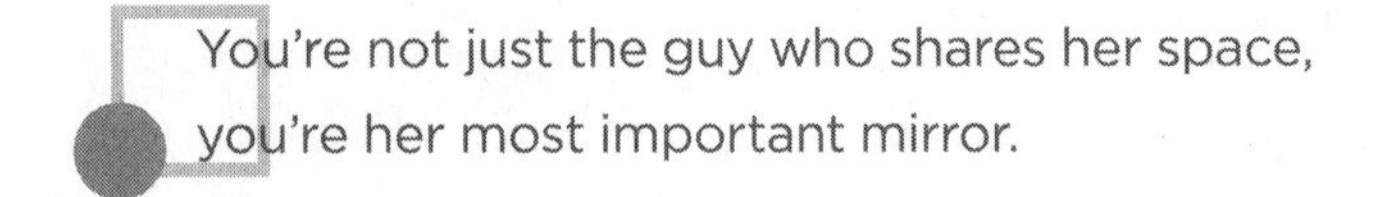

Say It

Just think of a few affirming words—"You look beautiful today" (or your own version)—and *say* them. That kind of compliment might not feel natural to you at first, but if you stick with it, it can eventually feel as familiar as "Pass the remote."

Whenever possible, your guy-mirror talk should be specific. "A lot of women are so desperate for specific, honest compliments," one wife told us. "We're dying of thirst for them. I think guys probably often think them but don't say them. But I hope they can learn to say them, because one compliment can carry me for a long way."

A key time to practice affirmation is when you've both noticed another attractive person. One woman told us, "To me, the confirmation I need is something like this: 'Yes, that other woman is cute, but you're beautiful, and *you're mine.*' Those words would be such a help to me in consciously tearing down the insecurity I carry around."

Say It Now

It is also important to train yourself to say it when she needs it. In other words, right away. Whenever you think it. Or if she's just gotten dressed up to go out, what she's looking for is the immediate, reflexive response that proves you've been wowed. But as this story from one couple we talked to shows, we men have to practice putting ourselves in that frame of mind lest we send the wrong message!

> Train yourself to say it when she needs it—right away.

HER: After I get ready to go out somewhere, there's sort of a thirty-second rule. If he hasn't noticed me in thirty seconds, I guess I don't look good enough for him. So, okay, we were going out last night. I take a lot of time getting ready and spiffy for him, and I think I look

> pretty hot. I come downstairs and he doesn't say anything. So instantly I'm a bit deflated. We walk out of the house and climb into the car, and as we're backing out of the driveway, he notices that the little metal insignia on the car hood is crooked. He stops the car and gets out to straighten it. He noticed that, but he didn't notice *me*?

HIM (laughing ruefully): Pray for me, Jeff!

Erase "Fine" from Your Response Options

"Fine" is not fine unless used in the sense, "She's so fine!" "Fine" is what you mumbled to Mom when she asked how school went.

The problem is, we misunderstand the real question. When the woman in our life asks "How do I look?" or "Is what I'm wearing okay?" we think she's wondering if she looks presentable. But that's not it at all. What she's looking for is reassurance that we think she is beautiful, stunning, and so-glad-she's-mine. And "fine" or "okay" are not even on the same planet as that.

Answer Her Real Question: "Do I Still Rock Your World?"

And that gives us the answer to how we handle that dreaded question, "Do these jeans make me look fat?"

Oh boy.

We all instinctively feel that there is *no* safe answer to this question. But in this case, she's not asking "Can I walk out the door in this?" Instead, she's feeling insecure about her body, about her beauty, and whether you still love and appreciate her. Most of the time, in fact, what she's asking is, "After twenty years of marriage and two kids, do I still rock your world?" If you answer *that* question well, you're good to go.

My advice? Say "Babe, you look gorgeous" and hold her hand all the way into the restaurant.

There will be times, of course, when your wife truly wants feedback. If that's the case, ask her *in advance* to help you know when she needs reassurance versus when she needs to know if an outfit looks good. An agreed-upon question or cue is all you need. For example, Shaunti has told me that if she says "Does this outfit work?" she really wants me to be candid, so she doesn't wear something that I don't think does her justice.

What If I Agree There's an Issue to Work On?

If your wife or girlfriend is struggling with a real issue (she's twenty-five pounds overweight) rather than being dissatisfied with something she can't healthfully change (she thinks her nose is too big), realize that she feels terrible about it already. Knowing you are disappointed makes it worse. On the other hand, *if* she's seriously talking about losing weight—and you think she's inviting your input—let her know you're on her side. A good sentence starter might be, "I love you no matter what. But if this bothers you, how can I help?" Then be willing to help. That might mean handling the soccer run so she can hit the gym or forgoing your nightly ice cream if it tempts her too much.

Whenever possible, make the effort with her. But whatever happens, keep on affirming her in those areas you *do* find beautiful, including her loveliness as a person.

Don't Take "No" for an Answer

By now, you might be thinking, *But I try to compliment my wife—and she always brushes it off.* It's pretty easy to give up, thinking she doesn't need affirmation or that there's no point in expending the energy if she's not going to believe it. But here's a pointer from Shaunti: take her reluctance as a sign that she needs the affirmation even more. Remember, her flaws loom large in her mind—even if you hardly notice them.

> Tell her—often—that you truly don't notice what she thinks of as flaws and that you find her beautiful.

For her, knowing that you find her lovely outside *and* inside will go a long way. We've all seen examples where an otherwise plain-looking woman became absolutely beautiful in our eyes because she had the "beauty of a gentle and quiet spirit," as the apostle Peter put it. If your wife is a lovely person but knows that her teeth are crooked or her post-childbearing stomach is no longer flat, tell her—often—that you truly don't notice what she thinks of as flaws. Tell her that her inner loveliness radiates through her, and that you and everyone else find her beautiful.

View Cost as an Investment

A lot of husbands struggle with their wives' desire to spend money on clothes, makeup, or beauty treatments. I hope by now you're seeing what's really happening here—she's trying to stay in the center of your field of vision and to bolster her own internal gauge of how she feels about herself.

No one is saying households should throw budget caution out the window. But what might appear a nonessential to us men might be a budget priority for her that she is willing to make trade-offs for. Here's a note Shaunti received on this topic:

> Please explain to the guys how important clothes are to women. Please try to explain how frumpy and unattractive we feel in old clothes, whether they are worn out or just out-of-date. A couple of my best friends struggle with this in their marriages; it's a common problem.

Now it's time to squarely address what may be the most important beauty connection of all. You and I can do an excellent job of reflecting our wife's beauty back to her and *still* cause enormous damage. How?

Fact 5: In my hand I hold a hammer.

THE HAMMER DROPS: LOOKING ELSEWHERE

We now know that women are powerfully affirmed by knowing that their husbands find them beautiful. But that power has a dark side. Because if a woman sees her husband's eyes *also* affirming the beauty of other women, she ceases to feel special. Suddenly, not only is she not affirmed, she's in competition with the world again—including for the attention of the one man she thought she already had. That's when the hammer hits the mirror that's you—the most important mirror in her life—and shatters it.

> If a woman sees her husband's eyes *also* affirming the beauty of other women, she ceases to feel special.

Now, because women are not as visually wired as we are, there are bound to be some misunderstandings here—some conflicts between what we consider innocent and what our women think. We may think, *My wife knows it's just a guy thing and I don't love this other woman I'm looking at.* Yes, sometimes it can simply be admiring beauty. And yes, God created a beautiful world—and populating it with attractive people is consistent with His artistry. But the challenge with looking at a beautiful woman is the speed at which admiration morphs into something else. Looking at the sweeping vista of the Rockies just doesn't run the risk of my next thought being *I wonder what those mountains would look like without all that snow on them.*

I urge you not to settle for what many in our culture consider acceptable compromises in this area. The New Testament sets a pretty high standard: "Do not conform any longer to the pattern of this world, but be transformed by the renewing of your mind." But that's because God's standard benefits you, not just her.

There are many practical, encouraging resources to help us in this area, including *Every Man's Battle* by Stephen Arterburn and Fred Stoeker. But I'm not going to spend the rest of this chapter talking about how we need to keep our thought lives pure, since most of us already know that. My main purpose is to help motivated, sensitive, and slightly clueless guys like you and me become more motivated, more sensitive, and slightly less clueless husbands by explaining the inner lives of the women we care about.

The hard truth is this: our wives and girlfriends *don't* just dismiss our sideways glances as a guy thing. Look at what one woman wrote us:

> I haven't been able to come to grips with my husband looking at other women. He is not into pornography, for which I am so thankful, but sometimes I see him looking for quite a bit longer than just a glance at other, younger women. I cannot describe the hurt I feel when he allows his eyes to take in every detail. I think otherwise very wonderful men don't stop to think about how this makes a woman feel. That figure my husband is looking at clarifies for me his deepest physical desires—and I look nothing like that. This leaves me feeling like I can never be what my loved one *really* wants.

It's News to Them...

I was also surprised at how many women had no idea that our visual wiring makes it difficult to not notice other women—and how many women have a really hard time with that knowledge. Remember, women *already* feel that they are in competition with every other beautiful woman—real or imagined—out there. Many women have told Shaunti and me that it's not that they walk around feeling violently suspicious of where we are looking as much as that they know they live in a culture saturated with options other than them. Shapelier options, racier options, younger options, easier options.

And now they know that the man they love is wired to notice every option. So when he does, it's hurtful.

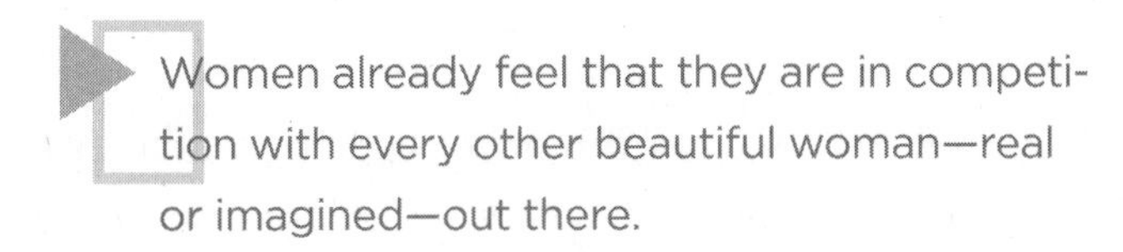

When the Mirror Shatters

On our survey for this book, although two-thirds of women said they'd be bothered if their man noticed a woman with a great body, only one out of four said they'd be hurt. But when we asked how they'd feel *if they knew their man's thoughts were lingering on that woman's body,* the number of women who said they'd be hurt jumped to three out of four, with even higher rates among women under age forty-five. (Shaunti suspects that these numbers would be even higher if women could actually see inside our heads and watch our thoughts like a movie. I do too.)

Imagine [a situation where a woman with a great body walked into a room and your husband glanced several times at her.] Now imagine that you could magically see inside your husband/significant other's head. If you were to find out that his thoughts were lingering on that woman's body, would you find it hurtful? (Choose one answer.)

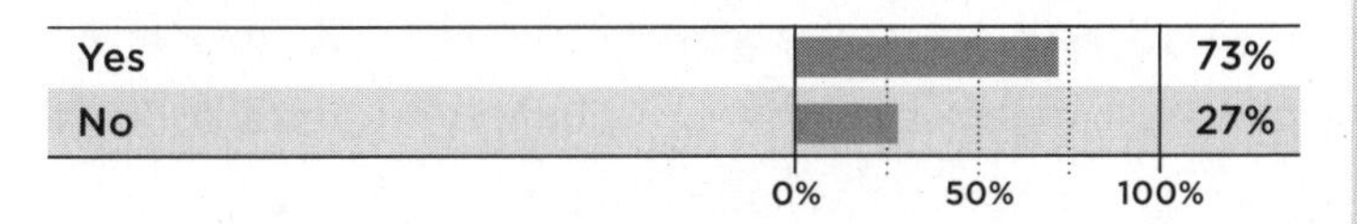

Truth is, most women can't comprehend why a man would choose or risk such damage. For many, lingering thoughts (and let's just admit it, lusting) were the same thing as cheating. "A woman whose husband doesn't control his looking and lusting will start to feel like a failure," one wife told us. "Why shouldn't she? Her beauty can no longer measure up to what her husband wants. His eyes speak volumes, so she has no choice but to doubt. But *she* wants to be found worthy in his eyes. *She* wants to be his beauty."

> "A woman whose husband doesn't control his looking and lusting will [feel she] can no longer measure up to what her husband wants."

As a man who, like you, wants to honor and show love to his wife, I find that woman's comment—and literally thousands more like it—very sobering. While most women don't mind if a husband or boyfriend is truly appreciating beauty (as in "What a beautiful girl!"), they experience pain if we look at, linger on, and lust after another attractive female. Their trust in their man's love gets badly shaken.

Shaking turns to breaking when the other woman or image obviously aims to *provoke* lust. That brings us to porn.

PORN SENDS HER A MESSAGE

"Let's face it," wrote one woman, "my husband can't control what woman will show up at what store or what street at a given time. It's not as though he's wishing that woman to appear. Porn, however, is different. Porn is a conscious choice. I think that when a man turns to porn, no matter how infrequently, it sends a clear message to his wife that she is inadequate. It says that no matter how she tries, she can't satisfy him sexually. Why should she bother trying?"

Unless a woman is naive about the power of porn or has become desensitized to it for other reasons, when her husband uses porn, it *feels* like cheating. And in truth, it *is* cheating. (Jesus's words come to mind here: "Anyone who looks at a woman lustfully has already committed adultery with her in his heart.") Even wives who don't equate pornography with adultery find the experience excruciating.

The fact is, for all men, this is an area where there has to be zero tolerance. Obviously that applies to pornography, but it also applies to lingering glances and lustful thoughts. We injure our wife when we look elsewhere for a thrill that we vowed to look for only in her. We break her trust. And we shatter our ability to reflect her beauty back to her.

WE CAN SEND HER ANOTHER MESSAGE

Since our wife needs to know that we find her beautiful, and she feels protected by knowing that we only have eyes for her, well, we have plenty of opportunities these days to send her that message.

In the mid-1990s, *Sports Illustrated* did a cover feature entitled "The Trials of David" on David Robinson, the MVP center for the San Antonio Spurs. One segment of the article described how Robinson handled himself as a professing Christian, husband, and father in the midst of the NBA's intense temptations. For example, during television breaks, he would sit on the bench and stare at the floor in order to avoid looking at the gyrating cheerleaders on the court.

The article also mentioned that, like all NBA players, Robinson was constantly approached by attractive women who wanted to talk to him and were probably offering more than just witty conversation. Apparently he would rather brusquely brush them off. When asked to comment on that seemingly rude practice, he said, in effect, "If any woman is going to get her feelings hurt, *it's not going to be my wife.*"[7]

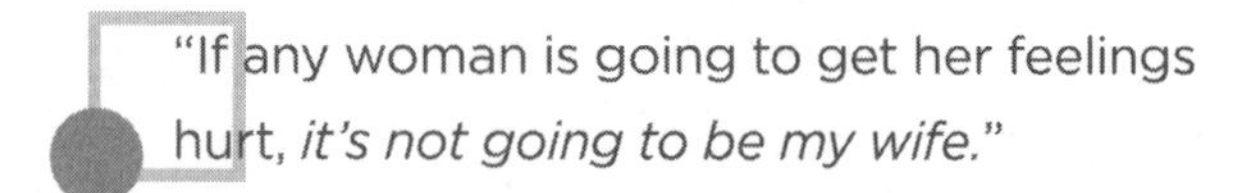

A protector and hero in action.

Each day your wife and mine hold out to us their intense, God-given, little-girl desire (and right) to be treasured. Each day she's threatened on all sides by an offensive and abusive world. And each day—with kind words and faithful eyes—we, too, can be our wife's protector and hero.

9 THE MAN SHE HAD HOPED TO MARRY

What the woman who loves you most, most wants you to know

In just a moment I'll share my biggest surprise from all my embedded-male research in interviews, surveys, and websites.

But before I do, I want to take you to a different data bank entirely: the mailbag of messages from wives and girlfriends who wrote and e-mailed Shaunti after reading *For Women Only.* Overwhelmingly, they relayed two things: how much they didn't know they didn't know and how much the relationship had changed once they understood their man's inner life—and started doing things differently.

THE CHANGE IN TWO THAT STARTS WITH ONE

At various points in this book, you may have found yourself saying, "But if she would only be *reasonable,* I wouldn't have to do all this stuff you're telling me!" We sympathize with that sentiment, because Shaunti and I have each felt it at one time or another in our *own* learning process!

So many of the women who wrote to Shaunti described the same feeling: "This is unfair. Why do I have to do all the work?" But they also described how they came out the other side. Look at this excerpt from one e-mail:

> I fought my urge to defend myself and prayed that God would open my heart to consider the possibility that it was me, not my husband, who needed to change. And of course I immediately realized that was true. I was frustrated to know that I had behaved this way for five years of our marriage. But by the end of the book, I "owned" it. And I also realized that if I had the power to destroy my marriage, I now have the power to change and build it up again!

Guys, we could say the same thing. We don't have to wait until she completely understands us to see positive results. Now that we have more clarity about several key areas of her inner life and needs, the ball is in our court. We've now seen that you can be the only person to change in your relationship and *still* expect great new beginnings. Your marriage is definitely worth your taking the first step.[8]

Which leads me to the biggest surprise of all.

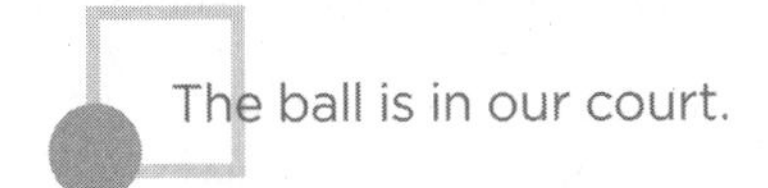

The One Most Important Thing...

As you can imagine, being an embedded male gave me lots of opportunities to be surprised. But nothing can compare to how I felt when I looked at the end of the survey. After two dozen multiple-choice questions, we gave the survey takers a blank space and asked, "What's the most important thing you wish your husband/significant other knew, but feel you haven't been able to explain in a way he understands?"

I assumed that the women would have plenty to say about what their husbands didn't understand, and in all honesty I had to gather my courage to look at the responses. And then I was astonished. Because the top thing that women wished their man knew was this:

- *You are my hero.*

Not always in those exact words, but invariably with that exact meaning. Over and over again, when women could say anything, they tried to express just how central their man was in their life, how much they admired, appreciated, and needed him, how much he made them happy, and how grateful they were for such a wonderful husband.

They were saying, in essence, that their husband really *is* the man they hoped he would be when they married him. Their average, ordinary guy—the person who sometimes leaves his fly down and the toilet seat up—*is* their knight in shining armor. Look at what this survey taker said she most wished her husband knew:

> He has made me the happiest woman in the world. I could have never asked for anything more. His love and support throughout our marriage is more than any woman could want. I am so lucky to have found him thirty-two years ago.

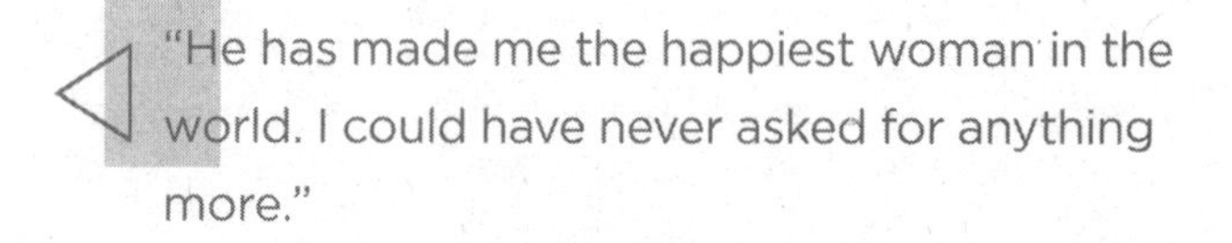

There's no way in this short space to give you the same sense of awe I felt as I sat at my computer and scrolled through so many similar survey responses. Here are just a few examples:

- How deep my love and respect is for him.
- How much I appreciate him.
- How much I care for his happiness, feelings, and well-being.
- How happy he makes me.
- How much I respect him as a person.
- I would trust him with my life.
- My husband means more to me than words can say. He is the true essence of what I dreamed a husband would be when I was a little girl.
- I dearly appreciate his hard work.
- I feel incredibly lucky to be with him today.
- When he puts himself down, it hurts me—no one should say bad things about my favorite guy.

THEY FEEL IT BUT DON'T ALWAYS KNOW HOW TO SHOW IT

I had been skeptical when Shaunti proposed this idea, but she suspected from her talks at women's groups around the country that *most* women really do feel great respect and appreciation for their husband or boyfriend but don't always *show* it. Often women simply don't realize that some of their words or actions actually convey a lack of trust, when, as she says, "that is not the way they feel *at all*."

So on the survey we decided to ask the question directly and see what happened. Shaunti guessed that at least nine out of ten women would jump at the chance to confirm that they *did* respect and appreciate their husband or boyfriend.

And she was right.

Is this statement true or false? "Although I may not always show it well, I do deeply need, respect, and desire my husband/significant other." (Choose one answer.)*

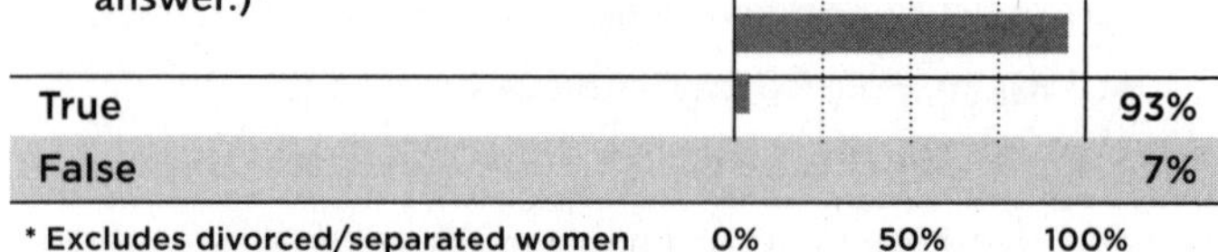

*** Excludes divorced/separated women (who still answered in the 80% range!).**

IN CLOSING...

I will leave you with this comment from one woman who spoke for many in trying to describe just how important her husband is to her:

> My husband smiles at me when he comes home from work and discovers the kids have drawn monsters on my legs with markers. He appreciates egg sandwiches and

SpaghettiO's more than a gourmet meal. He believes that I am a better mother, more talented, and a more virtuous person than I actually am.... His eternal optimism changes me ever so slightly, day after day, into something much more beautiful than I'd otherwise be. He's imperfect, puerile, and sloppy, yet strong, wise, and loving.

The fact that I get to live with him over the course of my lifetime is one of the biggest scams I've pulled off—I keep waiting for him to wake up, jump over the mound of unwashed clothes, and bolt out the door. But he sees even my imperfections as endearing. Over the past ten years, we've both changed. But the one thing that remains constant is my utter and unashamed need of him.

Not to mention, he's really good in the sack.

Acknowledgments

Thousands of people provided the input and assistance that were crucial to the writing and content of this book, and there is no way to adequately thank all of them in this short space. To all of these wonderful folks, we want to say thank you, and we ask forgiveness in advance for the many we will not be able to name personally.

First, we must deeply thank and acknowledge our prayer team, who did the most important work by covering us in prayer during the original research and writing and for this revised edition. You have our deepest gratitude, and we, in turn, pray for great blessings on each of your lives.

The professional survey of women that is at the core of this book was guided by the experienced hand of Chuck Cowan of Analytic Focus (analyticfocus.com) and performed by Kevin Sharp and the rest of the team at Decision Analyst (decision analyst.com). As in all of our other books, I thank this excellent team.

We promised to keep the identity of the interviewees and focus group participants confidential, so we cannot name them here. Please know how much we appreciate all of you. We also are so appreciative of the many conference organizers, women's ministry directors, marriage pastors, and others who invited us to speak, allowing us to test, refine, and deepen our findings over the years.

Several individuals went above and beyond in providing assistance and help as we originally investigated the topics covered in this book. We need to especially acknowledge counselors Chris and Susan Silver of Tree of Life Ministries and Atlanta-based sex therapists and experts Dr. Douglas Rosenau and Dr. Michael Sytsma.

We are very grateful for the team that has come alongside to support and encourage us personally and professionally during the writing of both editions of this book, especially Shaunti's amazing staff team, led by her exceptional staff director, Linda Crews. Special thanks to Jenny Reynolds, whose help on deciphering brain science has been invaluable for so many of these books. We are also indebted to our special friends Eric and Lisa Rice, whose input, collaboration, encouragement, and friendship have been invaluable.

We are not quite sure how to adequately thank our exceptional editors, David and Heather Kopp, who went way, *way* above and beyond the call of duty, particularly the unexpected duty of taking a huge manuscript and turning it into a book that someone might actually be willing to read. To both of you: we are so grateful for your professional skills, your encouragement, and your friendship. Thanks to editors Amy McDonell, Eric Stanford, and Laura Wright for their hard work on this revision. We are also immensely grateful to the rest of the WaterBrook Multnomah family, especially Steve Cobb, Ken Petersen, Carie Freimuth, and Allison O'Hara, for their incredible friendship, support, and commitment to excellence. You all are such a pleasure to work with! Special thanks to Don Jacobson at the original Multnomah, whose leadership and friendship started this whole thing for us.

We also must express our incredible gratitude to our parents, to whom this book is dedicated: Bill and Roberta Feldhahn, and Richard and Judy Reidinger. You know we could never have written this book without each of you, who rode to the rescue time and again to help with kids, household chores, and editing input while deadlines loomed. We love each of you very much and are immensely grateful for your presence in our lives.

To our children, thank you for being such great kids and so understanding when Mom or Dad had to be locked away with a computer for hours at a time. We adore you and are so proud of the godly young woman and man you are and are becoming. We are so grateful to be on the adventure of life with you!

Finally, and most important, we lift up all praise and honor to the One who truly deserves it. If there is any eyeopening power in this book, it is because of the anointing of the Lord, who cares for His children and wants their relationships to be filled with joy.

Notes

1. *The Parent Trap,* directed by Nancy Meyers (Burbank, CA: Walt Disney Pictures, 1998).
2. The brain science in this chapter is simplified from an extensive review of research published in multiple journals, articles, and books. For example, the information on the effect of the ratio of gray matter to white matter in the corpus callosum comes from a study by University of Pennsylvania neuropsychiatrists: Ruben C. Gur et al., "Sex Differences in Brain Gray and White Matter in Healthy Young Adults: Correlations with Cognitive Performance," *Journal of Neuroscience* 19, no. 10 (May 15, 1999): 4065–72, www.jneurosci.org/content/19/10/4065.full.pdf. For more details on the different brain wiring of men and women in this area, written in laymen's terms, see the "Emotions" chapter of Shaunti's book *The Male Factor: The Unwritten Rules, Misperceptions, and Secret Beliefs of Men in the Workplace* (New York: Broadway, 2009).
3. See Douglas E. Rosenau, *A Celebration of Sex* (Nashville: Thomas Nelson, 2002). He addresses the physiological issues in more detail.
4. If you find yourself in the 25 percent of marriages where your wife is the one wanting more, and you would like a

resource that includes a discussion of that pattern, we recommend *A Celebration of Sex* by Douglas E. Rosenau.

5. Full quote: "The biochemical urge we call the sex drive comes in two basic styles: aggressive and receptive. The aggressive sex drive is controlled not just by testosterone, as most people think, but by vasopressin, DHEA, serotonin, dopamine, and LHRH as well. The receptive sex drive... has been overlooked altogether.... Receptive doesn't necessarily mean passive [but] available, and perhaps willing, but without the initiative to pursue sex" (Theresa L. Crenshaw, *The Alchemy of Love and Lust: Discovering Our Sex Hormones and How They Determine Who We Love, When We Love, and How Often We Love* [New York: Putnam, 1996], 125).
6. John M. Gottman and Nan Silver, *The Seven Principles for Making Marriage Work* (New York: Crown, 1999), 205–6.
7. The full quote reads, "I made a rule when I got married.... I decided that if anyone's feelings are going to be hurt, they're not going to be my wife's. If I think [a woman] is acting inappropriately, I say so. It may sound harsh, but that's the way it is. My wife is not going to be the one to suffer." David Robinson quoted in Leigh Montville, "The Trials of David," *Sports Illustrated,* April 29, 1996, 95.

8. For men who want to learn about certain areas in more detail, we list additional resources at formenonlybook.com. You may want to start with Emerson Eggerichs, *Love and Respect* (Brentwood, TN: Integrity, 2004), particularly the chapters written for men.

Dig deeper!

Ideal for individuals or small groups, the *For Women Only, For Men Only and For Couples Only Video Study Pack* offers materials for women, for men, and for couples. This resource with DVDs and a participant's guide, fosters thoughtful interaction, enabling couples to communicate better and embrace each other's differences.

Shaunti Feldhahn Showed You How Men Think At Home —Now Find Out What They Think At Work

Do you know the unwritten rules of the workplace? *For Women Only in the Workplace* will equip you to be an effective Christian businesswoman no matter what your circumstances.

Read an excerpt from this book and more at
www.WaterBrookMultnomah.com